WHY PLATO MATTERS NOW

ANGIE HOBBS

BLOOMSBURY CONTINUUM
LONDON · OXFORD · NEW YORK · NEW DELHI · SYDNEY

BLOOMSBURY CONTINUUM
Bloomsbury Publishing Plc
50 Bedford Square, London, WC1B 3DP, UK
Bloomsbury Publishing Ireland Limited,
29 Earlsfort Terrace, Dublin 2, D02 AY28, Ireland

BLOOMSBURY, BLOOMSBURY CONTINUUM and the Diana logo are trademarks of
Bloomsbury Publishing Plc

First published in Great Britain 2025

Copyright © Angie Hobbs, 2025

Angie Hobbs has asserted her right under the Copyright, Designs and Patents Act, 1988, to be
identified as Author of this work

For legal purposes the Acknowledgements on p. 192 constitute an extension of this copyright page

All rights reserved. No part of this publication may be: i) reproduced or transmitted in any form,
electronic or mechanical, including photocopying, recording or by means of any information
storage or retrieval system without prior permission in writing from the publishers; or ii) used
or reproduced in any way for the training, development or operation of artificial intelligence
(AI) technologies, including generative AI technologies. The rights holders expressly reserve this
publication from the text and data mining exception as per Article 4(3) of the Digital Single
Market Directive (EU) 2019/790

Bloomsbury Publishing Plc does not have any control over, or responsibility for, any third-party
websites referred to or in this book. All internet addresses given in this book were correct at the
time of going to press. The author and publisher regret any inconvenience caused if addresses have
changed or sites have ceased to exist, but can accept no responsibility for any such changes

A catalogue record for this book is available from the British Library

Library of Congress Cataloging-in-Publication data has been applied for

ISBN: HB: 978-1-3994-0337-5; eBook: 978-1-3994-0339-9; ePDF: 978-1-3994-0341-2

2 4 6 8 10 9 7 5 3 1

Typeset by Deanta Global Publishing Services, Chennai, India
Printed and bound in Great Britain by CPI Group (UK) Ltd, Croydon CR0 4YY

To find out more about our authors and books visit www.bloomsbury.com
and sign up for our newsletters

For product safety related questions contact productsafety@bloomsbury.com

For Mike, the best brother anyone could have

Philosophy begins in wondering
Plato, *Theaetetus* 155d

Contents

Chronology	viii
Maps	x
Preface	xii
Introduction: Plato's Life and the Socratic Inheritance	xvi
1 The Dialogue Form	1
2 Harmony and the Good Life	23
3 Democracy, Demagoguery and Tyranny	51
4 The Ideal City and its Decline	77
5 Heroism, Celebrity and Money	101
6 Love and Friendship	121
7 Art, Censorship and Myth	151
Epilogue	169
Notes	170
References	185
Further Reading	190
Acknowledgements	192
Index	194

CHRONOLOGY

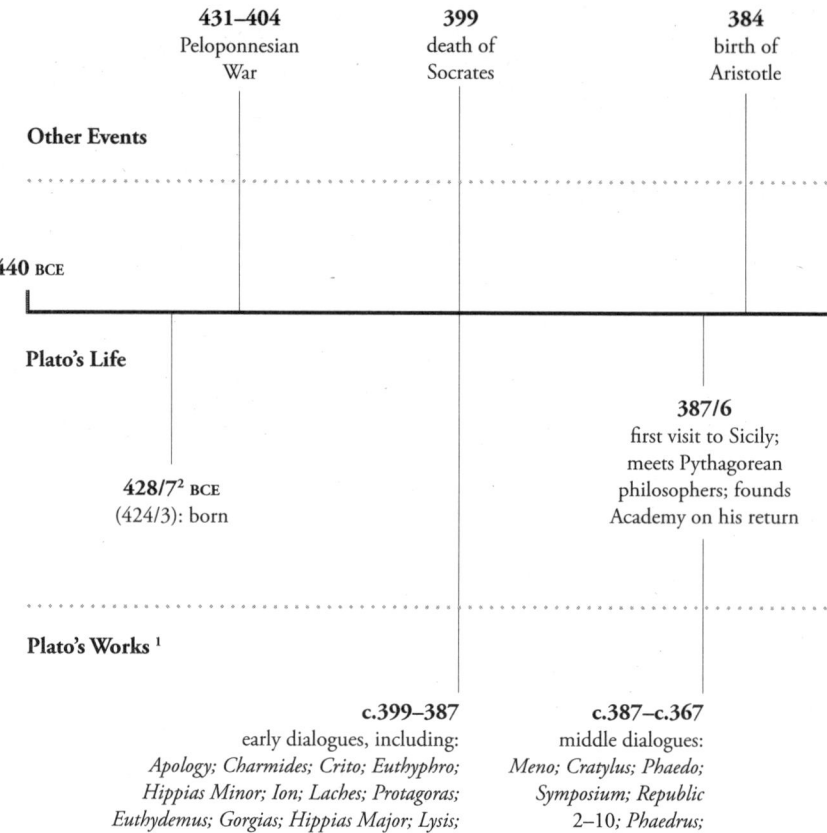

Referencing System
The referencing system in universal use to particular passages in Plato's works (e.g. *Republic* 473c) is that derived from the 1578 edition of the complete works of Plato compiled by a French printer and scholar, Henri Estienne, commonly known by his Latin name of Stephanus. *Republic* 473c, for example, refers to the third column of p. 473 of the Stephanus edition. However, when referring to passages in the *Republic* and *Laws*, I also reference the widely used Book numbers for those lengthy works, e.g. *Republic* 5.473c.

---

[1] We do not know for sure exactly when Plato wrote any dialogue, although in some cases a reference to a historical event indicates the earliest possible date of composition. I have followed the traditional (though not universally accepted) groupings into early, middle and late, both because I find them persuasive and for ease of navigation.

[2] Athenians did not number their years, but named them after one of the annual archons who administered the city. Archons were in place from (roughly) April to April, so we cannot always tell in precisely which numbered year an event took place. Some scholars argue for a later date of birth, around 424 BCE. For our purposes, nothing of substance hinges on this.

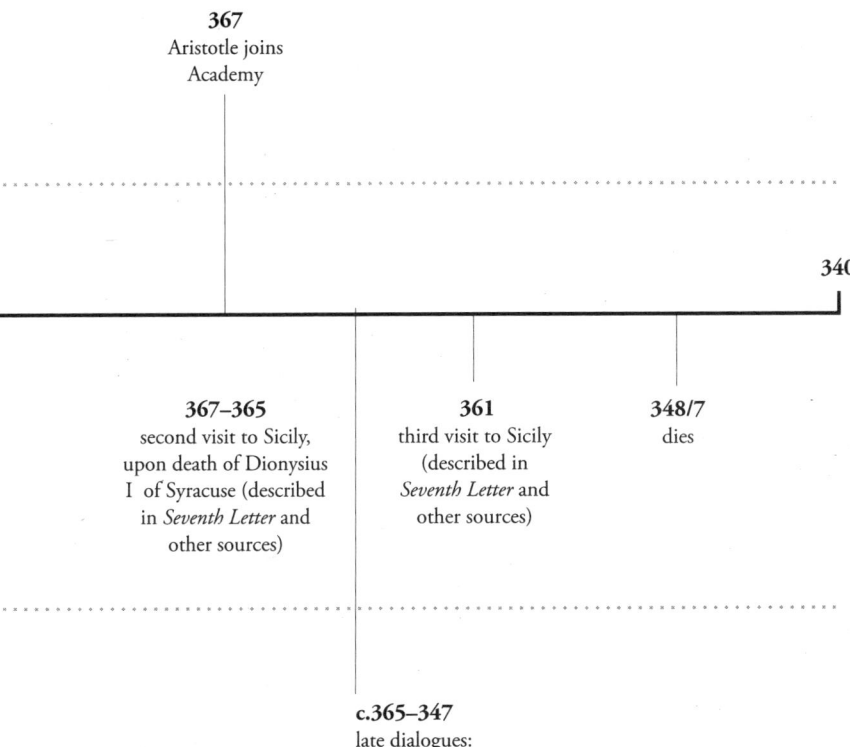

*The thirteen letters ascribed to Plato are not thought to be authentic, but the Seventh Letter in my view (though not all scholars agree) does appear to have been written by someone well-acquainted with Plato, and with good knowledge of the events described (although the summary of Plato's views is very odd). A possible author is his nephew Speusippus, writing shortly before or after Plato's death.

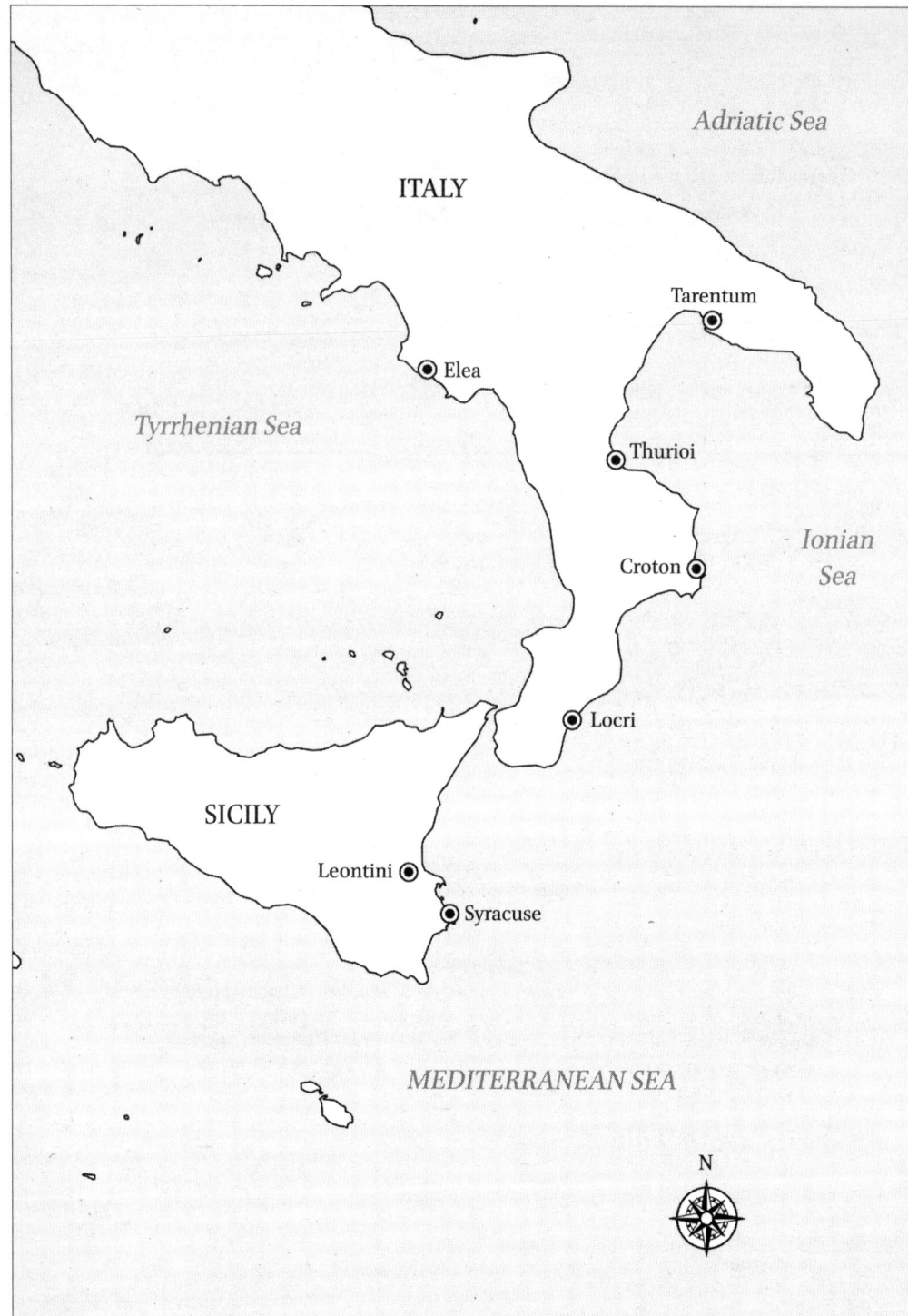

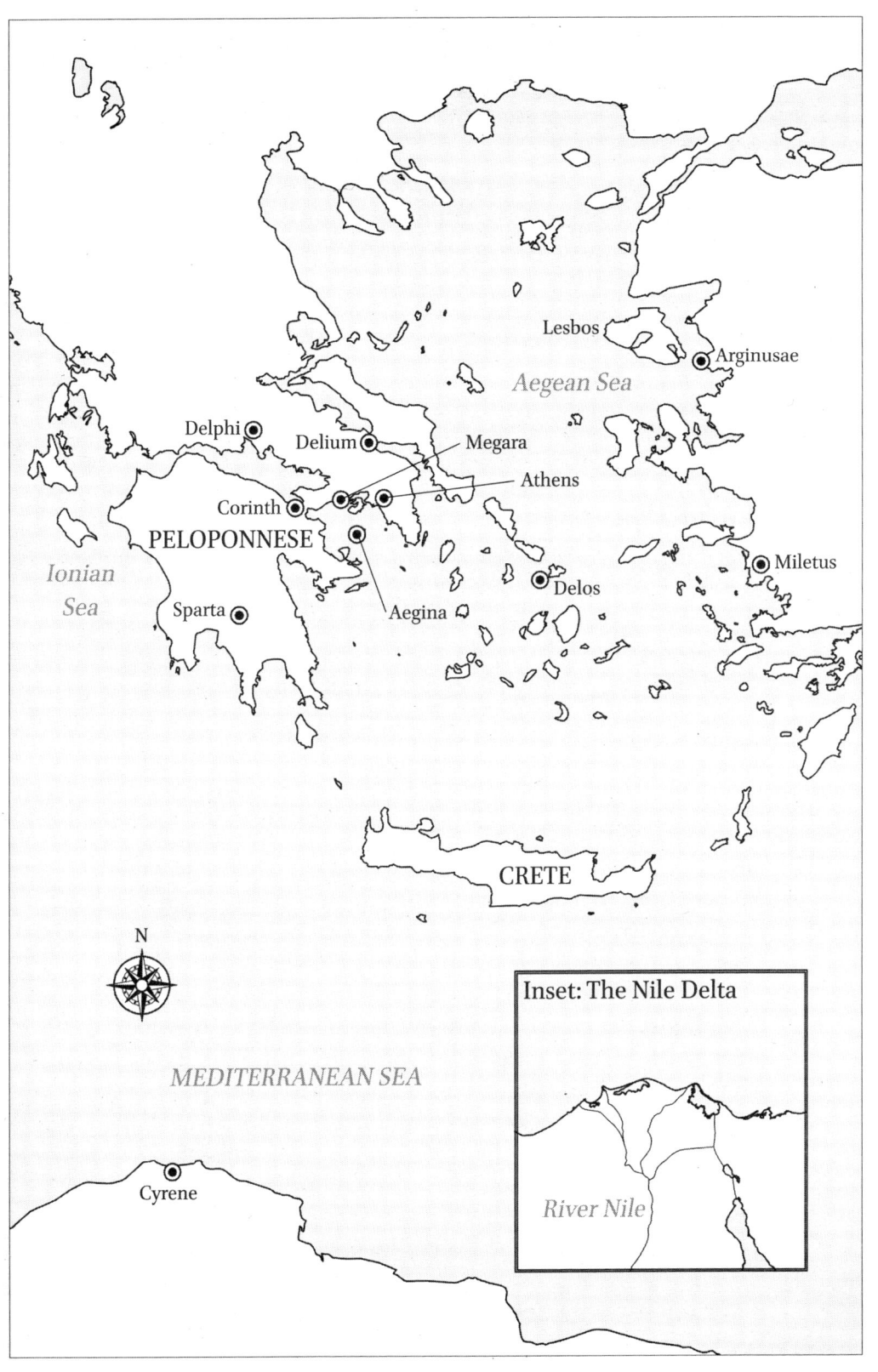

Preface

Plato has always mattered. The plethora of legends that quickly grew up around him is testimony to the fact that people immediately recognized the importance of his questions and ideas, and that their imaginations were captivated by the beauty, vitality and power of much of his writing. According to one tale, Socrates dreamed that a cygnet was sitting in his lap, and that it suddenly sprouted feathers and flew away, singing a sweet song; the very next day the young Plato was introduced to him and Socrates claimed that this youth was the cygnet of his dream.[1] Plato's eloquence clearly greatly impressed the ancients: Cicero also tells us of a story that when the infant Plato was sleeping in his cradle, bees settled on his lips, presaging his 'unique sweetness of speech'.[2]

Plato's ability to engage, delight and, at times, provoke and infuriate continued through the centuries: the Neoplatonists, St Augustine, Marsilio Ficino, St Thomas More, Karl Marx, Friedrich Nietzsche, Karl Popper, Isaiah Berlin, Iris Murdoch – all these and very many more enter into explicit or implicit dialogue with Plato, whether with approval or the reverse. As I try to show in this introduction to some – very far from all – of his key arguments, ideas, methods and images, the questions that Plato raises are with us still, and addressing both them and Plato's responses with seriousness (but not deference) can do much to clarify and enrich our own thinking, and help us work towards possible solutions to the issues of today. The aim of this book is to examine certain key ideas, arguments, and passages throughout Plato's works, together with the dialogue form and other literary devices in which and with which they are expressed, and to explore why someone in the twenty-first century should care about them. Why, precisely, does Plato still matter? How does he speak to our times?

The material selected comes from a variety of dialogues, written at different stages of Plato's career. I do not set out to argue for a particular chronology (although I will in fact be working with a fairly traditional rough grouping into early, middle and late, outlined in the (possible) Chronology on pp. VIII and IX). Plato's thought evolves over time, and certain key ideas of his middle dialogues, such as the Forms and the tripartite psychology of the *Republic*, *Timaeus* and *Phaedrus*, are reworked very considerably (or even abandoned) in later dialogues: Plato is always asking questions of himself. I do not, however, specifically address unitarian, developmentalist or revisionist views of his corpus; I am simply saying: these works are important and here are some of the reasons why. The emphasis is therefore on Plato now, but the history of how some of his works and ideas have been received will not be ignored, as some of the reasons he matters now depend on those receptions and interpretations, both accurate and inaccurate.

As we shall see, one of the reasons Plato matters is because of the challenges his works can present to those of us who try to defend (sometimes with difficulty) liberal democracy. The ideally just city that the character of Socrates proposes in the *Republic* is unquestionably run on authoritarian – indeed totalitarian – lines, and much the same can be said of the semi-ideal city described in detail by the main protagonist of Plato's last work, the *Laws*. I make no attempt to gloss over the fact that some of the views expressed by the character of Socrates (and the Athenian Stranger[3] in the *Laws*) may make many of us decidedly uncomfortable, and at times repel us; however, I do argue that even when the 'solutions' offered seem too extreme, again and again we find Plato the off-stage author asking the right questions. In the twenty-first century, many of the issues that he raises are vital still: demagoguery and tyranny; sophistry and fake news; censorship of the arts and the potential value and danger of myth-making; heroism and fame; love and friendship; what it might mean for an individual or a community to flourish.

We also need to be careful. As we shall be exploring in more detail, Plato should not be confused with any of the characters he creates in the dialogues, including Socrates and the Athenian Stranger: he cannot be assumed uncritically to endorse any of the opinions they express. The work that we know as the *Republic* (its Latin title, *res publica*, was given to it by Cicero; in Greek it was known as *Politeia*) would be *banned* in the ideally just city it outlines: it does not meet the censorship criteria of that city. Plato, the consummate artist and ironist, cannot have been unaware of this ultimate irony.

These vital nuances have often been missed by Plato's interpreters, and as a consequence accusations have been directed at him which he does not always deserve. Even more disturbingly, throughout the centuries there have been dangerous distortions of the views expressed in the dialogues – either through deliberate and cynical manipulation or through lazy, partial and selective reading, usually driven by the desire to make Plato fit a particular agenda. (Although I have of course inevitably had to select from Plato's extensive body of work, I have tried very hard not to project my own views onto him, although I accept that there is no view from nowhere, and that my selections reflect my particular interests.) For this reason too, Plato matters, and it is essential to go back to the texts and find out what he really said. When we do, we shall find not only that the right questions are usually being asked, but that in some cases the solutions themselves are genuinely helpful, even if we do not want to endorse them in their entirety. We shall find that Plato's tripartite psychology, for instance, or his view of *erōs* as a stream of desire, suggest useful ways of approaching contemporary problems.

Fortunately, many more of the influences of Plato's work have been positive, or at least neutral, and this evidence for why he matters – in theology, psychology and the arts as well as in almost every branch of philosophy and political thought – will also be touched on. In *Process and Reality* (1978: 39), A. N. Whitehead claims that the European philosophical tradition can best be characterized as a 'series of footnotes to Plato'. This is not true, but it is true that after Plato no philosopher in the West can fail to have been influenced by him, for better or worse, whether they are aware of it or not.

I fell in love with Plato when I was a student of 19, and have been reading his works, writing and broadcasting about them, and discussing them with undergraduates and graduates throughout the decades since. 'Philosophy begins in wondering, and nowhere else,' says Socrates in the *Theaetetus*;[4] Plato helped harness and nurture that sense of wonder in me, and I shall always be grateful to him. I still find his dialogues inexhaustibly rich, beautiful and thought-provoking. At times I find them disturbing, but they always provoke me into exploring why I am disturbed, and thus coming to a more precise and lucid understanding of the questions at stake. In what follows I concentrate on some of the characters, concepts, arguments, methodologies, images and myths which continue to fascinate me the most, and which I have found to be of the most fascination to generations of students. It is unashamedly a personal work. Being compelled by reasons of space to select from such a vast body of writings has at times been very difficult, and I have chosen to focus mainly (but by no means exclusively) on the less technical dialogues from Plato's early and middle periods; my hope is that the reader will be stimulated to explore some of the superb later dialogues for themselves and discover more of Plato's important and rewarding contributions to epistemology, logic and metaphysics. To this end I have included some editions and discussions of the later works in the Further Reading section. The chapters are designed to be read in order, each building on what has gone before; however, if a reader wishes to dip into a particular chapter, there are sufficient cross-references to enable it to make sense. Unless otherwise stated, all translations are my own (in some cases adapted from the translations cited in the Primary Sources).

In short, if we take the trouble to approach Plato with open eyes and minds, we will I believe find that many widely held prejudices and assumptions about him do not stand up to scrutiny. For all the undeniable challenges and justified concerns, he nevertheless has a very great deal to offer us now. We have perhaps never needed him more; it is time to look at his dialogues afresh.

Introduction: Plato's Life and the Socratic Inheritance

Plato was born c.428/427 BCE (possibly 424/423) into an aristocratic Athenian family in a period of profound political turbulence, and despite his own preference for a quiet and scholarly existence, his own life was also turbulent at times. In 431 a bitter civil war had broken out between the cities (sing. *polis*)[1] of Athens and Sparta, the Peloponnesian War, a vicious conflict that dragged on until Athens was comprehensively crushed in 404. At the beginning of the fifth century, Athens and Sparta had joined forces to ward off two invasion attempts by the mighty Persian Empire – a successful joint effort, the Persian armies being defeated at Marathon in 490, and then again at Salamis in 480 and Plataea and Mycale in 479. Once the Persians were overcome, however, the two great Greek powers vied for supremacy, and Sparta grew increasingly – and quite correctly – suspicious of Athenian empire-building, carried out under the guise of their heading a supposedly protective league, the Delian League, against future Persian threats.

Nor was civil war the only problem that Athens faced in the final third of the century. Cramped siege conditions fostered the outbreak of a devastating plague in 430 which killed, amongst many others, the democratic leader Pericles; and on top of all this there were simmering hostilities in Athens between supporters of a democratic system of government in which all adult male citizens – no females – participated directly, and those who wanted an

INTRODUCTION

oligarchic regime in which power resided with a wealthy few. Plato's own family was linked to both factions. His mother, Perictione, was related to two of the so-called Thirty Tyrants, a pro-Spartan oligarchy installed in Athens in 404 after Sparta's victory; however, her second husband, Plato's stepfather Pyrilampes, was a democrat and had been a friend of Pericles (Plato's father, Ariston, had died when Plato was young, and Pyrilampes too died when Plato was a teenager). Her family was also descended from Solon, who had laid the foundations for Athenian democracy in the early sixth century. It is hardly surprising that in his political philosophy Plato was to aim above all for civic harmony and the avoidance of internal strife.

Given his elite background, he was expected to have a career in politics, but as a young man he developed an interest in philosophy and, after initially learning about the philosophy of Heraclitus from Heraclitus' follower Cratylus (of which more anon), Plato became an associate of Socrates; during his twenties, he would also almost certainly have undertaken periods of active military service, as an aristocrat very possibly in the cavalry, though he may also have served as a hoplite. At some point during this period he – again almost certainly – underwent initiation into the sacred mysteries of the cult of the fertility goddess Demeter at Eleusis; he retained a keen interest in mystery religions all his life. In 404 the pro-Spartan oligarchy invited him to join them (not surprisingly in view of the family connections), but he decided to wait and see how they behaved. Their brutal excesses revolted him, and despite the family ties he refused to endorse them. When democracy was restored in Athens in 403, Plato was initially cautiously optimistic and felt that, on the whole, the democratic leaders behaved with moderation. However, in 399 came the accusations against Socrates, his friend and mentor, for 'corrupting the young, refusing to believe in the city's gods and introducing new divine beings'. The real reasons behind the accusations were a mixture of the political (some of the Thirty had associated with Socrates) and the personal (Socrates had annoyed many in authority by revealing through his questioning that they did not have the expertise they claimed). Plato attended the trial of Socrates and was amongst those who offered money to pay a fine for him. (This detail at *Apology* 38b is the second of only three occasions in the dialogues where Plato mentions himself by name, the first being *Apology* 34a, where Socrates simply states that Plato is present.) However, Socrates was condemned to death, and the third occasion where Plato names himself is in his account of Socrates' final hours in the *Phaedo*, where it is stated (59b) that Plato was not present in the prison that day. The narrator simply says: 'Plato, I think, was ill.' The 'I think' is telling: it suggests that illness was not the real reason for the traumatized Plato's absence. Shortly afterwards he left Athens in grief and disgust (and considerations of physical safety may also have been an issue), initially taking refuge with the philosopher Euclides and his circle at Megara. For the next 12 years Plato travelled extensively around the Greek world, and probably further afield as well to Egypt and Cyrene (in modern Libya), travels very probably still interspersed with periods of military service.[2] One of the most significant of these journeys was around 387,[3] when he visited the Greek colonies in southern Italy (Magna Graecia) to study mathematics and harmonics with the Pythagorean communities there. They were followers of the charismatic sixth-century sage Pythagoras, who combined serious scholarship with an ascetic and disciplined communal way of life and adherence to a set of religious beliefs, particularly concerning the immortality of the soul and its capacity to transmigrate, including into non-human animals (which his followers said was one of the chief reasons for their vegetarianism and refusal to practise animal sacrifice); their religious beliefs intertwined closely with the mystery Orphic cults of Greek culture in the West, and were of profound appeal to Plato, who was already, as noted, an Eleusinian initiate.[4] We will be returning to the Pythagoreans (and indeed Orphism) in later chapters; the crucial point for now is that in addition to their mystical side, Plato was also profoundly impressed by their scholarly work, particularly on geometric proportion – a concept that we will find figuring prominently in the *Gorgias* and elsewhere – and their belief that the cosmos is an ordered whole bound together by mathematical laws.

On this same trip circa 387, Plato also visited Sicily and had increasingly fractious dealings with the tyrant of Syracuse, Dionysius I – according to the admittedly unreliable third-century CE biographer Diogenes Laertius (3.18), he forcefully criticized tyranny to Dionysius' face. In any event his experiences at the court of Dionysius were later to inform his vivid portrayal of the evils of tyranny in the *Gorgias* and *Republic*. In chapters 3 and 4 we will see how Plato, while no fan of direct democracy (the only kind he knew), nevertheless thought tyranny a great deal worse, and issued a stark warning on how it can emerge, even (and perhaps especially) from democracies.

This first visit to Sicily was also of the utmost significance to Plato personally in that he appears to have fallen deeply in love with Dionysius I's brother-in-law, Dion, an attachment that was to last until Dion's assassination in 354, and to embroil Plato in considerable trouble on two subsequent trips to Sicily. In the moving and apparently authentic elegiac verses which Plato wrote for Dion on his untimely death, he cries out in pain: 'you who drove my heart mad with love'.[5]

On Plato's initial visit in 387, however, his relationship with Dionysius, always tense, deteriorated swiftly, and he departed soon for Athens. According to later and unverifiable reports, on the return journey he was sold into slavery on the island of Aegina at the orders of a vengeful Dionysius; happily for philosophy, he was ransomed either by a Cyrenean called Anniceris or by unnamed friends.[6] Once safely back in Athens, he seems to have made the decision to devote the rest of his life to philosophy, and not to go into politics – at least directly – and it is probably in this period that he wrote the *Gorgias*, an intensely personal, passionate, and at times angry defence of this choice. To put the choice into practice he acquired a plot of land outside the city walls, at the Colonus edge of a public training ground called the Academy – a grove dedicated to Hecademus (or Academus), an Attic hero in Greek mythology, and situated conveniently away from the scrutiny of the kind of public men who had put Socrates to death. Here he founded a research and teaching institute which also came to be known as the Academy, to the confusion of scholars ancient and modern alike.[7] Its members lived in communal fellowship – clear echoes of the Pythagorean communities which had so impressed him – and engaged not only in higher-order esoteric scholarship amongst themselves, but also in exoteric public lectures. Unusually for the time, but appropriately for a man who was to call for Philosopher-Queens as well as Philosopher-Kings in the *Republic*, women were allowed to attend at least the public lectures: Diogenes Laertius names two (Lastheneia of Mantineia and Axiothea of Phlius). The aim of the Academy was not simply to train philosophers, but to give future legislators and political advisors (and perhaps ambitiously also leaders) a philosophical foundation. Plato may not have embarked on a political career himself, but as Diogenes Laertius notes (3.23): 'his writings show that he was a statesman (*politikos*)'.

INTRODUCTION

An important part of Plato's mission was to distinguish the education he offered in philosophy from the training provided by the other main educators of the time, such as the rhetorician Isocrates and the sophists. Isocrates had set up his school in Athens circa 392, offering an education in rhetoric which – if Isocrates is the character Plato has in mind at *Euthydemus* 305c, as is commonly believed – lay in the borderlands between philosophy and politics, and the sophists were mainly itinerant, professional teachers of the skills needed to win an argument in public speaking and debate, sometimes irrespective of the truth. Not only did Plato not regard either Isocrates or the sophists as engaging in genuine, rigorous philosophy, but he also disapproved of the fact that they both charged fees (often high ones): Plato's private income allowed him the luxury of not charging for his teaching. He regarded both sophists and rhetoricians (and the orators they trained) as potentially – though not uniformly – dangerous, and they will appear throughout this work.

Plato remained at the Academy, writing and teaching, for the rest of his life, and some of his students became exceptional philosophers themselves: above all Aristotle who, aged 17, arrived from northern Greece to study with Plato in 367 and stayed working with him until Plato's death in 348/7. Unlike Aristotle, he never married or had children – his heart remained true to Dion – and he no longer travelled outside Greece apart from two more disastrous trips to Sicily in 367/366 and 361, seduced back by Dion on the death of Dionysius I to try to mould the young Dionysius II into the kind of Philosopher-Ruler that Plato had advocated in the *Republic* (probably written in the 370s). It was hopeless – Dionysius had some ability and a few good intentions, but was just too self-indulgent to be Philosopher-Ruler material – and the doomed attempt finally ended with Plato being quasi-imprisoned by him (he was certainly unable to leave his lodgings in the palace-fortress on Ortygia, an island in the bay of Syracuse). Plato only just escaped with his life, apparently having sent for help to his Pythagorean friend Archytas in Tarentum in southern Italy, who dispatched a fellow Pythagorean in a ship to prevail on Dionysius to let Plato go.[8] Once back in Athens, Plato prudently stayed put, and let his writing and teaching do the talking. He died on his birthday in 348/7, and his devoted students and colleagues buried him at the Academy.

PLATO AND SOCRATES

As we have seen, Socrates was not the only philosophical influence on Plato – as well as Heraclitus and his doctrine of flux, we shall also find the monism of Parmenides playing a key role – but Socrates was unquestionably the most important, shaping both the content and style of Plato's work. Socrates himself engaged in philosophy through the oral practice of elenchus – a technique of question-and-answer – with both individuals and small groups, generally outside in the agora and gymnasia of Athens (and sometimes indoors at drinking-parties, symposia), asking questions and showing how his interlocutors did not in fact understand what they claimed to know, and indeed often held contradictory beliefs. He refused to write anything down, saying (usually) that the only thing he knew was that he knew nothing; in addition, if the views attributed to

INTRODUCTION

the character of Socrates in Plato's *Phaedrus* (274c–277b) were also held by the historical Socrates, he did not think writing was a particularly good medium for the practice of philosophy: reliance on the written word weakens our powers of memory, and books always say the same things when you question them; you cannot engage in a proper debate with them.

Plato, of course, did choose to write, and we will be exploring the dialogue form that he chose – clearly the nearest form in writing to the oral techniques of his mentor – in chapter 1. In the majority of his dialogues, especially in those which are often grouped as 'early' and 'middle', 'Socrates' is the chief interlocutor. Indeed, one of the many reasons Plato matters is that in his dialogues he keeps the memory of Socrates alive through his vivid portrayal: his Socrates is always compelling, charismatic, ironic, provocative and utterly unique. (Xenophon's Socrates is more conservative and chattier; there is a strong suspicion that the military man, devoted but intellectually unambitious, did not fully understand Socrates' elusive complexity.) Plato's entire corpus – not just the *Apology*, which literally means 'defence' and in which he dramatizes Socrates' trial – can at one level be seen as an extended defence of his mentor's life and work, an extended critique of the Athenians for charging him and forcing his 'suicide' by hemlock in 399. However, this raises two questions of fundamental importance. Firstly, what is the relation between the character of 'Socrates' and the historic Socrates? Secondly, to what extent does Plato the off-stage author agree with the views he puts into the mouth of 'Socrates'? And these two questions give rise to a third question for anyone writing about Plato: is it ever permissible to say 'Plato believes that . . .' or 'Plato holds that . . .'? What should be the criteria for deciding when to write 'Socrates says . . .' and when to write 'Plato thinks . . .'?

In this work I adopt the following approach. As stated, the character of 'Socrates' in the dialogues is always a fictional construct and should never be understood as a precise attempt to recreate the historic Socrates. Nevertheless, the views put into the mouth of this fictional character may be more or less close to those of the historic Socrates, largely depending on Plato's own philosophical development. We know from a number of sources that the historic Socrates was almost exclusively concerned with ethical questions, questions regarding how to live and what sort of person to be; such examination matters because 'the unexamined life is not worth living'(*Apology* 38a). He was particularly intent on the search for definitions of key ethical terms: what is it that all instances of courageous acts or people, for instance, have in common? What is courage itself? What, *mutatis mutandis*, is temperance or moderation (*sōphrosunē*)? These ethical questions are the main focus of Plato's 'early' dialogues, and I agree with those who think that these dialogues are reasonably close to the teachings of the historic Socrates.

As the historic Socrates does not appear to have concerned himself particularly with questions of political theory, psychology, epistemology or metaphysics, we can fairly safely say that when Plato's Socrates enquires into these areas, he is representing the expanding interests of Plato himself; namely, Plato's increasing realization that in order to explore ethical questions about what constitutes a flourishing life, we need first to understand what constitutes the human *psychē*, and what social and political conditions are needed for it to achieve its full potential. And given that Plato further believes – again building on Socrates' legacy – that both individuals and societies can only flourish when reason is in control, he also comes to hold that these psychological and political questions can only be addressed if we understand what constitutes reality, truth and knowledge.

At no point, however, should we assume that Plato the off-stage author *uncritically* agrees with any of the views expressed by the character of Socrates (or indeed with the views of the main interlocutors in later dialogues, such as the Eleatic Stranger in the *Sophist* and *Statesman*, or the Athenian Stranger in the *Laws*). It is reasonable to suppose that Plato gives to Socrates or the Eleatic or Athenian Stranger views that he currently finds the most attractive; but he still always wants to scrutinize and question those views, sometimes through the medium of very bright and perceptive interlocutors.

INTRODUCTION

Does this mean that someone writing about Plato can never say with any confidence 'Plato thinks . . .', or 'Plato holds . . .'? Can no theories or arguments at all be ascribed to Plato himself? I think this is implausible. In what follows I use 'Socrates says . . .' for a specific quote or paraphrase from a dialogue. But when 'Socrates' (or the Eleatic or Athenian Stranger) expresses allegiance to a theory many times (as Socrates expresses allegiance to a belief in Forms, and the tripartite *psychē*, in the 'middle' dialogues), I think it is justified to ascribe such theories to Plato, *providing* we remember that Plato always wants us to question even his currently most cherished beliefs – indeed that he is always questioning them himself, and often developing or revising them. In some cases we also have independent evidence – from Aristotle, for example – that Plato did indeed hold that view, at least for a time, and was always willing to scrutinize it.

THE SOCRATIC INHERITANCE

What views, then, did Plato inherit from his mentor? Before Socrates, philosophers such as Thales, Heraclitus and Parmenides concentrated mainly on the nature of reality and truth and the structure of the universe, but as we have seen, Socrates directs his focus onto ethics. As Cicero later puts it in the *Tusculan Disputations* V 10-11: 'Socrates brought philosophy down from the heavens and placed it in towns . . . and homes.' His fundamental ethical question was perhaps the most basic of all, and was understood as such by Plato: at *Gorgias* 500c the character of Socrates says:

> So you see how our discussion concerns that which should be of the greatest importance to any person even if he has only a modicum of sense – that is to say, how one should live.

An almost identical claim is made at *Republic* 1.352d: 'our discussion is not about some trivial question, but about how one should live'. In each case the Greek formulation of 'how one should live' is almost exactly the same (as indeed it is at *Laches* 187e–188a);

it seems entirely reasonable to suppose that this is the formulation of the historical Socrates. It is a radical shift of focus – so much so, that philosophers before Socrates were later known collectively as the Presocratics.

So how did Socrates think we should live? He assumes that we all want to live a flourishing life. We will be saying more about flourishing in chapter 2, but for now we can simply note that the Greek term, *eudaimonia*, is more objective than our 'happiness': it may include subjective feelings of happiness and enjoyment, but it is generally more to do with the fulfilment of potential, the actualization of our faculties. The assumption that we all desire this may be too hasty, and there will almost certainly be exceptions, but on the whole it is not an unreasonable one. More controversial is Socrates' next move: that the flourishing life is the virtuous life. His argument is that the soul is far more precious than the body or external goods such as wealth or social standing: indeed, wealth and even health can only do me any good if I exercise them virtuously. The welfare of my utterly precious soul is entirely up to me. Other people can only damage or take away my external goods, or harm (or indeed kill) my body; I am the only person who can harm my soul, and I do this by acting viciously. Harming others, therefore, harms me far more than them.

The consequences that flow from this are profound. The injunction not to harm others applies in *all* circumstances: even if someone wrongs me, I should not return wrong for wrong, as I would be harming myself most of all. In saying this, Socrates is thus radically rejecting the law of revenge that forms part of the ethical code of the Homeric heroes (and indeed the Old Testament): 'help your friends and harm your enemies'. It has often been noted that in this he appears to anticipate Jesus' injunction never to return wrong for wrong in the Sermon on the Mount (Matthew 5:38–9).

What, then, is this all-important virtue on which the welfare of my soul depends? It is knowledge, knowledge of the human good, and all the individual virtues – such as wisdom, justice, courage and moderation – are united in this knowledge (the Delphic maxim 'Know thyself' plays a crucial role in Socrates' conception of

INTRODUCTION

moderation in particular). But what exactly does this 'unity of the virtues' mean? Does Socrates simply mean that all the individual virtues are interdependent, that if you have one you have them all? Or is he making the even stronger claim that they are all, literally, *one thing*, namely knowledge of the human good (although this knowledge may manifest differently in different circumstances – hence the different names)? There is keen scholarly debate about this, but either way, if virtue is knowledge, then vice is ignorance. It therefore also follows that no one does wrong willingly and furthermore that there can be no conflict of desires, and no weakness of the will: if you are able to find out what the best thing to do is, you will do it.

We will find Plato developing, and in some cases altering, this Socratic inheritance in a number of ways, particularly in respect of developing a more complex psychology and epistemology, and in searching for a metaphysical grounding for Socrates' search for the definitions of ethical and aesthetic terms. But Plato never loses sight of the basic ethical framework: how should I live and what sort of person do I want to be?

I

The Dialogue Form

We have seen how Plato never speaks in his own voice – indeed only referring to himself three times in all his works – but creates dramatic dialogues involving a rich and varied cast of characters, and that in this he is approximating as closely as he can in written form to Socrates' oral technique of question-and-answer (elenchus). We have also drawn attention to *Phaedrus* 274c–277b. In it the character of Socrates recounts a supposedly Egyptian tale – the myth of Theuth – in which the invention of the art of writing is critiqued for impairing our ability to train our memories; Socrates adds to this the charge that books always say the same thing: you cannot *debate* with a book. If the historic Socrates also held such views, then they may have influenced his decision not to write himself at least as much as his professions to lack knowledge. Plato may have felt that inventing a form of philosophic dialogue was the best way of trying to meet these challenges to the art of writing while still keeping the legacy of Socrates alive (the irony that the shortcomings of writing are of course here written down will be touched on below).

It is a radical invention: before him philosophers had written in paradoxes and aphorisms (Heraclitus), paradoxes (Zeno), epic hexameters (Parmenides) and – so far as we can tell from the fragments – prose monologue (Anaxagoras). It is now time to examine in more detail why Plato feels this form is so appropriate to his own overall ethical approach, and to examine how he employs dialogue to model helpful and unhelpful ways of engaging in debate, and the contemporary relevancies of such models.

However, in order to do this we first need to say something about the nature of dialogue in general and its role in Athenian society in particular: we need to consider the environment in which Plato is writing. What constitutes genuine dialogue? According to the *Oxford English Dictionary* (1989), 'dialogue' can connote the normative 'valuable or constructive discussion' as well as the descriptive 'conversation . . . between two or more persons' (and the literary genre which depicts such a conversation). There could, therefore, be a significant discrepancy between ideal and actual dialogue: the realization of the ideal will depend greatly on context.

One of the key factors will be the respective power relations between the participants. In the notorious 'Melian Dialogue' in Thucydides' razor-sharp *History of the Peloponnesian War* (5.85–113), ambassadors from Athens in 416 BCE seek to persuade the reluctant islanders of Melos (a Spartan colony) to submit to what is in effect the Athenian empire. The interchange takes place with over 3,000 Athenian and allied forces amassed offshore. In this intimidating setting, the Athenians brusquely inform the Melians that it is a 'law of nature' that the strong do what they want and the weak endure what they must – hardly a foundation for an open and equitable exchange.

Thucydides is clearly inviting us to consider the true nature of the Athenians' commitment to dialogue, at least in international affairs. Even in domestic Athenian politics, however, the picture is complex. In general, democratic Athens conducted much of its business through debate, in the Assembly and law courts, and its ideals of *isēgoria*, equality of speech, and *parrhēsia*, frankness of speech, officially at least applied to all citizens (admittedly only freeborn adult males). The theatre, too, not only staged dialogue but endorsed it as a cultural practice. As Socrates himself admits in the *Apology* (37c–d) and *Crito* (51c–53a), it is only in Athens that he can imagine being allowed to practise his brand of oral philosophy in the public squares and spaces. Yet this same democracy sentenced Socrates to death in 399, and it is reasonable to suppose that behind the official charges of corrupting the young, rejecting the city's gods, and introducing new divine beings lay a deep resentment at the way Socrates engaged in dialogue, interrogating self-appointed (and indeed sometimes city-appointed) experts, and deflating their pretensions to knowledge (*Apology* 22a–c).

Socrates' activities contain their own tensions between democracy and dialogue. His preferred technique of question-and-answer was ideally conducted with a single interlocutor at a time, as *Protagoras* 338a and *Gorgias* 474a–b emphasize; he dismisses the sophist Gorgias' practice of eloquent rhetorical displays to large crowds as not conducive to real philosophic progress.[1] In consequence, although Socrates' methods could not easily have flourished outside a democratic context, he was generally only able to employ them on a few of the leisured elite (*Apology* 23c).

When we turn to Plato himself, the ironies and complexities multiply. Despite the fact that, as we shall see, he was often highly critical of the extreme form of direct democracy he witnessed at Athens, his works could not have been written anywhere else in anything like their present shape: they are informed not just by his contact with Socrates, but by all the many and varied philosophers and teachers (both serious and specious) who flocked to the cultural hub of Athens from all over the Greek world, and flourished in its culture of vigorous debate and (relative) freedom of speech.[2] It is significant that after his many years of wandering it is to Athens that Plato returned to set up his Academy: it could not plausibly have been established in any other city. In addition, and again despite his profound reservations about democracy, his works reached, and were designed to reach, a much wider audience than Socrates' oral conversations.

Furthermore, in his middle-period dialogues especially, Plato allows interlocutors to question Socrates' methodology, and while they are of course questioning the fictional character, there is every reason to think that the questions are addressed to the practices of the historic Socrates too. Socratic cross-questioning and refutation may be very effective at exposing contradictions and clearing away false beliefs, but can they make positive contributions to the topic at hand? This is certainly the charge made by the (admittedly hostile) sophist Thrasymachus in *Republic* Book I (336c–d), and it is noticeable that the remaining nine books of the *Republic* contain much longer speeches by Socrates and make substantive contributions of lasting importance to ethics, political theory, psychology, aesthetics, epistemology and metaphysics; as many commentators have noted, the methodology develops from Socratic elenchus to Platonic dialectic.[3] The *Republic* does far more than simply expose fallacies and, as we have seen, in a further intricacy it would be banned in the ideal city it describes as it does not meet the censorship criteria of that city. Plato's dialogues, in short, arise out of the culture of democratic Athens, offer a robust critique of that culture and would be outlawed by the Philosopher-Rulers he appears – in the *Republic* at least – to advocate instead.

Nevertheless, despite these complexities – and we might add that 'dialogues' composed by a single author are still in a sense monologues – there is no doubt that the dialogue form is utterly central to Plato's work: he deploys it variously as a vehicle for teaching; for attracting readers to the philosophic life; and for making philosophic discoveries (and in this last respect it is notable that in the *Theaetetus*, a late middle-period dialogue, *thinking* is depicted as engaging in dialogue with oneself 189e–190a). Indeed, charges that the character of Socrates sometimes asks 'leading' questions[4] can usually – though not always – be resolved if we stop to consider whether Socrates at this point is aiming to prompt his interlocutor in a certain direction, or undertaking a genuine investigation with them. In order to explore how Plato deploys the form, it will be helpful to make a distinction between the dialogue form as a *whole*, including scene-setting, characterization, imagery, irony and other literary techniques, and the debates between the main speaker – usually but not always Socrates – and his interlocutors.

THE DIALOGUE FORM

THE DIALOGUE FORM AS A WHOLE

Let us begin by considering the dialogue form as a whole. Firstly, it is vivid, immediately engaging and attractive: it draws readers in. Once drawn in, the – at least superficially – open-ended questioning allows readers, including readers in the distant future, to enter the debate for themselves, to scrutinize and assess and ask questions of their own. In short, it compels readers to engage in active interpretation and reflection, to philosophize for themselves rather than just reading about the views of others. The irony of raising the shortcomings of writing in a written dialogue in the *Phaedrus* is a case in point – Plato often deploys irony to stimulate active thought and response: he does not simply *depict* dialogue between the various characters; he writes in a way designed to *promote* dialogue with present and future readers.

Furthermore, he provides constant evidence that he believes philosophical progress can only result from such active, internal, strenuous engagement. Consider, for example, this passage from near the beginning of the *Symposium* (175c–d), the drinking-party at which a wide cast of vibrant characters discuss the nature of erotic love, including a student of rhetoric, a student of sophistry, a tragic playwright, a comic playwright and a doctor. Socrates has finally arrived, very late, having stopped off on the way to think in a neighbour's porch, and the host of the party, the tragic playwright Agathon, invites Socrates to sit beside him:

> so that I can have the benefit of contact with that bit of wisdom of yours, which came to you in the porch.

Ah, replies Socrates:

> it would be good if wisdom were the kind of thing that could flow out of the one of us who is fuller into the one who is emptier, simply through our touching each other, as water will flow through wool from the fuller cup into the emptier.

The clear message – which nevertheless Agathon never fully understands – is that he is going to have to do the hard philosophical work for himself.

The dialogue form also fits in perfectly with Plato's overall framework of an ethics (and politics) of flourishing, *eudaimonia*. We shall be discussing this framework in more detail in the next chapter, but we have already noted that for Plato – following the historical Socrates – the fundamental ethical question is 'how should one live?', and that this in turn involves reflection on what sort of person one should be. The dialogue form enables Plato to show the intricate connections between character, belief and life: what you think and believe both stems from and in turn helps to shape who you are and how you live. It also enables Plato to show how your life is in addition a *test* of your professed belief: if you won't live it, you don't truly believe it. The very wide variety of characters in the dialogues serve as models for our inspection, interrogation and reflection. Do we want to adopt a particular character as at least a partial role model or life model, or does the character rather serve as a warning, a character and life to reject?

Plato makes skilful use in this respect of the time difference between his writing of a dialogue in the fourth century and its dramatic setting (usually in the late fifth century when Socrates was still alive). He can rely on the fact that many of his readers know what happened to the characters after the dialogue closes. The interlocutors themselves, of course, are usually blissfully unaware of these additional layers of meaning in the words that Plato puts into their mouths and actions; his technique allows us both to glimpse their lives at a particular moment, and also to gather a sense of how they later turn out. A particularly powerful example of this technique is Plato's treatment in the *Symposium* of the glamorous, charismatic and dissolute Alcibiades: politician, general and all-round hell-raiser, who drunkenly disrupts the drinking-party, and gives a passionate account of his unrequited love for Socrates. We shall be exploring this account of *erōs* in chapter 6; the point here is to see how Plato employs the troubled future history of the historic Alcibiades to cast a shadow over his behaviour and words in a dialogue set in 416.

As a young man, renowned for his beauty and sexual allure, Alcibiades had shown great intellectual promise and Socrates had tried to help him make the most of his considerable gifts, but – as Alcibiades freely admits in his blazingly honest speech (216b–c) – he disliked Socrates' criticisms and kept running away from philosophy to the seductive adulations of the adoring crowd. At the time of the drinking-party described in the *Symposium*, he is about 34 and his life is already starting to unravel: he arrives late, having been carousing elsewhere, and so drunk that he has to be supported in by a female pipe-player and others. Shortly after the date of the fictional party, the real Alcibiades persuaded the Athenians to undertake an imperialistic expedition to Sicily, and was appointed one of the three generals who were to lead it. Yet one night during preparations for the expedition, the *hermai*, heads of the messenger god Hermes on a plinth with a phallus, were mutilated throughout Athens, and Alcibiades was one of those accused of sacrilege: the *hermai* stood in the porches of people's homes and temples and were regarded as providing protection. He was also charged with other defacements of statues after having had too much to drink, and of profaning the religious Eleusinian mysteries at private parties (Thucydides 6.27–8).[5] Alcibiades wanted the trial to take place immediately as he (correctly) guessed that the charges would only increase, but no: he was ordered to set sail for Sicily and face trial on his return. However, as soon as he arrived in Sicily, he was commanded back to Athens; on the return journey he escaped and defected to Sparta, the arch-enemy of Athens in the ongoing Peloponnesian War.

In the following ten years his life descended into increasing chaos, as Alcibiades flip-flopped between Sparta, Athens and Persia, and democratic and oligarchic factions. He soon fell out of favour with the Spartan king (he was rumoured to have been conducting an affair with the queen), and in 412 he defected again, this time to the Persian Tissaphernes, satrap of Lydia and Ionia. In 411, however, he managed to get himself reinstated as general by the beleaguered Athenians, and initially he helped them win some successes, but when the Athenian naval defeat by Sparta at Notium in 406 was – perhaps unfairly – blamed on him, he left for the Thracian Chersonese (the modern peninsula of Gallipoli) in disgust, and after the Athenians further rejected his advice before the battle of Aegospotami the following year, he sought refuge again in the Persian Achaemenid Empire. But the refuge proved to be short-lived: although the circumstances of his death are murky, it appears that in 404, aged 45, he was killed by Persian assassins in Phrygia, probably sent by Pharnabazus, satrap of Hellespontine Phrygia, at the behest of the Spartans.

It is hard to overstate just how famous Alcibiades was in Athens, and the rough outline of this roller-coaster history of his (largely) wasted talent and untimely death would have been well-known to Plato's readers, and he skilfully and obliquely alludes to them in the *Symposium*. He twice has Alcibiades compare Socrates to a statue of the satyr Silenus (215a–b and 216e–217a), knowing that this would remind his readers of the charge that Alcibiades had mutilated the *hermai* statues; it also suggests that Alcibiades' future behaviour will amount to an attack on Socrates too. At 215b, too, Plato pointedly has Alcibiades call the statuaries' shops which contain the Silenus figures *hermoglupheia*, places for the carving of *hermai*; it is the only known use of the word and again seems to be an allusion to the pending desecration. The same would also appear to be true of 217a, where Alcibiades refers to his (now largely former) youthful beauty as his *hermaion*, his gift from Hermes: the suggestion here is that Alcibiades will not only go on to damage Socrates, but himself as well.

The overall effect of these subtle allusions is to highlight Alcibiades' ingratitude: even if he was not directly involved in the attacks on the *hermai* – and Plato does not commit himself – he certainly betrayed Athens in other ways, and these verified betrayals could easily be considered a rejection of both his natural talents – his *hermaion*, his gift from Hermes – and the benefits he received from his other potential mediator between the mortal and divine, the daimonic (*Symposium* 219a) Socrates. This rejection will, Plato suggests, bring about Alcibiades' untimely death: at 216a Alcibiades says that he habitually runs away from Socrates and his challenges as fast as he can, 'so that I do not grow old sitting beside him'. He of course did not grow old anywhere; and although Socrates reached 70, he may well have lived considerably longer had not his former association with Alcibiades been one of the factors that helped to bring about his indictment and conviction.[6] Plato appears to have Alcibiades unwittingly refer to this too: at 216c Alcibiades says of Socrates that 'on many occasions I would gladly see him departed from this world'; while at 219c Plato actually has Alcibiades calling the other symposiasts 'jurors', and claiming that their task is to judge between him and Socrates. The irony on Plato's part, of course, is that Alcibiades will not live to see either the results of the judging or of his wish.

An earlier example in the *Symposium* of the ironic foreshadowing of Socrates' death occurs at 175e, just after the interchange between Agathon and Socrates cited above on how wisdom is acquired. Agathon teases Socrates:

> You criminal mocker! . . . A little later you and I shall go to court over this matter of wisdom, and Dionysus shall be our judge.

Although Agathon is entirely unaware of the implications of his words, Plato is suggesting that the Athenian people who will try and convict Socrates in 399 are as drunken and capriciously unreliable as Dionysus, god of wine and disorder.

Through all these literary techniques, Plato is attempting to engage not just our rational minds, but our emotions too: he wants to effect real change in our whole *psychē* and thereby, as Socrates bluntly puts it in the *Protagoras* (356e), to 'save our lives'. Exactly how these changes are supposed to take effect will depend on the theory of human psychology explicit or implicit in the dialogue in question, and that is a topic we will be considering in the next chapter. However, the general point is immediately clear: the literary dialogue form is the perfect vehicle for affecting both our rational and non-rational faculties, and Plato employs all of his formidable arsenal of literary skills to achieve these changes: characterization; ironic foreshadowing and, as we will see throughout, the creation of potent images, similes and myths – myths which will prove to be of the utmost importance to a number of contemporary concerns and one of the main reasons why Plato still matters so profoundly.

HOW TO DEBATE: MODELLING GOOD AND BAD DIALOGUE

Equally important will be the opportunities the dialogue form provides Plato for modelling how to engage (and not engage) in philosophic discussion. What lessons can we learn about how best to engage in dialogue, including – and perhaps particularly – those with whom we disagree?

The first requirement is simply to be prepared to take part, as the *Republic* makes clear. As we will see in chapter 3, the initial discussion in Book 1 between Socrates and the old man Cephalus about the nature of justice ends abruptly when Cephalus loses interest and leaves to make a sacrifice. Of those interlocutors of Socrates who do stick around, who does Plato present as positive models for engaging in dialogue: what are the essential qualities? Ideally, they need to show goodwill, and at the very least be prepared to take part in an open, honest, collaborative exchange, rather than seeking to 'win' the debate by whatever means. These conditions apply whether the aim of Socrates in a particular interchange is exploratory or pedagogical – whether he sees it as a joint search for truth or an attempt to help a less experienced interlocutor learn and understand. In this respect, as we saw briefly in the Introduction, Plato frequently draws a marked contrast between the philosopher, motivated by a deep love of wisdom, and the professional sophist, driven by a desire simply to defeat his interlocutor – an interlocutor viewed not as a friendly partner but as an opponent. This key distinction is explored by Plato in, for example, the *Euthydemus*, *Republic* 6.489d–496a and, indeed, in the *Sophist* itself. In the *Apology*, Socrates claims that one of the reasons for the general prejudice against him in Athens is that he has often been mistaken for a sophist (18b);[7] it is hardly surprising that Plato is so determined to differentiate sophistry from true philosophy.

The *Euthydemus* nicely illustrates the contrast in approaches. The dialogue opens with Socrates telling his old friend Crito about a recent encounter he has had with two sophists, Euthydemus and Dionysodorus, who have 'acquired a faculty for wielding words as their weapons and readily confuting any argument, whether it is true or false' (272a–b). What the sophists practise is not Socratic elenchus (or Platonic dialectic), but the combat sport of eristic, a style of argument which aims not at truth but at the 'defeat' of the other side. We shall be returning to them shortly, but the *Euthydemus* also gives us an excellent illustration of a well-intentioned interlocutor in the youthful Cleinias, who answers all questions – whether from Socrates or the two sophists – honestly and 'fearlessly' (275c). Furthermore, his answers are admirably brief: we have already seen how, in the *Gorgias*, Socrates criticizes the sophist Gorgias for making lengthy rhetorical displays which cannot easily be interrogated; he makes a similar charge against lengthy oratory in the *Protagoras* (329a–b), though he is fair-minded enough to clarify that although the sophist Protagoras has indeed just given a very long speech, he is also capable of answering questions concisely.

Cleinias is keen, honest, good-humoured and able enough – albeit a bit naïve (*euēthēs* 279d) – though not necessarily a budding intellectual. Theaetetus (in the *Theaetetus*, on the nature of knowledge), however, definitely is an intellectual, a brilliant teenage pupil of the distinguished mathematician Theodorus from Cyrene (the historical Theaetetus went on to make original and important contributions to solid geometry and the theory of irrationals); he is clearly presented by Plato as a positive exemplar of how to engage in rigorous enquiry with Socrates, exploring in depth whether knowledge is a) perception, or b) true judgement, or c) true judgement with an account. What of Socrates' role as questioner in all this? In the *Euthydemus*, he explicitly says that his interchange with Cleinias on the relation between virtue and faring well is to be understood as a blueprint (*paradeigma* 282d) of a genuinely hortatory argument rather than combative eristic: he is sincerely trying to help Cleinias clarify his thinking and truly *understand* what is being said.

Although beneficial dialogue needs to take place between honest, engaged and well-intentioned interlocutors, it can still be challenging. Cleinias and Theaetetus are young and readily amenable to Socrates' suggestions; much tougher, but still admirable, interlocutors are Plato's two older brothers, who are present in Cephalus' house in the *Republic*: they definitely take on the role of probing 'critical friends' and sometimes even of a sceptical devil's advocate. Come on, says Glaucon, at the end of Book 1, show me that it really pays *me* to be just, even if I am mistakenly accused of injustice and tortured for it; and in what follows he often greets Socrates' proposals with an astringent or sardonic comment. Adeimantus, meanwhile, doggedly queries the practicality of the ideally just city that Socrates envisages. As a result we have the impression in the *Republic* that Socrates is not simply trying to teach and exhort, but that he is engaged with Glaucon and Adeimantus especially (less so with the others there) in a genuine collaborative enterprise, aiming at substantive philosophic progress.

In all varieties of 'good' debate, however, *persuading* one's interlocutor (rather than bulldozing them into submission) is key. Real understanding needs to be checked at each stage, and there needs to be genuine agreement, both rational and emotional, for philosophic progress to be made; this is one of the main reasons why, in the early dialogues at least, Socrates prefers questions and answers to be relatively short (though we will certainly see his responses getting longer as Plato develops his own psychological, epistemological and metaphysical theories). Indeed, in Plato's last work, the *Laws*, the main speaker (the Athenian Stranger here rather than Socrates) says it is vital that a persuasive prelude should introduce every law as it is only through such preludes that the lawgiver(s) can hope to elicit true consent from those they govern (719e–723d). The Athenian Stranger remains true to his word:

each law is introduced by a much longer preamble, which aims to inform and persuade the citizens that the law is necessary.

Persuasion is possible because of two views which appear so consistently throughout the dialogues that it is hard to think they are not Plato's own. The first is that there is a rational controlling intelligence (*nous*), and the cosmos is divinely and providentially ordered.[8] The second fundamental belief is that human reason is akin to this divine controlling reason.[9] There is a small spark of cosmic fire within humans (*Philebus* 29b–c); it is the divine element within us, and it follows that humans both can and should try to hone their rational powers: this is the essence of the 'assimilation to God' as far as is humanly possible, which we are told is our chief human task.[10] The lyric poet Pindar, writing in the fifth century, may have claimed that mortals should restrict themselves to mortal thoughts and affairs,[11] and that trying to exceed these boundaries is hubristic and dangerous, but for Plato it is our divinely appointed task to exercise our divinely sourced reason, and engaging in rational, reflective, persuasive dialogue is one very important way of doing this. Indeed, the reason-honing benefits of taking part in such a dialogue may accrue to both parties even if persuasion does not end up taking place.

It is also very important to note that Plato does not regard any topic as off-limits. One should not be concerned about others making fun of our ideas, as Socrates emphasizes in the *Republic* when he proposes (457a–b) that women should also not only exercise, but exercise naked, just as men currently do: if their improved fitness can be of benefit to the *polis*, then that is all that matters. Everything and anything can be questioned and reflected on, including matters of divinity and religion. *Pace* Stephen Hawking,[12] in Plato there is no inevitable conflict, or even tension, between religious belief and philosophy, or religious belief and science: it is a key part of our divinely appointed task to raise questions, including about the nature of the divine, and the proper human attitude towards it. Witness the seminal discussion in the *Euthyphro* about whether things are to be called holy because they are loved by god, or whether god loves things because they are holy (9e–10a). As the dialogue unfolds, it is strongly implied that the latter is the case; and it is further implied that holiness is the assistance humans provide to the gods in producing the noble product of human virtue – which would in turn suggest that Socrates' practice of questioning his fellow humans to help them understand the nature and importance of virtue is itself a holy task.[13] Indeed, in the *Apology*, Socrates portrays his work of engaging Athenians in debate about key ethical concepts as the fulfilment of a divine mission from Apollo (e.g. 23b, 30a).

There are, however, philosophical positions which Plato thinks would rule out the possibility of dialogue if they were true; it is not that the positions are off-limits for discussion – indeed Plato has his characters discussing them, in as far as that is logically possible – but the positions gesture to worlds in which discussion, and perhaps language itself, would struggle to exist. One of these views[14] is the dictum of the sophist Protagoras that 'human is the measure of all things; of things that are, that they are, and of things that are not, that they are not'. Interpretations of this dictum – the so-called Man/Measure – are many, but we need only concern ourselves here with what appears to be the interpretation of the character of Socrates in the *Theaetetus*. Here Socrates suggests that if Protagoras means that we each create our own separate reality, then we will quickly end up in a solipsistic world in which there is no shared truth and debate is not even possible (at one point he depicts an imaginary Protagoras popping up, disagreeing with Socrates, and then running off again without waiting to hear Socrates' response [171d]).

We should also note that the importance of engaging in dialogue does not mean that agreement can necessarily be reached: at *Crito* 49c, for example, Socrates says that it is simply not possible to reach agreement with those who think that one should return wrong for wrong.

HOW NOT TO DO IT: MODELLING BAD DIALOGUE

As we have already seen, Plato clarifies how to engage in fruitful debate not just by modelling willing and honest participants, but

THE DIALOGUE FORM

tricky ones too: we can learn as much from the bad examples as from the good. Above all, he makes it clear that aiming at victory over one's interlocutor – an interlocutor viewed as an opponent rather than a partner – is absolutely not the way to do it: such a pugilistic attitude will definitely not be conducive to the intellectual or moral improvement of any of the participants (even if we, the readers, can learn something from such prickly exchanges). In the early and middle periods of his career at least, Plato often seems to search out the most hostile opponents for Socrates that he can find. In the *Gorgias*, the sophist-educated and aspiring democratic politician Callicles bursts explosively into the debate at 481b. Socrates has just managed to extract a grudging agreement from another interlocutor, Polus, that if doing wrong is more shameful than suffering it, it is more harmful for the agent as well: indeed, doing wrong is so harmful to the agent's soul that if we do err we should hurry to the law courts and denounce ourselves as fast as we can, just punishment being the only means of spiritual purification. Callicles is incensed, and rudely accuses Socrates (482e) of resorting to vulgar demagoguery, relying on solely conventional notions of what is shameful or fair in order to win his argument, and ignoring the true, 'natural' meanings of these terms. He goes on to deliver a scathing attack on philosophers, contemptuously dismissing them as utterly ignorant of how things really stand: they are boys amongst men and slaves amongst the free.

We shall be exploring the substance of the interchange between Socrates and Callicles in chapter 3; for now we need only note that Callicles' hostility and scorn obstructs any real possibility of learning on his part. He is bright and educated enough to follow Socrates' line of argument in what follows, but he becomes increasingly terse and sulky, and at one point (505d) he says that Socrates needs to find someone else to engage in debate, or indeed just continue talking by himself, answering his own questions. However, at least Callicles does resume the discussion, and stays to the end, even if he does not appear to have really understood what Socrates is saying. An even more aggressive case is that of the sophist Thrasymachus in *Republic* Book I, who has become increasingly frustrated by Socrates' exposure of the fallacies in his interlocutors' attempts to define the nature of justice. When Socrates asks whether anyone has a new suggestion to offer, Thrasymachus 'gathered himself together and sprang on us like a wild beast, as if he wanted to tear us in pieces' (1.336b). He angrily accuses Socrates of talking simple-minded rubbish, and being childish; he also says that Socrates only pretends to be ignorant because he wants to avoid giving a straight answer. Socrates protests, and says that it is very difficult to give a straight answer to Thrasymachus because:

> You ask someone for a definition of twelve, and add 'And I don't want to be told that it is twice six, or three times four, or six times two, or four times three; that sort of nonsense won't do.' You know perfectly well that no one would answer you on those terms.

Thrasymachus then says that he will give them his own definition of justice, *providing* they pay him his usual fee.[15] Again, we will examine Thrasymachus' view of justice as nothing more than 'the interest of the stronger' (and not usually in the interest of the individual citizen) and Socrates' response in chapter 3; our focus here is on Thrasymachus' combative manner of engaging in discussion, and how it does not benefit him. He, too, becomes increasingly sullen when his position is critiqued by Socrates, as he can see no point in debate other than victory over one's opponents (his limited outlook is highlighted by the fact that he assumes Socrates must be equally competitive). Even though Socrates' arguments against Thrasymachus are in fact themselves questionable – a point we shall also be touching on in chapter 3 – Thrasymachus at least thinks he has been 'defeated' and at 1.354a says sarcastically that Socrates should enjoy his 'festive treat'. After this he only speaks once (in 5.450a–b), although he is referred to as still present at 6.498c–d, and indeed Socrates says there, rather bafflingly, that he and Thrasymachus have recently 'become friends'. However, even though he stays, there is no indication that he genuinely learns anything, either about the true nature of justice, or about how to conduct debate.

Callicles and Thrasymachus are vivid and memorable characters, and as such have clear pedagogic value: once again, it is important to distinguish what *they* learn (very little) compared with what *we* learn from such interchanges. And what we can learn is not just about how not to engage in dialogue; we can also learn about the topics under discussion. As we will see in chapters 3 and 4, Plato deftly shows us, through Callicles and Thrasymachus, three things of the utmost importance about the topics at hand: firstly, why the nature of justice (and virtue as a whole) is so important and how it relates to well-being; secondly, why the views of Callicles and Thrasymachus are so challenging and, thirdly, how one might set about responding to those challenges.

More generally, and just as importantly, Plato shows us how critical it is at least to try to engage in dialogue, even with – perhaps especially with – those with whom we disagree, and who may well be hostile towards us. Attempts at engagement may not always work – the cases of Callicles and Thrasymachus suggest not – but they just might, and, crucially, the dangerous views held need to be publicly aired and debated and not remain underground. As we will shortly see, such a message is of profound importance to current political, religious and cultural divisions. First, however, we need to consider the threat to genuine dialogue posed by a rather different kind of sophist – the one who is still absolutely intent on victory rather than truth, but rather than trying to bludgeon their interlocutor into submission through aggression, is prepared to use any kind of verbal or argumentative trick to win. For all their faults, at least Callicles and Thrasymachus are honest about what they really think, and indeed Socrates commends them for it. The verbal tricksters present an even graver challenge because they have no interest in honesty, just victory by any means.[16]

Particularly egregious examples are Dionysodorus and Euthydemus in the *Euthydemus*, who unsettle the willing but inexperienced young Cleinias through unscrupulous wordplay. Euthydemus asks Cleinias which sort of men are those who learn: the wise or the ignorant? While Cleinias is gathering his thoughts, Dionysodorus whispers to Socrates that whichever way Cleinias answers, he will be confuted. And this is precisely what happens, through a play on two meanings of 'learning': the Greek term (*to manthanein*) can be applied both to those who have yet to acquire knowledge, and those who have already acquired it. Euthydemus also plays with two meanings of '*amathēs*', which can simply bear the meaning of 'unlearned in', or the definitely pejorative 'foolish' or 'stupid'. Cleinias is understandably confused, and Euthydemus tries a second assault: do learners learn what they know, or what they do not know? Again, while Cleinias hesitates, Dionysodorus gleefully whispers to Socrates: 'All our questions are like that. They leave no escape.' Poor Cleinias is defeated again, through the same play on words, but this time Socrates comes to his aid, explaining the verbal tricks that have been deployed on him, and saying – in a light tone but clearly with serious intent – that the two sophists are just playing with him:

> I call it play because, even if one were to learn many or even all of such tricks, one would not know anything more of the true state of the matters at hand, but only be able to play games with people, owing to difference in sense of the words, by tripping them up and overturning them (278b).

Towards the end of the dialogue (303d), Socrates tells his friend Crito that most people would consider it a greater disgrace to refute others by means of such specious tricks than be refuted themselves.

One final point: although Euthydemus and Dionysodorus initially appear to be genial enough, if unattractively mocking of the bamboozled Cleinias and disdainful towards Socrates, Dionysodorus does not like it at all when another participant in the discussion, Ctesippus, makes fun of him and contradicts him. Dionysodorus claims that Ctesippus is being abusive, but Ctesippus says no: Dionysodorus must not confuse contradiction with abuse (285d). For dialogue to work, and real philosophic progress to be made, we must be able to cope with being challenged.

CONTEMPORARY APPLICATIONS

One does not have to share Plato's view that our individual human reason is a microcosm of a rationally ordered cosmos to appreciate the profound potential benefits of his views on, and practice of, dialogue: we can learn far more from the interchanges than some of the interlocutors themselves, and one of the main things we can learn is precisely how to see through the smoke-and-mirrors of a contemporary Euthydemus. An ability to spot fallacious arguments and verbal skulduggery is clearly of the utmost value in exposing the fraudulent claims of today's snake-oil salesmen and women, be they unscrupulous advertisers, politicians, journalists, conspiracy theorists, social-media influencers, or self-styled religious and cultural leaders.

Furthermore, the positive models Plato provides of how to engage in honest, collaborative dialogue, genuinely aimed at finding out the truth, can help us see how to interact with people of perhaps very different political views and address the current unhelpful polarization in politics and culture around the world. Plato gives us the tools to help combat the damaging and dangerous silos and 'culture wars', often confected – and certainly greatly exaggerated – by a few for their own political and economic advancement.

Similar lessons can be applied to debates between those expressing different religious views, or between those of faith and those of none. We have already seen that Plato thinks there is nothing sacrilegious about discussing matters of religion and the divine – quite the reverse – but just as with political and cultural debates, it can be done well or badly. The broad principles about how to engage constructively in dialogue apply to all religious debates, including those which focus explicitly on current religious conflicts, and which deal with specific features of the religions involved. However, it is also worth pointing out the obvious but often overlooked fact that although Plato himself was deeply religious, he did not adhere to any of the current dominant world religions;[17] he is thus not directly implicated in any of the current conflicts in which participants claim allegiance to one of those religions. The texts of his dialogues can therefore in addition function to some extent as a shared cultural resource and offer us an inclusive space and a platform for debating general religious and ethical issues without the participants in the debate feeling so keenly that their specific beliefs and identities are being immediately threatened.

It is of course true that Plato's dialogues have often been regarded as foundational to Western rationalism, and not all wish to situate themselves within such a tradition. However, as we shall see, the non-rational is also of fundamental importance in Plato. As for 'Western', it is worth pointing out that not all Greek (or Roman) philosophers were born or lived within the boundaries of the current 'West', and not all were white, a useful reminder that geographic and national boundaries have always been fluid, as have notions of 'tribe' and 'ethnicity'. Furthermore, we owe the preservation of much of the Greek corpus to Islamic scholars such as Al-Farabi or Ibn Rushd (Averroes), who also did much to enrich the tradition with their own original thought.

Nevertheless, even if we do feel under verbal attack, we should still try to engage; this is the clear message of Socrates' attempts to convince Callicles and Thrasymachus. Such dialogic engagement may not always work, but if we do not even try then the opportunities for misunderstanding, mistrust, division and hatred will only grow, and the chances of descent into warfare will be increased. At the time of writing in 2024, brutal alternatives to dialogue are on vivid and horrific display around the globe. It is true that, while in the *Apology* Plato shows Socrates conversing with everyone and anyone (as was almost certainly the practice of the historical Socrates), later in his career Plato has Socrates say in the *Phaedrus* (276e–277a) that the dialectician needs to find an 'appropriate soul' in whom to sow the seeds of knowledgeable discourse.[18] But the focus here is on finding a genuinely promising student of philosophy, who can nurture the seeds to fruition and in turn pass the seeds of the fruits on to the next generation; there is no suggestion that we should cease to engage with a more general audience, and indeed Plato continued to give public lectures at the Academy throughout his life as well as undertaking more specialist work with his students and research associates.

Another field which can benefit greatly from Plato's use of the dialogue form as a whole, and the models he gives us of how to debate well and badly, is that of education – not surprising, given that Plato's research, writing and teaching were inextricably interlinked. In an encouraging number of cases around the world, Plato's deployment of dialogue, based at least to some extent on the oral practices of the historic Socrates, is already informing educational theory and practice in both formal and informal educational settings. The Philosophy for Children (P4C) movement is diverse in its sources and approaches, although the pragmatist philosopher John Dewey is key to many of them; but Plato and Socrates are central too: witness the powerful and moving documentary *Young Plato*, in which an inspirational headmaster in an all-boys primary school in post-conflict Belfast employs ancient Greek philosophy to instil a habit of critical thinking to encourage the boys to see beyond sectarian boundaries. Nor are Platonic dialogue (and dialectic) and Socratic elenchus only finding pedagogic applications in schools: the Philosophy in Prison initiative, for example, also owes much to both.

In all these settings and formats, appropriately updated and adapted versions of Plato's (and Socrates') methodology can facilitate real engagement, questioning and reflection, which in turn can lead to a deeper understanding of the topic at hand than can be achieved by simply 'teaching to the test'. When practised successfully, lessons based on this methodology can be very enjoyable, and this in itself creates fertile ground for engagement and deeper understanding as well as being good in its own right; furthermore, all these benefits – including the enjoyment – may happily accrue to the teachers too. Just as importantly, participants can learn *how* to discuss and debate, and, if necessary, how to disagree in a way which remains respectful even if the disagreement is profound. Given the deeply damaging polarization in many current adult political, cultural and religious debates, the importance of a training in constructive dialogic practices from an early age cannot be overestimated, and is another reason why Plato still matters so much.

2

Harmony and the Good Life

EUDAIMONIA AND THE ETHICS OF FLOURISHING

If, then, these are Plato's dialogic techniques, what does he do with them? We have seen that he inherits from the historic Socrates an ethical approach based on the questions 'how should one live?' and 'what sort of person should one be?', and that – whether rightly or not – Socrates thought we would all agree that we want to live a flourishing life and flourish as a person, and that 'flourishing' (*eudaimonia*) is a more objective concept than happiness or pleasure. As he puts it to his old friend Crito while awaiting his death in prison: 'it is not living, but living well which we ought to consider the most important' (*Crito* 48b). But what does this actually mean? What is a good life and is it the good or the bad people who get to live it?

The literal meaning of *eudaimonia* is 'protected by a benevolent guardian spirit, a benevolent *daimōn*',[1] and in Plato (and Aristotle) it usually at least involves the excellent realization of our mental and physical faculties.[2] This will of course require careful analysis of what our faculties actually are and what their excellent realization looks like, and this in turn will lead to consideration of what social and political conditions are needed for this fulfilment. We will be examining Plato's thoughts on these questions in the *Republic* below, but we can immediately see that one of the potential strengths of an eudaimonist foundation for ethics is that we can always try to exercise our faculties in the best way available in the circumstances, even when *feeling* happy is neither possible nor appropriate. At a time of terrible conflicts in Ukraine, and in Gaza and Israel and the Sudan and many other countries, it would simply not be appropriate – indeed decidedly disturbing – to watch footage of the horrific suffering and feel cheered; and for those actually enduring the suffering, cheer is clearly an even rarer option. But we can always ask ourselves: 'In these very difficult circumstances, how can I nevertheless best exercise my various faculties in ways which foster both my good and the good of the community as far as those circumstances allow?'

It is an *agent*-centred approach, at least capable of taking on board the complexities of the lived human experience. It differs from (and to my mind is more compelling than) act-centred theories, such as those based on duties and rights (e.g. Kant), or utilitarian consequences (e.g. Bentham and, with caveats, Mill).[3] It considers the whole person, living a whole life, and as such invites us to reflect on the structure, shape and narrative of a well-lived life. It is thus an ethical approach which has particular connections with aesthetics, and with stories – this is another reason why Plato's dialogue form is particularly appropriate to his fundamental approach to ethics: he depicts and alludes to historical, fictional and mythical characters to help us appreciate which can serve as models of flourishing, and, just as saliently, which are models to avoid. We may, of course, want to ask whether there is a temptation to try to impose an artificial order on the mess of daily existence, but, as we have already begun to see, Plato's colourfully varied cast brilliantly illustrate chaotic as well as ordered lives: his portrait of Alcibiades is a vivid example of the former. And in any case there is a separate question about whether it might be possible for living agents to sculpt some genuine order out of the mess, as opposed to a philosopher-artist simply attempting to impose an artificial order on given material at one remove.

THE FLOURISHING CITY AND *PSYCHĒ*

By the time of writing the *Republic*, Plato has come to realize that the issue of what comprises *eudaimonia* can only properly be addressed through a psychological theory more sophisticated than that offered (or perhaps more accurately implied) by his mentor Socrates, and that this psychology in turn will raise fundamental questions concerning the true nature of reality and how we come to know about it. Although, as we shall see, it is a psychology (and underlying metaphysics and epistemology) which poses serious challenges, it is also one which offers rich possibilities for tackling contemporary concerns and problems, and so it is worth exploring in some depth.

In *Republic* 1.352b–354b, Socrates argues that everything has its own particular function and corresponding excellence, and that the function of the *psychē* is to live, and its excellence is justice. It is not a persuasive argument, as it plays on two meanings of 'good' and 'well' ('beneficial' or 'fine'/'honourable'),[4] and Glaucon and Adeimantus are alert to this, demanding that Socrates show that it really does pay the individual agent to be just. However, the passage is a useful illustration of the fundamental point that 'living well' is understood by those present as mostly an *objective* concept, suggestive of the excellent actualization of our particular faculties.

For a detailed psychological theory to underpin the claim that living well equates to living justly and virtuously we need to wait until *Republic* Book 4. To appreciate it, however, we have to say a little about the context in which it is introduced. In Book 1, the sophist Thrasymachus (whom we shall be considering in more detail in the next chapter) claims that as (conventional) justice is simply the 'interest of the stronger', it follows that injustice usually serves the individual better than justice; justice is only for naïve fools. Glaucon and Adeimantus elaborate on this,[5] and they challenge Socrates to show that justice really is to the individual's advantage. Socrates replies that we cannot know whether justice really benefits the agent until we know what it is, and it will be easier to spot justice if we start by looking for it on the larger canvas of an ideally just *polis*. He therefore proceeds to construct a picture of an ideally just community based on the need for economic exchange and the principle that each person should perform only one job: specialization both accords with what he claims to be the natural distribution of skills, and allows the citizens to concentrate on perfecting their particular task. Initially this community consists of just one class: everyone is both a producer and a consumer of goods and services; Glaucon, however, scornfully protests that such a life would be fit only for pigs, and in response Socrates allows the introduction of more sophisticated pleasures. This has detrimental consequences: as the community expands it comes into conflict with its neighbours, and an army is required. On the principle that no one should perform more than one job, this army will form a separate class, called Guardians (374a–e).

We will be discussing the Guardians, and indeed the whole political set-up in the *Republic*, in more detail in chapter 4. Here we need only consider the ideally just *polis* as an introduction to the psychology of Book 4. From 2.376c–3.412a, Socrates lays down strictures for the early education of the Guardians: it is vital that the potentially aggressive instincts necessary for fighting foreign enemies are carefully controlled by a programme of literary and musical studies (collectively called *mousikē*, and explored below) and physical training, so that the Guardians do not turn against their own people in peacetime. At 3.412b, Socrates then proceeds to divide the Guardian class itself into two: those responsible for military, policing and executive duties are now termed Auxiliaries (3.414b), and are to assist an elite group of Rulers, whose task is to plan and care for the good of the city as a whole. The virtues of the city are located in the functions performed by the three classes and in the relations between them. It is owing to the wisdom of its Rulers that the city as a whole will be wise, and owing to the courage of its Auxiliaries that the city as a whole is courageous. Moderation or temperance (*sōphrosunē*) in the city results when all three classes agree about who ought to rule, and the appetites and desires of the majority of the citizens are controlled by the rational desires and wisdom of the Rulers; *sōphrosunē* is thus a kind of harmony or concord (4.430e) and, unlike wisdom or courage, belongs to all three classes. Finally, justice is the condition which makes all the other virtues possible: the condition that each individual perform their own job and not interfere with anyone else. And if each person is performing their own job, then, even more critically, each class will also be performing its proper function. It is this maintenance of the proper divisions between the classes that can strictly be termed justice in the city (4.434c).

Justice, therefore, appears on this account to be in Socrates' view unquestionably beneficial to the city: it makes for peace and security, wise ruling and harmony between the classes. Without it, he says, the city would simply fall apart. But the challenge of Glaucon and Adeimantus, and of Thrasymachus before them, was directed at justice in the *individual*: can Socrates show that justice in the individual operates in a similar way? Can he show that the individual's *psyche* is also somehow divided into three parts? My intention is not to analyse the validity of the analogy in any detail, but rather try to appreciate why Plato thinks the notion of psychic harmony can only properly be understood by placing it in a political and social setting.[6]

THE TRIPARTITE *PSYCHE* AND PSYCHIC HEALTH

In *Republic* 4.435e, Socrates claims that three basic character traits exist in humanity at large: love of learning, a spirited element and a money-loving element. His next step should be to try to show that, albeit in varying degrees, each trait exists in every individual. He omits this step, however, but he does include the following one: namely to try to show that the individual does not display each trait in the same part[7] of themselves, but that the three traits are evidence for three divisions in the individual human *psyche*. He does this by appealing to the evident phenomenon of psychic conflict: 'One and the same thing cannot act or be affected in opposite ways at the same time in the same part of itself and in relation to the same object' (4.436b). As we may simultaneously have an impulse towards and an aversion from the same thing, these contradictory desires must arise in different parts of the *psyche*. Socrates then proceeds to give examples of different kinds of psychic conflict, which he claims show that there are three main 'parts' – or perhaps more accurately 'faculties' – in the individual, embodied human *psyche*:

reason, analogous to the Rulers; a spirited element (*thumoeides*), analogous to the Auxiliaries; and the appetites, analogous to the Producers. We later learn (9.580d–581b) that each faculty also has its own particular desires: reason desires truth and reality; the *thumoeides* desires honour and success; and the appetites desire physical satisfactions and material comforts and the money that may be needed to acquire them. Socrates' arguments for these three faculties are controversial,[8] but here we need only concern ourselves with the supposed conclusion, namely the theory of the tripartite *psychē*, and the way Socrates employs it to identify the state of *eudaimonia* and the state of *aretē* (excellence or virtue). The individual, he claims, will be wise if reason is in control, ruling for the good of the whole *psychē*; courageous if the *thumoeides* supports the decrees of reason; and temperate if all three faculties are in 'friendly and harmonious agreement' that reason should rule, and there is no civil war amongst them. Justice – as in the city – will be the condition that makes all this possible, namely that each psychic faculty perform its own specific function (4.441c–442d). Socrates sums up in a key passage from 4.443c–444a; it is so fundamental to our inquiry that it is worth quoting in full:

> Justice, therefore, we may say, is a principle of this kind; its real concern is not with external actions, but with a person's inward self, their true concern and interest. The just person will not allow the three elements which make up their inward self to trespass on each other's functions or interfere with each other, but, by keeping all three in tune, like the notes of a scale (high, middle, and low, and any others there be), will in the truest sense set their house to rights, attain self-mastery and order, and live on good terms with themselves. When they have bound these elements into a disciplined and harmonious whole, and so become fully one instead of many, they will be ready for action of any kind, whether it concerns their personal or financial welfare, whether it is political or private; and they will reckon and call any of these actions just and honourable if it contributes to and helps to maintain this disposition, and will call the knowledge which

controls such action wisdom. Similarly, they will call unjust any action destructive of this disposition, and the opinions which control such action ignorance.

As justice in the city brought about peace, security and concord, so justice in the individual allows them to keep 'all three elements in tune, like the notes of a scale'. The just person can live at peace with themselves, and channel all their energies into achieving their overall goals, because they have become 'fully one instead of many, self-controlled and harmonious'. Injustice, on the other hand, is a 'kind of civil war' (4.444b), which occurs when the elements of the mind are 'confused and displaced'.

Justice is therefore, Socrates concludes, unquestionably to the benefit of the individual as well as the city, and injustice is unquestionably to the individual's detriment. Indeed, there is an exact analogy between health and sickness in the body and in the *psychē* (4.444c). Exactly as 'health is produced by establishing a natural relation of control and subordination among the constituents of the body, disease by establishing an unnatural relation', so 'justice is produced by establishing in the *psychē* a similar natural relation of control and subordination among its constituents, and injustice by establishing an unnatural one'. Consequently 'it seems, then, that excellence (*aretē*) is a kind of psychic health or beauty or fitness, and defect a kind of illness or deformity or weakness', and each is the result of one's practice, good and bad. Glaucon and Socrates go on to agree that we all want psychic health at least as much as we want physical health; there is therefore a very strong implication that this state of psychic harmony can also be identified with flourishing, with *eudaimonia*: Glaucon certainly says that our lives would not be worth living if our psychic harmony disintegrated, and Socrates concurs. In contemptuously dismissing the value of justice, Thrasymachus was also unwittingly dismissing the value of psychic health and flourishing. If he had known what he was talking about, he would not have said what he did.

It is hard to overstate what a pivotal moment this is in the history of Western thought. It is the first time that the concept of 'psychic health' (or 'mental health', *hygieia . . . psychēs*) appears in our extant sources, and we shall be looking at connections with Freud shortly. The identification of both *eudaimonia* and *aretē* with the same internal state of psychic health is a real turning point: justice no longer primarily consists in external actions – as the previous speakers had conceived it – but is a profound internal state. Amongst Socrates' interlocutors, Glaucon and Adeimantus at least fully understand the importance of the theory: at 504a, Adeimantus says that the analysis of the tripartite *psychē* is fundamental to the entire discussion. It is true that in 10.611–612 there is a suggestion that the true self is to be identified with reason alone, but this seems to refer to which faculty will live on after the death of the body; there is nothing to indicate that the embodied *psychē* is anything other than tripartite.

PSYCHIC HARMONY

The key to understanding this ideal internal state is the musical terminology that Plato deliberately employs: flourishing and excellence are a matter of psychic *harmony*. Psychic harmony, and the grace and beauty of life that flow from it, are utterly foundational to the moral and political programme of the entire dialogue. At *Republic* 9.588a, for instance, the just person is said to be superior to the unjust person in terms of 'grace and beauty of life', while at 9.591d we are told that the just person attunes the harmony of their body to the harmony of their *psychē*, since they are the 'true *mousikos*', the person truly living in accord with the Muses.

Three key points need to be emphasized immediately. Firstly, harmony of *psychē* and life is viewed as both aesthetically and morally beautiful. Secondly, this beauty is also portrayed as *beneficial* to the agent: as we have seen, the beautiful psychic harmony that comprises justice also comprises the flourishing, the *eudaimonia*, of the agent. And, thirdly, as this psychic health manifests itself in being 'one instead of many', it is naturally suggestive of a *whole* person, living a *whole* life – and that in turn leads again to the view that a person and their life can be seen and assessed in terms of narrative shape.

Given how much therefore depends on the notion of harmony here, it is vital that we consider what it entails. The original meaning of *harmonia* is a 'joining', or 'fitting-together'; the expert practitioners are carpenters. However, it swiftly takes on two musical meanings (and we should note that neither of these meanings embraces complex harmony as we understand it today). Its primary musical sense refers to the building blocks of melody: a tuning or fitting-together of notes, a pattern of pitches and intervals – in other words, a scale. We have already seen how Plato was impressed by the work on geometric proportion undertaken by the Pythagoreans whom he visited in southern Italy; his imagination was particularly fired by their discovery that these building blocks of melody could be analysed in terms of mathematical ratios and patterns. He was also intrigued by their supposition that these same ratios and patterns might govern the cosmos as a whole: in the fifth century, Philolaus had argued that the cosmos is a true *harmonia*,[9] and in the fourth century Plato's friend Archytas (a former pupil of Philolaus) was the first person on record to talk of 'geometrical proportion' (fr. 2); he may therefore have been the originator of the distinction between 'geometrical equality' and 'arithmetical equality' that we shall see in the next chapter playing such an important role in the *Gorgias*.[10]

The Pythagorean approach to *harmonia* is based on *quantitative* analysis. But there was also a *qualitative* approach pioneered by a mysterious fifth-century sophist called Damon, a friend and advisor to the statesman Pericles and friend of Socrates (and one of the sophists whom Plato respected). Damon claimed that there were special types of scale – special patterns of tuning – associated with particular characteristics and emotional effects. These patterns of tuning are named after particular ethnic groups (for example, the Dorian, Phrygian, Lydian and Ionian), and when used in this sense *harmoniai* are usually translated as 'modes' (e.g. *Republic* 3.398d–399c).

Whichever of these two musical senses of *harmonia* Plato has uppermost in mind in any particular passage, the same fundamental point holds: when he is talking about the *psychē* being in a state of internal harmony, he is talking about it being in tune.

THE *KALON* AND EARLY EDUCATION

What, then, is the theoretical underpinning of Plato's notion of psychic harmony in both quantitative and qualitative senses? The answer lies in the concept of the *kalon*, a term which embraces both outward aesthetic beauty and inner moral beauty, moral nobility. It exerts a strong power of attraction even before reason has fully developed; it merits admiration and praise. But what connects outer and inner beauty? The answer again lies in mathematics: both kinds of beauty arise from the 'correct' mathematical proportions and ratios that, as we saw in the Introduction, Plato believes structure the entire cosmos (*Gorgias* 508a–b; *Timaeus* 36a, 87c, 90c–d). For Plato, what is *kalon* is always an objective matter; he accepts that people will differ in their opinions about what is beautiful, but he firmly holds that some people will simply be wrong, and others right.

The crucial importance of the *kalon* in forming the tastes and character of the young child is made clear in a key passage from *Republic* 3.400c–403c, a passage which sums up the primary education of the future Guardians (the future Rulers and Auxiliaries). Socrates has already emphasized at 2.377b that young children are particularly impressionable and mimetic. He now highlights how artistic and aesthetic influences can be absorbed and emulated not only through formal education in *mousikē* (poetry and music), but also informally through immersion in the human-made environment. True, objective outer beauty is created by those who possess true, objective inner moral beauty – a moral beauty which is the internalization of reason, of *logos*. Furthermore, even though the formal identification of psychic harmony with both *eudaimonia* and *aretē* does not occur until the Book 4 passage cited above, it is already emphasized here that there is an intimate connection between beauty (both aesthetic and moral) and the good and beneficial. Socrates is claiming, firstly, that immersion in aesthetic beauty will help inculcate moral beauty in the child and that this is to the benefit of the child; and, secondly, that a child who can appreciate aesthetic beauty, and convert it into inner moral beauty, will naturally welcome the development of reason when they are a little older, and the understanding reason offers of *why* both outer and inner beauty are beneficial to our psychological health. As a result: 'we must look for artists and craftsmen capable of perceiving the real nature of what is beautiful (*kalon*), and then our young men[11] living as it were in a healthy climate, will benefit because all the works they see and hear influence them for good, like the healthy breezes from wholesome places . . .' (3.401c–d).

He continues:

> . . . That . . . is why this nurture in the arts is crucial. For rhythm and harmony penetrate deeply into the mind and take a most powerful hold on it, and, if the upbringing is good, bring and impart grace and beauty; if it is bad, the reverse. And moreover the proper upbringing we propose to give will make a man quick to perceive the shortcomings of works of art or nature, whose ugliness he will rightly dislike; anything beautiful he will welcome gladly, will take into his *psychē* and so grow into a truly fine person; anything ugly he will rightly condemn and dislike, even when he is still young and cannot understand the reason for so doing, while when reason comes he will recognize and welcome it as a familiar friend because of his upbringing.

The proportions that account for beauty can be appreciated by very young children, long before they understand the mathematics behind them (if indeed they ever do). Children can respond to beauty from birth and absorb it into different layers of their *psychai*; beauty can thus profoundly shape the development of a child's character. And as outer and inner beauty naturally attract us and inspire love and desire, the early-education programme outlined by Socrates in the *Republic* is summed up at 3.403a as the proper guidance in our capacity to love – a key point that we will be exploring in chapter 6.

THE ROLE OF THE *THUMOEIDES*

How is this pre-rational penetration of the *psychē* by beauty to be brought about? The 'middle part' of the tripartite *psychē*, the *thumoeides*, has a vital role to play in the achievement of psychic harmony. Although the innate reasoning capabilities of young children are not yet fully realized, the *thumoeides* is robustly active from birth, and because it desires honour and success, it is naturally inclined towards those characters, actions and works of art which are already honoured and praised in the surrounding society. It has a natural sensitivity towards those things, people and actions which its society calls *kala*, fine and beautiful, and if this sensitivity is guided towards true *kala*, then the *thumoeides* will be able to perform its proper function of being the ally of the reasoning faculty. Although *Republic* 3.410b–412a makes it clear that education in the arts (*mousikē*) is mainly aimed at training reason, while physical training (*gymnastikē*) is mainly aimed at the *thumoeides*, a properly guided *thumoeides* can nevertheless do much to pave the way for the proper development of reason.

Republic 3.411b–412a is particularly important here in that it vividly describes the power of aural and visual stimuli to penetrate deep into the *psychē*, and the consequent need to achieve the correct balance between *mousikē* and *gymnastikē* in early education. Too much *mousikē*, or *mousikē* in the wrong harmonic mode, slackens and eventually destroys the 'sinews of the *psychē*', leaving the young person weak and cowardly. Excessive physical training, on the other hand, makes those same psychic sinews too taut and brittle: it is vital that the reasoning faculty and the *thumoeides* are tuned to the right pitch. The educator who can do this, who can correctly tune the *psychē*, is therefore, Socrates says, able to produce music of far more significance to the *polis* than any artist.

Plato's conception of the *thumoeides* is of profound significance, and one of the many reasons he still matters.[12] It is a faculty that is often overlooked in discussions of his work, but his specific deployment of characters, both as participants in the dialogues and as examples alluded to, is often guided by whether he regards their

HARMONY AND THE GOOD LIFE

thumoeides to be in a healthy or unhealthy state: does the character honour the right things, and seek the right kind of success? If the yearning for honour is one of our deepest needs, then the easiest route to attaining it is to emulate those whom our society already honours. This is another reason why Plato's ethics of flourishing leads swiftly to a forensic examination of society's current heroes (such as Achilles and Odysseus), and why he realizes that he needs to create new heroes, such as Socrates; we shall be exploring these rich and complex issues in chapter 5. Psychic harmony, in other words, will almost always need the right political and social conditions for its achievement; it will almost always require a society which honours the right role models. In the *Republic*, as we will see in chapter 4, Plato comes to the drastic conclusion that new, suitable role models will need a new society to endorse them, and in which they can more easily be emulated.

REASON AND THE FORMS

What does it mean to welcome reason as a friend? We have seen that reason desires truth and reality and in *Republic* Book 5 Socrates argues that the world of phenomena around us which we perceive with our senses – the phenomenal world – is not truly real; the only things that are truly real are what he calls the perfect, unchanging, non-sensible *Forms* of Goodness and Beauty and Justice and so on, and in Book 10 he includes Forms of both animate and inanimate objects as well. It is the Form of Beauty, for instance, that connects all the beautiful things and people and acts in this world, and it allows us to arrive at our concept of beauty. The Form itself, however, is more than the concept; it would exist even if there were no humans to apprehend it.[13] The world we perceive with our senses is simply a shadowy copy of reality; it is only the intelligible realm of the perfect Forms that is truly real.

We shall be discussing the Forms and their political implications in more depth in chapter 4. For now, I simply want to argue that Plato's theory of psychic harmony, flourishing and virtue is of real value and applicability now even if – perhaps especially if – one does *not* believe in the Forms (at any rate as they are described in the *Republic*). Plato's views on psychic harmony, and how it is to be achieved through early immersion in beauty, certainly raise serious concerns, and we shall be considering some of them shortly. These concerns, however, should not prevent us from seeing what a rich theory it is, and how, with appropriate modifications, it can help us address some substantive contemporary issues.

PSYCHIC HARMONY AND MENTAL HEALTH

Firstly, we should note that it presents a very *positive* and value-imbued conception of psychological health, which involves far more than the mere absence of illness or disease; Plato would not be sympathetic to many contemporary attempts to articulate and defend supposedly value-free conceptions of either physical or mental functioning (when they are articulated at all), whether that functioning is directed at individual survival or the reproduction of the species.[14] However, as illness and disease are then often conceived in terms of the absence of health, the argument quickly becomes circular, confused and unhelpful. For Plato, the understanding and achievement of both physical and psychological health involve nothing less than a full and conscious appreciation of what it is to be human. Of course, the reason much of modern healthcare avoids such value-imbued terminology is because it also wants to avoid being prescriptive: the aim is the delivery of healthcare divested of the values of particular health practitioners. Plato's theory clearly challenges this understandable and well-meaning approach, but in a way which I think it is at least useful to ponder. Perhaps all conceptions of both mental and physical health are in fact *inevitably* imbued with values and norms, whether consciously or not – values and norms which ultimately depend on the speaker's conception of what it is to be a human and live a fully human life; and these conceptions vary hugely, geographically, historically and culturally. To take just one example: someone behaving in such a way that would nowadays have people calling urgently for an ambulance might in a previous century have had them regarded as a saint. Whichever model of mental health you select or assume, there will always somewhere be someone who disputes it, someone who argues that they cannot, or choose not, to reproduce, or to exercise all their faculties, or to function in ways that their surroundings would seem to require; they may not even choose to survive. If this is the case, then perhaps Plato is simply being honest about bringing to light what is usually concealed. We might then do well to take seriously the fundamental message that we cannot know how to treat a sick or unbalanced human until we have a clear idea of what it means to be a healthy one, and we cannot know this until we have an understanding of what it means to be a human being at all.

As Plato also believes that humans need to live within society out of economic, political and ethical necessity, he holds in consequence that the full psychic health of an individual cannot be properly considered, let alone achieved, outside the appropriate political, social and artistic conditions: true, positive health is by no means just a matter for the medical profession. We need to create a culture and society that actively promote the notion of psychic harmony and help prevent fragmentation, disharmony and illness – a society, in short, that focuses on prevention at least as much as cure. The inevitable consequence of this, both challenging and liberating, is that healthcare professionals cannot work in isolation, but must work in conjunction with, amongst others, educators, architects, urban planners, artists and politicians. Here too, even if we have decided reservations about Plato's prescriptions, and the objective – indeed absolute – values and norms that underpin them, his ideas deserve our serious consideration.

REASON AND FREEDOM

To appreciate this more fully we need to delve a little deeper into precisely why Socrates in the *Republic* claims that only reason is able to rule for the good of the *psychē* as a whole, and why as a result psychic harmony and health can only be achieved if reason is in control. We have seen how all three parts of the *psychē* possess their own objects of desire: the appetites for physical satisfactions and money; the *thumoeides* for honour, victory and success; and reason for truth and reality. However, only the person in whom reason rules, claims Socrates, has the intelligence, knowledge and experience of all the desires to make an informed choice about their relative value and consequently judge which way of life is the most pleasurable (*Republic* 582a–d). Simply being content with our current life is not enough: we also need to know whether our life would be pleasanter and we would flourish more fully if we were experiencing a different kind of pleasure and life, and only reason, Socrates says, has access to this knowledge. This is largely because only reason can apprehend the perfect, immutable, non-sensible explanatory principles that are the Forms.; above all it is the only faculty that can apprehend the Form of the Good. It is this argument in Book 9 which explains why in Book 4 Socrates claims that reason is the only part that is concerned for the good of the *psychē* as a whole (441e). It is the job of reason to assess the desires of each part and seek to satisfy the 'truest and best' of those desires (9.586e–587a) and, in so doing, it will quite properly give priority to its own desires for knowledge and reality. This is partly because, in a highly contentious move, Socrates claims that only the pleasures of reason are truly real because only they are directed towards real objects – namely the Forms (9.583b–587a). The appetites, on the other hand, are naturally greedy and insatiable and, if left to their own devices without rational control, will rapidly lead to an upsetting of our ideal internal balance. They always want more and they focus obsessively on their object without paying regard to that object's true worth (4.437e–438a). In contrast, the kind of order which stems from rational control imitates the order of the realm of the Forms (6.500c–e).

Such a theory clearly gives rise again to the question raised above: namely, can such views have anything of value to say to those of us who do not believe in the Forms (at least as they are articulated here), and who do not subscribe to the view that pleasures (as opposed to the objects that give rise to pleasure) can be more or less real? Again, I believe the answer is yes, and one of the most important reasons why this is so is the strong link that Plato has Socrates make between reason and freedom. This connection is possible because Plato is not here primarily concerned with freedom in the sense of lack of interference from others (although he is perfectly well aware that that is how the term is often interpreted),[15] or with freedom in the (possibly incoherent) sense of 'could have done otherwise'; what Plato is interested in is freedom in the sense of acting in accordance with one's true wishes, where 'true wishes' are not the whims of the moment (for which Plato usually employs the term *epithumia*, or the phrase '*moi dokei* + infinitive', 'it seems (good) to me to . . .'), but arise as a result of informed reflection on the nature of one's best overall interests (for which Plato often uses the term *boulēsis*).[16]

At *Republic* 9.577e, for example, we are told that the *psychē* which is tyrannized by the rule of one of the irrational desires will be 'least able to do what, as a whole, it wishes (*boulomai*), because it is under the compulsive drive of madness, and so full of confusion and remorse'. In contrast, rational, informed wishes are wishes that we *want* to have, that accord with what are now termed second-order desires;[17] and they are wishes that only reason can enable us to form or approve. For Plato, the psychic harmony that only reason can create and which is constitutive of both flourishing and moral excellence is, precisely, the state of psychic freedom. Neither (what we might distinguish as) the morally wicked person nor the mentally unwell person is free: both are in the grip of irrational desires and obsessions, and in extreme cases of moral wickedness (such as the tyrant, as we will see in chapter 4), wickedness and mental illness will coincide in culpable mania.

This fundamental link claimed between reason and freedom has been of profound significance in the history of Western philosophy and political thought, and is one of the chief reasons why Plato still matters, even if we do not subscribe to the Forms or a belief in 'true' or 'false' pleasures. However, we may still want to ask whether Plato himself thinks this freedom is available to all, or only applies to the Philosopher-Rulers, and within the context of the ideal city. The answer is nuanced. In the *Republic*, certainly, perfect freedom will only be possible for the perfectly rational Philosopher-Rulers, and this perfect rationality can only be achieved by training in the ideal education system and immersion in ideal artistic and cultural conditions. However, we should also remember that the conversation between Socrates, Glaucon, Adeimantus and the rest itself takes place within the very different social and political environment of Socrates' Athens. The conception of psychic harmony that Socrates proposes may look rather different, and be achieved rather differently (if in Plato's eyes necessarily imperfectly), when transposed from the ideally just city to a far more compromised world in which no ideally rational beings exist. The fact that Socrates argues that ideally rational harmony and perfect freedom can only exist in an ideally rational city does not mean that Plato thinks the concept has no use or application if imperfectly realized in an imperfect city or society.

This possibility, however, still compels us to question the relation between reason and its environment. On the one hand, reason can allow us to scrutinize the values of our culture and liberate us from simply being the product of our genes and that culture; on the other hand, reason can only do this if it is sufficiently trained, and this sufficient training will of course depend on the practices of that same culture, and who has access to them. This will also hold true in imperfect cultures where the education of reason falls short of Plato's ideal. In the *Republic*, Socrates is admirably clear about this: whether reason can take an objective overview of all the desires of the *psychē* will depend not just on its existence, but on its ability to function properly as ruler. If the *thumoeides* or appetitive part is in control, and reason is weak and undeveloped (smothered by the barnacles of its temporary incarnation, as Socrates puts it graphically in 10.611b–e), then the fundamental ethical questions either will not be asked at all, or will be answered according not to rational but to thumoeidic or appetitive objectives. And given that the precise nature of these thumoeidic and appetitive objectives is formed by the immediate cultural and physical environment, the answers of the enslaved reason will be similarly confined. In the depictions of imperfect cities and individuals in *Republic* Books 8 and 9, Plato gives us some vivid and depressing portraits of what happens to reason when it is stunted or perverted by its environment. The links between individual and city go much deeper than the surface analogy might suggest.

So the pressing question we need to ask is what degree of freedom does Plato think reason can achieve outside of the perfect education system and setting of the ideal city? However, I think the answer should encourage us. Given that he feels very free to critique Athens, and the historic Socrates did the same, it is clear that Plato believes a significant amount of freedom can be achieved even in imperfect circumstances. This further strengthens the possibility of contemporary modifications and applications of his notions of psychic harmony and an ethics of flourishing.

PLATO, FREUD AND ARISTOTLE

Before considering such modified applications, however, we should also take note of the fact that, even if Plato is not always acknowledged as the source, his conception of psychic harmony has been very influential, and two of the thinkers he influenced *are* acknowledged explicitly (whether with approval or not) in contemporary discussions of psychological well-being: namely, Freud and Aristotle. Freud had a profound admiration for, in his terminology, 'divine' Plato and considerable – albeit apparently fragmentary – knowledge of some of his works, particularly the *Symposium* and parts of the *Republic* and *Phaedrus*.[18] Such respect is particularly illuminating in that Freud's thinking developed in part from extensive clinical practice, a resource which Plato clearly did not possess. Although Freud does not explicitly say that his tripartition of ego, superego and id was influenced by Plato's tripartition of reason, the *thumoeides* and the appetites, the connections between the two tripartitions suggest that there is at least a case to be made for subliminal influence;[19] we may particularly note the central importance in both thinkers of the notion of a healthy *psychē*/psyche being harmonious and integrated, as opposed to the discordant fragmentation of a psyche in ill health. Freud *does* explicitly remark on the similarities between his concept of the libido and Plato's conception of *erōs* as a stream of erotic energy which can be guided onto different objects, and we will be discussing this in chapter 6.

However, perhaps the most profound and lasting influence of Plato's theory of psychic harmony, *eudaimonia* and virtue was on Aristotle, his student (and later research associate) at the Academy. Contemporary versions of an ethics of flourishing and virtue usually reference Aristotle rather than Plato, but in fact, although there are significant differences between Plato's and Aristotle's ethical foundations – Aristotle does not subscribe to the theory of Forms, for instance, and his tripartite psychology is rather different – in many other respects Aristotle's ethics of flourishing and virtue builds on Plato's model. It, too, is agent-centred and focuses on the excellent actualization of our various faculties, the objective fulfilment of our potential. Both Plato's and Aristotle's versions have overlapping contemporary applications (though here we will of course concentrate on Plato). But both, too, raise serious questions and very similar challenges; before considering the contemporary potential of Plato's original version of an ethics of flourishing, therefore, we need to be transparent about the further difficulties his version presents and ask whether they, too, can be addressed.

PLATO'S ETHICS OF FLOURISHING: THE CHALLENGES

The threat of repression
An immediate task is to probe Plato harder on why he thinks that psychic harmony can only exist if reason is in control. Despite the links he claims between reason and freedom, it certainly seems to be an undemocratic model, to say the least: just as the Producers have no political voice in the city, so the appetites have only a minimal say in shaping the agent's life. When reason is in control, the best the non-rational desires can hope for is that reason will satisfy the 'best and truest' amongst them (*Republic* 9.586e–587a). Plato, no great fan of direct democracy, may not be particularly bothered by such a charge, but it may well give us pause for thought. Might not

the control of reason lead to damaging repression of many of our appetites and desires? Might not Plato be creating the conditions for mental illness rather than mental health?[20]

Plato has a response to such a charge, however, and it is one of which Freud approved: Plato suggests that there is an important difference between the dangerous *blocking* of desire and its *rechannelling* onto different objects. At *Republic* 6.485d, Socrates says that 'we know that if someone's desires set strongly in one direction, they are correspondingly less strong in other directions, like a stream whose water has been diverted into another channel'. We will see in chapter 6 how this passage connects to Diotima's account of the Ladder of Love in the *Symposium*; to anticipate briefly, if reason directs operations well, those appetites which it deems inappropriate to satisfy will not simply be blocked and thwarted, with potentially disastrous results, but diverted onto more wholesome and constructive objects and goals. As we will see, in practice the picture is rather more complicated and talk of rechannelling can sometimes be undercut by the language of repression. However, although the hydraulic model may not satisfy all the questions we may have about putting reason in control, it does go some way to answering one of the most important concerns.

Political and psychiatric abuse
An even more problematic charge stems from the identification of moral goodness with psychic harmony and health, and moral badness with psychic disharmony and illness. Would this not open the door to political and psychiatric abuse, of the kind we see, for example, in Alexander Solzhenitsyn's works, or Ken Kesey's novel *One Flew Over the Cuckoo's Nest* (and Miloš Forman's film)? Furthermore, even if the politician or doctor is genuinely well-intentioned, skilled and well-informed, some may still protest that the need for each individual to direct their own life – the need for autonomy – is simply too important to be overridden by professional expertise. Can these dangers and problems be averted? Although it is not possible to go into detail here (we will consider the topic a little more in chapter 4), I think perhaps they

can, through an account of psychological health and the rule of reason which emphasizes the importance of personal autonomy. However, this would then appear to conflict with the requirement in the *Republic* that the Producer and Auxiliary classes submit to the rational rule of the Philosopher-Rulers. Plato's psychological model can certainly be usefully modified, but to do so it will need to be taken out of the context of the ideally just city that Socrates describes.

A hierarchy of flourishing
The requirement that Producers and Auxiliaries submit to the superior reason of the Philosopher-Rulers stems from the fact that in the *Republic* Socrates speaks as if there is *one* ideal norm of psychic harmony, perfectly exemplified by the Philosopher-Rulers, which will result in a hierarchy of the kind of *eudaimonia* that individuals can achieve: Producers and Auxiliaries will indeed achieve the best lives of which they are capable, but such lives will still embody an objectively lower grade of flourishing than those of the Philosopher-Rulers. Slaves, and the mentally or physically disabled, will achieve lower grades still.[21] This will rightly make most of us feel decidedly queasy. If the notion of the actualization of potential is individualized, however, then the flourishing of an individual could depend not on where they fit into a single hierarchy, but the degree to which they are actualizing their *individual* capabilities. In other words, the modification would comprise an ethic founded on a notion of good *lives*, rather than on a single norm of the good *life* – but again an ethic which will require the model of psychic harmony to be removed from the setting of the ideal city. However, there will still need to be robust political and social support if individualized fulfilment is to be realized.

Education in beauty
What of the programme suggested in *Republic* Book 3 for achieving this harmony through immersing the young child in a beautiful environment? Clearly if the beautiful works of art and artefacts that Socrates describes ultimately derive their beauty from the Form of

Beauty then this will immediately present a stumbling block to all those who do not believe in the Forms, at least as they are usually thought to be presented in the *Republic*. But even if we decide to disregard the Forms, we are still left with the undeniable fact that Plato views goodness and beauty as objective, and, again, this is plainly not a view that would be universally (or perhaps even widely) accepted – though proponents of a subjective view of beauty might still be asked to account for the fact that people's subjective views of what is and is not beautiful can display considerable levels of agreement. Many may also question Plato's preference for aesthetic beauty perceived through the senses which can operate at a distance – sight and hearing – over beauty which is appreciated through direct physical contact, through touch and taste.[22] Furthermore, it is not just that beauty for Plato is a matter of objective perfection, but also (as we will be exploring in chapter 6) that this perfection is *homogeneous*: there is only one kind of beauty, greater or lesser in degree depending on the extent to which it participates in the Form. Is there to be no room for individual artistic expression and experimentation?

There is also another, very serious, challenge which applies to the connection Plato makes between aesthetics and ethics, and which does not depend on the contingency of a warped political or medical regime abusing definitions of moral goodness and health. What of the well-attested fact that many very wicked people, who have committed the most terrible atrocities, have claimed – and are still claiming – to take pleasure in the arts? Joseph Goebbels, minister of propaganda for the German Third Reich under Hitler, was a cultured man who enjoyed literature and music (although his tastes were principally for Germanic works, which makes one wonder whether he was chiefly responding to artistic quality or the nationality of the artist). Clearly his exposure to artistic beauty and his aesthetic experiences did not make him into a good person, or someone we would point to as a fine example of mental health. Is there any possible Platonic response to such a grave charge?

One response might be to say that such people were not sufficiently immersed in beauty from early enough in childhood – but this strikes me as a rather lazy answer, and surely inadequate: it is not hard to find examples of wicked people who grew up in cultured homes. Another easy – and again perhaps also lazy – answer would be to say that Plato would not allow the music of, for example, Wagner or Schubert to count as genuinely, objectively beautiful. But this is also unsatisfying: Plato might well have been appalled by the mixed media and dubious morals of opera, and even Schubert might have been dismissed as too extravagantly emotional, but it is hard to see what he would have objected to in the mathematical perfection of Bach, for instance, or the purity of Arvo Pärt.[23]

I think a more satisfying response to this very serious challenge may lie in Plato's tripartite psychology itself, and in particular the crucial passages quoted above from *Republic* 3.401d–402a and 3.411b–412a. Plato could reasonably ask *how deeply* has the music – or whatever art form – penetrated into the individual's *psychē*? Is the sound simply being enjoyed by the appetitive element at a surface level, or is it also penetrating and shaping the spirited (thumoeidic) and, critically, the reasoning elements? Socrates certainly claims that rhythm and harmony can impart grace and beauty if they penetrate the *psychē* deeply – but he also claims that this will only happen if the upbringing and education of an individual are good. A child could grow up with some access to beauty but still not be introduced to it in a way that allows deep psychic penetration to occur. And if Plato were to claim that in some cases beauty is simply not penetrating beyond a superficial level, he could have a point. If someone planning and executing the destruction of a peaceful city and its innocent civilians claims to take pleasure in, for example, Beethoven's 'Ode to Joy', but still continues with their wanton annihilation immediately after hearing it, then I think we can justly say that at some deeper level they have simply failed to appreciate and internalize the music and its rousing call for human friendship and unity.[24]

CONTEMPORARY APPLICATIONS

However, although there can be Platonic responses to some of the difficulties and challenges, few people now would want to adopt

Plato's ethics (and politics) of flourishing with any exactitude. Nevertheless, I still want to argue that, as the foundation of an ethical approach based on flourishing and virtue, there is much in his views on *eudaimonia* and *aretē* from which we can learn, and which we can update and apply to contemporary concerns, even if we do not believe in the Forms and the conception of goodness and beauty as absolutes, or the single hierarchy of *eudaimonia* that results. One point about which I think Plato is profoundly right is his understanding that an ethics of flourishing and virtue is achieved much more easily in the appropriate social and cultural conditions (even if we disagree with his interpretation of 'appropriate') — both in respect of education and also because certain virtues (such as justice) require a social context in order to be exercised. In other words, an ethics of flourishing cannot be divorced from a (small 'p', and sometimes large 'P') politics of flourishing. If we take from Plato the basic notion that individual flourishing involves the excellent actualization and harmonization of our faculties, and that this involves, if not identification, then at least very close links between flourishing and the various intellectual and moral virtues, then we can clearly see that an ethics of flourishing and virtue depends to a considerable extent on a politics of flourishing and virtue. Therefore, I believe that there are three areas in particular where a modified version of Plato's basic approach can be very helpful in addressing contemporary issues: education; healthcare; and urban and environmental planning.

Education
When considering the value of Plato to current pedagogy, I think it is helpful to distinguish the lessons we can apply to educational theory and practice in general from the specific study of some of his work by older schoolchildren and students. In respect of the former, in addition to the very clear message that education will need political support, both from national and local government and from the local community (the modern *polis*), it is also clear that the *aim* of education should be to enable children and young people to actualize all their faculties: intellectual, imaginative,

affective and physical. The fact that this may seem obvious is proof of the extent to which an ethics of flourishing which has its roots in Plato has influenced pedagogical practice. Perhaps slightly less obvious (and less palatable to some) is the further point that, if you agree with Plato that rationally guided emotional responses lead to morally appropriate choices and actions, then such intellectual and emotional development will necessarily involve character training too. If you further adopt his dialogic method that we discussed in chapter 1, then this method will form part of that training: recent studies have shown that philosophy provision in schools employing a dialogic method can increase confidence and a variety of social skills, including the ability to listen.[25] Above all, of course, the dialogic method enables students to *learn*: as we also saw in chapter 1, true learning for Plato has to be an internal and active process. As Socrates memorably puts it at *Republic* 7.518b–d, the educator cannot just put knowledge into a pupil's mind; the task of the educator is to turn the mind of the pupil in the direction of the light.

A vital point to note is that, if education is conceived within the context of a flourishing life, then it should assist the actualization of our faculties not only as a preparation for adulthood but also because the years of school attendance form a substantial part of any individual's life (and in some tragic cases, the whole of it). These years should be a time of flourishing in themselves: stimulating, fun and fulfilling (and this general point is also a good argument for including the study of some of Plato's dialogues by older pupils, as the dialogues tap into young people's natural curiosity, imagination and zest). These stimulating and enjoyable years of schooling should in addition help the young person start to form an idea of a flourishing life – what kind of shape and narrative it might take, and the links between individual and communal narratives.

Given these links between an ethics of *eudaimonia* and the idea of the shape or structure of a life, it follows that all the dimensions of a flourishing life – ethical, aesthetic and political – will again be greatly assisted through hearing, enacting and discussing *stories*: the form taken by the narrative of a different life is itself a part of that narrative. For young people raised on Harry Potter, Dr Who, *Game of Thrones*, *Lord of the Rings* and so on, fantastical leaps through time and space are an enticing challenge, not an obstacle. The task of the educator is to ensure that a rich variety of narratives, of characters and lives, is provided for reflection and discussion;[26] it is only by considering the narrative as a whole that young people can start to get a sense of what a flourishing or a stunted or warped life might look like, and what kind of intellectual, emotional and physical faculties need to be developed, and what intellectual and moral virtues fostered, in order to help a person enjoy a flourishing life and avoid a stunted one. Again, for older pupils, Plato's dialogues can be a valuable resource in this respect, inviting interpretation, questions and debate.

Healthcare
We have already considered the value of considering Plato's challenge to claims that conceptions of health should, or even could, be value-free: we have seen how, for Plato, all conceptions of psychic (and indeed physical) health are necessarily normative, and, whether we are aware of it or not, stem from our conception of what it is to be human. We have also considered the importance of his claim that both psychic and physical health can only be achieved, maintained and restored through the harmonization of our faculties, and that this requires a combination of different practitioners: educators, artists, designers and urban planners as well as those working directly in healthcare. In addition to these general points, however, I believe that Plato's ethics of flourishing can assist with very specific questions. In 2022, for instance, I was invited to write an Ethics Review of the UK's NHS Strategy Unit *Report on Strategies to Reduce Inequalities in Access to Planned Care*, and I found Plato's ethical approach very helpful at various stages of the care pathway, particularly in respect of the prioritization of waiting lists.[27] During the pandemic I also noted in a variety of forums how Plato's approach might be of use to policymakers in tackling one of the toughest ethical questions with which governments were confronted: namely, is it the task of a government to save life, or save quality of life?

Urban and environmental planning

There are a number of other fields in which Plato's ethics and politics of flourishing can offer a helpful resource for tackling contemporary issues, but I would particularly single out urban planning – and indeed farmed and wild environmental planning as a whole. We cannot know how to design our public spaces, or how to arrange for the best balance between farmed and wild in our rural environments, until we have a notion of what it might be for all the present and future inhabitants of those spaces (non-human animals and plants as well as humans) to flourish. This will of course involve extending Plato's theories beyond the human realm to include all living beings, and I am excited to see how such work progresses, and to assist it where I can. We have seen how Plato makes it crystal clear that, in order to achieve even only human flourishing, education, healthcare, art and urban and environmental planning are inextricably intertwined. In the centuries since he wrote, we have seen accumulating and now overwhelming evidence of how human flourishing – both individual and communal – is also inextricably intertwined with that of all living beings, and the earth and environment that supports us all. We need all the tools at our disposal to help us think through and tackle these grave and urgent problems, and Plato, I submit, can be of real assistance.

3

Democracy, Demagoguery and Tyranny

GORGIAS: THE POWER OF RHETORIC

We have seen how individual flourishing depends on a broader social and political context. It is now time to focus on this broader context in its own right, and there is no better place to start than the *Gorgias*, written, as we have also seen, around 487/6 , shortly after Plato's return from studying mathematics and harmonic theory with the Pythagorean communities in southern Italy. It is an extraordinary work, a heartfelt and sometimes angry defence of his own decision finally to abandon all thoughts of a formal political career in favour of philosophy. It had an immediate impact. The statesman, rhetorician and scholar Themistius, writing in the fourth century CE, claims that the dialogue had such a powerful effect on a farmer near Corinth that he 'forthwith left his fields and vines and committing his soul to Plato sowed and raised his teacher's doctrines for crops'.

Gorgias was a *rhētor* from Sicily, a term which embraces both teachers of rhetoric and orators, and he was renowned and widely respected in both departments. He was famous for his lengthy and flamboyant oratorical displays, lavishly adorned with flourishes of metaphor, rhyme and assonance. He had the highest opinion of rhetoric, claiming it could 'enchant, persuade and change the souls of men', and his opinion of his own abilities was hardly less elevated: there is a story that he dedicated a statue *of himself* to

Apollo at Delphi. In the dialogue he is on a visit to Athens and being treated as a superstar; he has just given one of his famed displays, but Socrates says he would rather engage him in conversation: in particular Socrates wants to know what rhetoric actually is and what it does.

Gorgias replies that rhetoric is concerned wholly with speech and is productive of persuasion in public gatherings, whether in the law courts or the Assembly or anywhere else, and it is immediately clear from his account that rhetoric will be of particular relevance in democracies such as Athens, where political influence and social standing depend on being able to hold sway at such gatherings. He goes on to emphasize that the art (as he terms it) of rhetoric endows its practitioners with freedom and power over others: in *Gorgias* 452e he actually uses the language of enslavement. Indeed, even if the orator is ignorant of a subject, he will be more persuasive than the expert, providing he is addressing people who are also ignorant. Gorgias casually acknowledges that rhetoric produces beliefs rather than knowledge, and equally casually admits that some orators abuse their powers,[1] but he says that teachers of rhetoric should not be blamed for the misdeeds of their students.

However, he also says that rhetoric deals particularly with the just and the unjust, with right and wrong, and that teachers of rhetoric *know* about the just and unjust and impart this knowledge to their students, and furthermore that those same students who have learned about the just and unjust must be just themselves, as those who have learned about building are builders and those who have learned about medicine are medical men. Socrates raises an objection: if this is the case, how then could orators also abuse their powers and act unjustly? However, the elderly Gorgias is tired, and allows his headstrong student Polus to take over.

If he felt so inclined, Gorgias could easily escape the logical inconsistency by rejecting either the claim that teachers of rhetoric teach right and wrong, or the claim that the person who knows justice themselves be just. Polus will in fact say that Gorgias should reject the first of these claims (as Gorgias does in fact do at *Meno* 95c). However, in the *Gorgias*, Gorgias is very keen to present rhetoric, teachers of rhetoric and the orators who practise rhetoric in the best possible light, and is reluctant to give up either of these claims – as Socrates probably knows. Nevertheless, this first interchange between Socrates and Gorgias is highly illuminating. It makes absolutely clear that the real subjects of the dialogue are power and freedom: what is the true nature of each; who really possesses them; and how do they interrelate? It also makes crystal clear the connection between rhetoric and sophistry: both can (ab)use words and act as a kind of harmful magic, distorting and obscuring the truth.

POLUS: FLATTERIES, ARTS AND FREEDOM

After saying that Gorgias should never have claimed that teachers of rhetoric teach right and wrong, Polus challenges Socrates to say what he, Socrates, takes the art (*technē*) of rhetoric to be. Socrates denies categorically that it is an art at all. He makes a key distinction between a true art and what he terms a flattery or knack which panders to the unreflective desires of the audience, and does not aim at what would be genuinely good for them but simply at their immediate gratification. Orators, and teachers of rhetoric, are simply panders, and through employing flatteries fall under the same general head as cooks, cosmeticians and sophists, whereas doctors, physical trainers and legislators practise genuine arts aimed at the good of those they address and treat. This general point is then clarified through a distinction between body and soul, and what truly tends to the good of each: physical training and medicine aim at the genuine good of the body; whereas cosmetic adornment and cookery are their counterpart flatteries which aim solely at pleasure. Similarly, legislation and justice aim at the true good of the soul, whereas their fake counterparts, sophistry and oratory, aim only at its gratification.

Polus protests, claiming vociferously that far from being mere flatterers, orators have as much power as tyrants to get people to do what they – the orators – wish them to do. Socrates, however, equally strongly denies that either tyrants or orators are truly powerful, because they can only do what *seems* to them to be best (*dokei autois beltista*, 467b), what they feel like doing, and not what they actually *choose* (*ha boulontai*),[2] since we would all choose what is actually best for us, and orators and tyrants do not know what that is – they do not understand the human good. They do not realize that by harming others they are damaging their own souls. Suffering wrong at the hands of others can only damage our bodies or material possessions; it is only by doing wrong ourselves that we can harm our souls.

It is a critical passage (466b–469e), and although Socrates concentrates on the freedom – or lack of it – of the tyrant and orator, it is also clear that the freedom of those deceived by the flatteries of oratory would also be badly undermined, in that they would not have the accurate information required to make a genuine choice (the circumscribed freedom of those living under tyranny is obvious).[3] Polus, however, is unconvinced: initially he appears to agree with Socrates' line of reasoning, but when asked to agree with the conclusion, that the tyrant is pitiable, he baulks and cites Archelaus, the murderous and scheming tyrant of Macedon. In Polus' view, Archelaus is *eudaimōn* and has a fabulous and enviable life.

No, says Socrates, he is utterly wretched, although his situation would be improved a little if he were punished for his crimes. What he and Polus are discussing are matters on which it is most honourable to have knowledge, and most shameful to lack it, namely who is flourishing (*eudaimōn*) and who is not (472c). Polus holds out, arguing that while it might be more *shameful* to do wrong than to suffer it, suffering wrong is much *worse*: what is shameful is different from what is harmful for the agent, and what is honourable and fine (*kalon*) is different from what is good and beneficial (*agathon*) for the agent. Socrates disagrees, arguing that if something is more shameful it must be more harmful for the agent, and if something is more honourable it must be more beneficial. He does this by pretty slippery means:

i) First, he defines the honourable (*kalon*) as something which either gives pleasure or brings benefit.

ii) He then defines its opposite, the shameful (*aischron*), as something which either gives pain or brings harm.
iii) So if doing wrong is more shameful than suffering it, it must either be more painful, or more harmful, or both.
iv) Since doing wrong is clearly not more painful than suffering it, it must be more harmful.

It is a slippery argument because a) the definition of the *kalon*, the honourable and beautiful, is too narrow, and b) it fails to address the utterly crucial question of *to whom* the pleasure or benefit is supposed to accrue. Polus has challenged Socrates to show that behaving unjustly to others will harm *the agent*, and by implication he has challenged Socrates to demonstrate that treating others justly will be to the agent's benefit.

Polus, however, does not spot these shortcomings – which may, of course, be a deliberate ruse on Plato's part, to prompt us to spot them for ourselves. Either way, Polus grudgingly agrees, but his claim that there can be a sharp divergence between honourable and beneficial courses of action from the agent's point of view is not really defeated, and it will require the more sophisticated psychology of the *Republic* to tackle it. In the *Gorgias*, Polus reluctantly lets Socrates forge ahead: the best thing, Socrates argues, is not to do wrong at all; however, if you do err, then you should turn yourself in forthwith and plead to be punished: this would be a good use of one's rhetorical skill and lead to the only means of purifying one's soul.

CALLICLES: MAN AND SUPERMAN

At this point Callicles – whom we met briefly in chapter 1 – can bear it no longer: really Socrates, he exclaims, are you joking or do you seriously intend to turn all of human life upside down? Polus, says Callicles, only got into difficulties because he was fool enough to kowtow to convention (*nomos*) and say that doing wrong was more shameful than suffering it: in fact it is suffering wrong that is more shameful because it shows that you are too weak to stand up for yourself and your own, and in nature (*physis*) weakness is the mark of the inferior being. The man who submits to wrong is not really a proper man at all (483b), but a mere slave; the real man – unlike Socrates,[4] Callicles focuses solely on the male – is the man with the natural ability to protect himself and his own and not be wronged in the first place. Laws and customs only say that doing wrong is more shameful than suffering it because they are made by the naturally weak majority to protect themselves against the naturally stronger few: this craven majority proclaim that equality of both power and wealth is fine and just because equality is the most they can possibly expect.

However, continues Callicles, if we look not to convention but to nature, we will see that in fact it is naturally right and fine for those who are superior in courage, 'manliness' and practical competence to rule the inferior and have more than an equal share of goods proportional to their superiority. This is not simply a brute fact but a prescription: it is the 'law of nature' as both the non-human animal world and relations between cities and peoples show. Strong men are like lions and the laws and conventions are the lions' chains; such men should, if at all possible, break free from such dishonourable imprisonment and 'trample underfoot all our rules and tricks and charms and laws which are all against nature'. Then the 'justice of nature' can finally blaze forth, and we will see in operation the poet Pindar's law of natural force, which declares that in the myth of his labours Heracles is justified in taking the cows of Geryones simply because he is the stronger of the two (484a–c).

Having set up his ideal of the superman, Callicles launches into a blistering attack on philosophers, whom he regards as pathetically lacking in such leonine attributes. While it is fine for a boy to dabble a little in philosophy, to continue with philosophic studies as an adult is ridiculous and unmanly: the adult philosopher is hopelessly ignorant of the ways of the world, and entirely inexperienced in the pleasures, desires and characters of men. If he ever has to engage in public affairs, he is bound to make a fool of himself, and he is equally bound to be lacking in manliness, since he spends his days huddled in corners with a few youths and avoids the social centres where men win glory. Utterly inexperienced in the characters of men, he is unable to protect himself or his own if wrongfully accused, he is a boy amongst men and a slave amongst the free. He would be much better off abandoning his philosophic fripperies and nonsense and instead emulate men of substance and renown.

Socrates proceeds to ask Callicles to say more clearly what he means in claiming that natural rulers should have more than the ruled, given that everyone is – or should be – both a ruler and a ruled, in that it is the task of reason to rule one's desires. Callicles is incensed: those who restrain their desires are simple-minded fools, and like those who allow others to harm them are in their lack of freedom no better off than slaves. The naturally fine (*kalon*) and just course of action is to let one's desires grow as great as possible and satisfy each in turn when it reaches its peak. The man who can do this, who has both powerful desires and the courage and manliness (*andreia*) and practical intelligence to satisfy them, is the man who 'lives rightly', and true *aretē* and *eudaimonia* consist in the luxury, licentiousness and liberty of such a man's happy existence. Most people, however, lack the ability to live like this, and so, just as in the political sphere, they invent a hypocritical code which calls moderation a virtue, and decry as shameful the magnificent rampageousness of the naturally superior few. The reality is that such conventional systems of morality are simply masks to conceal the impotence and unmanliness (*anandria*) of the servile masses, who willingly submit to the despotism of their artificial laws and censures. The craven agreements of these pathetic creatures are all against nature and not worth a jot.

Callicles thus thinks he believes that his political doctrine of might is right entails a private doctrine of unqualified hedonism: if one *can* do whatever one wants, whether in public or private life, it is right and noble that one *should*. Socrates, however, is able to demonstrate that he is not an unqualified hedonist at all, as he does not in fact consider all pleasures as equally good and fine: the clinching argument (497d–499b) is when Socrates asks him whether he approves of the pleasures of the coward, delighted to see the enemy retreating. Callicles admits that he wants to be able to distinguish between the cowardly and the courageous, and between bad and good men generally, and that therefore not all pleasures are good, and pleasure itself cannot be the same as the good.[5]

If unqualified hedonism does not in fact follow from a political 'might is right' position, however, then defeating unqualified hedonism will not defeat 'might is right'; Callicles' basic political position remains, and we need to gain a better understanding of the philosophic backdrop and political implications of his forceful opening speech. In terms of its backdrop, the key point is that it needs to be understood within the context of the late fifth- and early fourth-century debate – particularly amongst the sophists – about the relation (both actual and ideal) between *nomos* ('law' or 'convention') and *physis* ('nature'). Do laws and conventions help us express our true nature, or do they suppress it? Are they the glue that binds society together, as the sophist Protagoras believes, or, as Callicles holds, unacceptable chains? If *nomos* and *physis* appear to be pulling us in different directions, which should we follow? In the fragments of his work that survive, the sophist Antiphon appears to argue that, so long as we can get away with it, we should follow *physis*: *nomoi* are repressive shackles. The position taken by Callicles appears to be even more radical: he does not employ *nomos* solely in a conventional sense, but brings the two terms together, proclaiming the existence of a 'law of nature' in opposition to the laws promoting equality made by the democratic majority.

In doing this, he thus presents a particular challenge to Socrates as, unlike Polus, Callicles formally *agrees* with Socrates' harmonization of the fine and honourable (*kalon*) and the beneficial (*agathon*): he does indeed hold that virtue/excellence (*aretē*) and performing fine deeds will bring the agent personal benefit. The trouble is that he interprets both in ways which Socrates thinks are profoundly misguided. In this opening speech Callicles conceives of benefit solely in terms of power over others and material wealth (as we have seen, physical pleasure is later included too), and he then conceives of the *kalon* and natural *aretē* solely in terms of what will promote this conception of personal benefit, of personal well-being. The brand of egoism that Callicles advocates is not only psychological; it is also normative. Any political or social infringement on this notion of individual well-being is an unacceptable restriction on personal liberty and reduces the supposedly 'free' man to the condition of a slave. Plato makes vividly clear the contrast between the two visions for how we should live: when Callicles upbraids Socrates for not understanding the characters of men, the implication is that it is he, Callicles, who truly understands human nature.

The position taken by Callicles may be radical, but he is by no means alone at this time in his admiration for raw power and his belief that relations between cities and peoples as well as non-human animals support his views: we shall shortly find some similarities (though not identity) between his position and that of the sophist Thrasymachus in *Republic* Book 1. And the reason that Plato feels it so important to scrutinize and challenge this family of views is that he is acutely aware that the pressures of the Peloponnesian War brought them into the mainstream of both political debate and practice in Athens, as the magnificent *History* of Thucydides disturbingly shows. In Thucydides' account[6] in 3.38–48 of the Mytilenaean Debate in 427, the demagogue Cleon initially persuaded the Athenian Assembly to put to death all the male inhabitants of rebellious Mytilene on Lesbos, and to enslave the women and children.[7] In that case more judicious counsel happily prevailed and the city was spared. In 416–415, however, the inhabitants of the island of Melos were not so fortunate. Although they had originally been a Spartan colony, they had taken a neutral stance in the war, and in 416 the Athenians demanded that they surrender and pay tribute. The Melians refused and the Athenians laid siege; when the Melians finally surrendered the following winter, the Athenians killed all the men and enslaved the women and children, an atrocity widely believed to have been part of the motivation for Euripides' harrowing anti-war play, the *Trojan Women*, first staged in 415.

In Book 5.85–111 of his *History*, as we touched on in chapter 1, Thucydides dramatizes a dialogue just before the siege, in which the Athenians try to persuade the Melians to surrender. The words Thucydides puts into the Athenians' mouths are chilling. Here is 5.89:

> ...You know as well as we do that, when these matters are discussed by practical people, the standard of justice depends on the equality of power to compel and that in fact the strong do what they have the power to do and the weak accept what they have to accept.

The world view depicted a little further on in 5.105 is even bleaker:

> ...It is a general and necessary law (*nomos*) of nature (*physis*) to rule whatever one can. This is not a law that we made ourselves, nor were we the first to act upon it when it was made. We found it already in existence, and we shall leave it to exist for ever among those who come after us. We are merely acting in accordance with it, and we know that you or anybody else with the same power would be acting in precisely the same way.

As we shall see, Plato refuses to accept such a cynically impoverished view of human nature and human potential. We shall find him resisting with powerful arguments and ideas, although the abuses of state power around the globe at the time of writing (2024) suggest we are not yet paying sufficient attention.

Even on their own terms, however, Callicles' views can be challenged and prompt an array of questions. Is he justified in appealing to 'how things are' in the behaviour of non-human animals and relations between cities and peoples to support his claim? Is he not, perhaps, making an unjustified appeal from an (alleged) fact to a value? Has he really thought through the social and political implications of his views? Would there be just one superman per society or more than one? If more than one, how would the supermen interact? And if a superman (or supermen) actually did gain control, would not the laws they made have to command respect, and would this not then break down the sharp antithesis that Callicles thinks he wants to draw between nature and (conventional) law? Even this antithesis, however, is muddied by Callicles' desire to win social success and honours – honours that will to a large extent depend on his conforming to the socially accepted *nomoi*.

Nevertheless, despite these unanswered issues, Callicles is undeniably an important figure. There is persuasive evidence that his appropriately forceful espousal of raw power made a profound impression on Nietzsche.[8] Nietzsche cited Callicles' speeches with approval in his early lectures on Greek philosophy while teaching at Basel, and he praises the sophists in general for possessing 'the courage of all strong spirits to know their own immorality' (*Will to Power*, 429). The similarities are certainly striking: Callicles' contemptuous dissection of conventional morality is closely akin to that in *The Genealogy of Morals*, *Thus Spake Zarathustra* and *Beyond Good and Evil*, and the creation of an alternative ethic based on *physis* rather than (conventional) *nomos* is an ongoing project through all Nietzsche's work. It is also arresting how Nietzsche portrays true nobility in the form of a magnificent and untameable 'blond beast', and the coming overman (*Übermensch*) as a 'laughing lion'. Whatever the degree of the influence on Nietzsche, however, there is no doubt that Callicles challenges us to think hard about the origins and nature of conventional morality – is it in fact a cover for self-interest and would it matter if it were? – and he also raises critical questions about the nature of 'manliness' that are particularly pertinent given current debates about male online influencers and toxic versus healthy notions of masculinity.

Callicles also prompts us to scrutinize the nature of democracy and its vulnerability to demagogues who in fact wish to subvert it to their own ends. In 515a, Socrates notes how Callicles is just embarking on a political career in democratic Athens, and at 481d–e, Socrates emphasizes how when speaking to the crowd Callicles says whatever he thinks the crowd wants to hear. Yet in this private conversation – adroitly made public by Plato – Callicles reveals himself again and again to be utterly contemptuous of the *dēmos*, whom he regards as composed of individually inferior men who can only gain strength through numbers, and who misuse that collective strength to enchain the superior few. Plato makes it absolutely clear that Callicles, far from being committed to democracy, is in fact a demagogue and aspiring *autocrat*: although Plato mischievously has Callicles criticizing Socrates for demagoguery (482c), he makes it plain that the term in fact applies to Callicles himself, who wilfully misuses rhetoric in the hope of gaining power. What Callicles would have done with that power if he had been successful we can only guess – though Plato gives us very strong and disturbing hints – as we hear nothing of Callicles outside this dialogue. It is possible, of course, that Plato invented him (though this would have been highly unusual, and the detail Plato bestows on his portrait suggests he did in fact exist);[9] it is more likely that Plato selected someone whose youthful promise was known to have come to nothing as a warning against moral and intellectual indiscipline (and indeed there is a strong suggestion at 519a that the *dēmos* will later seize on Callicles, as they will turn against Alcibiades: neither can afford to be so dismissive of the source of the honours that they seek).

Plato's message is profound and lasting: if you misuse rhetoric and sophistry you will corrupt democracy and provide the perfect breeding ground for tyranny. Even if the historical Callicles did not succeed, a character like Callicles may emerge who will persuade the people to vote them in by democratic means and then use their position to try to destroy democracy. Plato knew that words really matter. It is not by chance that the *Gorgias* made such an immediate impact and has continued to resonate so deeply ever since.

SOCRATES' RESPONSE: ON NOT NEGLECTING GEOMETRY

How does Socrates respond to this serious challenge? As we saw briefly in the Introduction and chapter 2, his answer builds on Plato's mathematical studies with the Pythagorean communities in southern Italy. In *Gorgias* 503–5 he constructs an embryonic theory of psychic order: just as it is the presence of structure and order which distinguishes a good house, ship or body, so it is structure and order which distinguish the good *psychē* from the bad one. It is these structures and orderings of the *psychē* which are termed 'lawful' (*nomima*) and 'law' (*nomos*), and which constitute justice and temperance. To say that a body is structured and ordered is to say that it is healthy and strong, and such qualities are clearly beneficial to those who possess them. We may therefore infer that a well-structured and orderly *psychē* – namely a just and temperate one which respects the conventional *nomoi* – will also be to the agent's benefit.

This embryonic psychological theory correctly targets the supposed antithesis which Callicles asserts between *nomos* and *physis*: *nomos* is in fact here claimed by Socrates to be simply the external expression of a natural inner order; indeed, in 507–8, Socrates further claims that this natural psychic order is in itself a microcosm of the order of the entire cosmos:

> And wise men[10] say . . . that heaven and earth and gods and men are held together by communion and friendship, by orderliness (*kosmiotēs*), temperance and justice; and that is the reason, my friend, why they call the whole of this world by the name of order (*kosmos*), not of disorder or dissoluteness. Now you . . . do not give proper attention to this . . . but have failed to observe the great power of geometrical equality amongst both gods and men: you hold that grabbing more than your fair share is what one ought to practise, because you neglect geometry.

There is a story from later antiquity that over the entrance to the Academy there was a sign that read 'Let no one enter here who has not studied geometry.' Whether the tale is true or not – and I very much hope that it is – it certainly reflects the core of Plato's thought. This cosmos is beautiful, harmonious and good precisely because it is arranged on mathematical principles, on the ratios and proportions that underpin all the mathematical sciences, including geometry.

CALLICLES UNCHAINED

It is an appealing picture, but although by this point Callicles has mostly lapsed into sullen silence, it is not clear that he is really convinced, and neither is it clear why he should be. It is true that Socrates has been able to demonstrate to Callicles that his 'might is right' political views do not in fact translate into the unqualified private hedonism that he initially supposes, but 'might is right' itself retains its potency. Plato needs a more sophisticated psychology and corresponding theory of human flourishing to tackle both it and Callicles properly. The psychology of the *Gorgias* is still vague and muddled: at times a crude distinction between reason and desires is drawn; at other times Socrates makes an even more basic distinction between *psychē* and body.[11] There is certainly no mention of what the *Republic* will term the *thumoeides*, and Socrates really needs it: it would help him expose the tension noted above in Callicles' attitude to conventional *nomoi* and provide an apparatus for connecting reason and the material desires. It is not surprising, therefore, that Plato feels the need to take on a related political doctrine to that of Callicles in *Republic* Book 1, this time voiced by the combative and sarcastic sophist Thrasymachus. While there is debate about whether Callicles was a real historical figure, there is no such doubt about Thrasymachus: there is independent evidence that he was active in the late fifth century BCE. And although his position differs from that of Callicles in ways we shall explore, Thrasymachus still adheres to the supremacy of force.

THRASYMACHUS AND THE 'RULE OF THE STRONGER'

To appreciate the full impact of Thrasymachus' explosive entry into the *Republic*, we need briefly to outline the discussion about the nature of justice that precedes it. The dialogue opens with Socrates and one of Plato's brothers, Glaucon, walking down from Athens to the harbour at Piraeus to witness the festival of the Thracian goddess Bendis, newly introduced to Athens by migrant Thracian workers, and quickly embraced by some native Athenians (and in this deft touch Plato subtly shows us that, contrary to the charge made against him at his trial, it is not Socrates introducing new divine beings into Athens but the Athenians themselves). After seeing the procession and saying their prayers they are on their way back up to town when they are greeted by a businessman, Polemarchus, and several of his friends, including another of Plato's brothers, Adeimantus. Polemarchus invites Socrates and Glaucon to join them all for discussion in his home nearby, where he lives with his father, the wealthy Syracusan Cephalus. Socrates and Glaucon agree, and Socrates asks Cephalus what he thinks is the greatest advantage of being rich. Cephalus replies that wealth makes it easier to be just and do the right thing (the Greek term for justice, *dikaiosunē*, is broader than the modern English term): money enables you to make fitting sacrifices to the gods and, in your interactions with your fellow men, it allows you the luxury of telling the truth and returning what you have borrowed. Socrates objects that this may not always be the right thing to do: what if you borrow a weapon from a friend who subsequently goes mad and then asks for it back? Surely it would not be right to return it in those circumstances? Cephalus agrees, but is not interested in pursuing the discussion – he has a sacrifice to make – and hands over to his son Polemarchus.

Polemarchus claims that justice is giving others their due, which in practice means helping one's friends and harming one's enemies (the code of heroes such as Achilles and Odysseus in Homer's epic poems, the *Iliad* and *Odyssey*). But, says Socrates, can we not be mistaken about who really are our true friends and enemies? Polemarchus admits this, and refines his definition to say that justice is helping the friend who both seems and is genuinely good, and harming the enemy who both seems and is genuinely bad. Socrates is still not happy: surely the truly good and just man never harms *anyone*?[12]

This is the point (*Republic* 336b) at which Thrasymachus tears into the debate 'like a wild beast'. This is all pious and simple-minded rubbish,[13] he declares: justice is simply the 'interest of the stronger'. In every city (*polis*) it is the stronger person who, or the stronger party which, by definition, wields political power, and this ruling person or group makes the laws in his or its own interest and calls obedience to these laws 'justice'. This is true whether the government is a tyranny, aristocracy, democracy or anything else. What is termed 'justice' is simply a cynical cover for the self-interest of the ruler or rulers, and the subject who obeys these 'just' laws is simply furthering the interest of those in power and is a fool to go along with it if he can escape detection and punishment.

Initially it appears that Thrasymachus is conceiving of justice in legalistic terms: what is called 'justice' is simply what the laws prescribe. However, when Socrates points out that rulers may be mistaken about their true interest, and in consequence prescribe laws that are *not*, in fact, in their interest, Thrasymachus modifies the articulation of his view, and says that obedience to the laws will only constitute justice when they really are to the advantage of the rulers. Indeed, he claims, a ruler is only strictly acting *as* a ruler when he[14] does correctly frame the laws to his advantage; the man may make a mistake, but the ruler never can.

In this modification, Thrasymachus clearly presents ruling as an art or skill (*technē*), and this gives Socrates his chance. Is not every art directed at the good of its subject matter? Medicine looks to the good of the body; the equestrian art to the good of the horse; and the art of ruling to the good of the ruled. But Thrasymachus is scornful. Rulers, he declares, are like shepherds: they may appear to care for their flock, but this is only to fatten them up and thus get a higher price for them at market. Indeed, this exploitative behaviour is equally observable in the private as well as the public sphere. What is termed 'injustice' is simply the ruthless pursuit of one's own interests, and it pays the individual far better than 'justice', conceived as treating others decently and fairly. Injustice can even be regarded as a virtue (*aretē*), the virtue of prudent good sense, while justice is for naïve fools. We may despise the petty criminal, but when injustice is practised on a sufficiently grand scale by, for example, a tyrant, we merely call the tyrant happy and fortunate. We would all be tyrants if we could.

It might initially appear that in his second main statement Thrasymachus is contradicting his opening one. If justice is simply the interest of the stronger party, then surely the tyrant who supremely promotes his own self-interest is supremely just? Yet Thrasymachus clearly states that the tyrant is supremely *un*just (and admirably so). Some have argued that Thrasymachus is operating with two notions of justice, the conventional and the natural (as Callicles does), but a simpler reading suggests that a conventional notion of justice is retained throughout. Injustice is ruthlessly promoting your own desires at the expense of others, whereas justice is giving others their due. In theory each can be practised by both rulers and ruled (as indeed Thrasymachus admits in his second statement); in practice, however, opportunities for injustice will mostly be available to the rulers, whereas the ruled will generally have to accept the imposition of justice. In other words, the initial statement that justice is the interest of the stronger is not to be taken as a complete definition, but as a description of how justice operates in the world of *realpolitik*.

Thrasymachus admits that for the ruled the practice of injustice may sometimes be an unsuccessful means of satisfying one's desires (one may get caught and imprisoned), and this leaves open the possibility that in some circumstances justice would be the more pragmatic course of action. This raises questions about his claim that injustice is prudent good sense and the just are duped fools. His fundamental problem is an unacknowledged ambivalence towards the usefulness of justice as an institution. In his initial statement, the institution of justice is supposed to benefit rulers alone, providing they are genuine rulers who know where their true interests lie; yet in his second statement he suggests that all individuals benefit from the existence of justice, so long as they do not have to practise it themselves and merely benefit from others being just towards them. But it simply does not make sense to say that the institution of justice will benefit every individual providing they do not take part in it: if no one participates, the institution will be destroyed altogether and no one will benefit from it at all.

However, in other respects Thrasymachus does offer a coherent and consistent ideal. His ideal man – again, the focus is very much on the male – is the man who successfully promotes his own interests. This may well involve acting unjustly, but not always – a key consideration will be his political status, whether he is one of the rulers or one of the ruled. It would of course, in the view of Thrasymachus, be greatly preferable to be one of the rulers: underlying his ideal male is a notion of *eudaimonia*, of flourishing, conceived starkly in terms of the appropriation and possession of material wealth and power over others.

Such a position is clearly akin to that of Callicles, but before we consider their similarities (and differences), and the relevance of both to contemporary affairs, it is interesting to note how Plato's thinking on the relation between morality and the law appears to have developed since the *Crito*, a dialogue which purports to depict Socrates' discussion of the issue while imprisoned and awaiting execution in 399. Crito and Socrates have been friends since boyhood but, unlike Socrates, the adult Crito is wealthy and tries to persuade Socrates to let him use his money to help Socrates escape from prison. Socrates responds courteously, but says no: to escape would be to violate the implicit agreement he has made to abide by the laws of Athens, an agreement shown by the fact that he has chosen to spend all his life in the city and benefit from those same laws. Even if the laws are now being misapplied in his particular case, that is still no reason to break his agreement. Furthermore, to disobey the laws would be to undermine their authority – effectively destroying them.

The position of Socrates in the *Crito* was almost certainly the position of the historical Socrates. Yet the debate between Socrates and Thrasymachus shows that Plato now views the relation between the law and doing the right thing as considerably more complex. Thrasymachus, as we have seen, starts out by appearing to equate 'justice' with simply obeying the laws – laws, however, which have in all cases been cynically made by whoever is in power to further their own narrow interests. When Socrates reminds him that rulers are sometimes mistaken about where their true interests lie, Thrasymachus abandons this legalistic position and says that justice is only to be equated with obeying the law when the rulers have made laws which do indeed further their interests. It might be thought that Thrasymachus' cynicism nevertheless cannot trouble the lofty view of the laws voiced in the *Crito*, which assumes that laws have been made for the general good. I am not so sure: even if Plato wants us to reject Thrasymachus' cynical outlook, the whole discussion nevertheless raises the fundamental question: does any moral authority the law might possess depend on who makes it, how they make it, and to whose benefit? It is intriguing that in the account of the ideally just city to come – an account which for better or worse has had such a profound impact on political theory and practice – law is hardly mentioned at all. The main focus is always on education.

CALLICLES AND THRASYMACHUS

How similar is Thrasymachus' position to that of Callicles? In one respect, there is a notable difference. Although they both greatly admire strength, they diverge significantly in their understanding of who possesses it, of who is to be classed as 'the stronger'. For Thrasymachus, 'the stronger' refers solely to whichever person or political party is actually in power, providing they really do know where their true interests lie; whereas for Callicles, 'the stronger' refers to those who are by nature more courageous, 'manly' and competent, and these men may or may not hold political sway. So for Thrasymachus the stronger may consist of the democratic majority, providing that majority is currently in government; Callicles, on the other hand, contemptuously dismisses all supporters of democracy – whether in power or not – as naturally weak and self-serving. It is for this reason that it is only Callicles who draws a contrast between conventional and natural justice; in Thrasymachus' eyes, 'justice' can only ever be a matter of convention, one invented by those in political power to further their own interests. For Callicles, conventional justice is a device of the weak majority to suppress the naturally stronger few, whereas

Thrasymachus portrays conventional justice as a device of the *de facto* strong – the rulers – to exploit the weak (the ruled).

All this is true, yet the connection between their two positions lies deeper. Both share a profound admiration for the ruthless and effective pursuit of self-interest, and both, critically, conceive of this self-interest solely in terms of material wealth, power over others, and freedom from interference – in Plato's tripartite psychology, in terms solely of the two non-rational (and, unless properly trained and controlled, irrational) psychic faculties, the appetites and the spirited element (*thumoeides*). Plato recognizes this deeper connection, and illustrates it by linking their two positions with the same quote from the lyric poet Pindar. We have seen how at *Gorgias* 484b Callicles proclaims that, if the naturally leonine man can break free from the chains of convention, then the 'justice of nature' will be able to blaze forth, and we will see in operation Pindar's law of natural force, which declares that Heracles is justified in taking the cows of Geryones simply because he is the stronger. Although Thrasymachus himself does not cite these lines of Pindar, they *are* referred to by the Athenian Stranger at *Laws* 4.714e–715a, when he is discussing the view that justice is simply the 'interest of the stronger' – precisely, of course, the view of Thrasymachus. Earlier, at *Laws* 3.690b, the fundamental underlying link between the positions of Callicles and Thrasymachus is laid bare when the Athenian Stranger employs the same Pindar quote when considering the basic belief that the stronger should rule and the weaker be ruled.

DEMOCRACY AND TYRANNY

Given the current rise of authoritarians and dictators around the globe, and their popularity with some, it clearly behoves us to consider the views of Callicles and Thrasymachus with great care. Those of us who do not share such views still need (indeed, particularly need) to understand their appeal, and appreciate both the underlying connections and the nuanced differences between them. Callicles, the aspiring democrat so dismissive of democracy, shows how when democratic guards are down, and popular rhetoric is misused, democracy can itself be an uncomfortably suitable breeding-ground for tyranny. Thrasymachus challenges us to admit that we would all be tyrants if we could. If we want to protest, how best to do that? Both Callicles and Thrasymachus compel us to reflect on current moral conventions and ask what really grounds them. Both equally compel us to consider the formal laws of our country: who made them and how were they made? Were they made responsibly for the good of all, or selfishly and cynically to further the perceived interests of a particular group? What do we owe to our national laws, particularly if we believe them to have been poorly made? To what extent would breaking a particular law undermine the rule of law altogether?

In respect of the misuse of rhetoric, both Callicles and Thrasymachus also demonstrate the slippery dangers of subverting (whether wilfully or otherwise) the use of general moral terms. As we have seen, Callicles is happy formally to agree with Socrates' harmonization of the *agathon* and the *kalon*: he does indeed agree that performing fine (*kala*) deeds will bring personal benefit. The problem is that he interprets both concepts in ways which Socrates cannot accept. He dismisses conventional justice and decency as simple-minded foolishness. Thrasymachus goes even further, proclaiming that what is conventionally regarded as injustice (the only kind of injustice in his eyes) is positively an *aretē*, the virtue of prudent good sense; (conventional) justice is again dismissed contemptuously as naïve foolishness. This subversion of the ordinarily accepted application of moral terms is something that the historian Thucydides highlights in his blistering account of the civil war in Corcyra (modern Corfu) in 427:

> Thoughtless daring was now regarded as the courage (*andreia*) one would expect to find in a party member; prudent delay was a specious cloak for cowardice; moderation was just an attempt to disguise one's unmanliness (*anandros*); ability to understand a question from all sides meant that one was totally unfitted for action.[15]

It is almost certain that Plato was well-acquainted with Thucydides' *History*, and in any case he would wholeheartedly agree: for both Thucydides and Plato, the corruption of moral language both presages and accompanies the corruption of morals.[16]

SOCRATES' RESPONSE TO THRASYMACHUS

The attempts by Socrates in *Republic* Book 1 to counter Thrasymachus are all unsatisfying.[17] This may well be a deliberate strategy on Plato's part, as they all show the need to go beyond the resources offered by the historic Socrates and provide the much more sophisticated psychology and accompanying theory of flourishing which in chapter 2 we saw offered by (the character of) Socrates in *Republic* Book 4, and which are undoubtedly the original work of the mature Plato. The first three arguments in *Republic* Book 1 rely on a conception of the virtue of justice as a craft or skill (*technē*), and we have already seen Thrasymachus scornfully dismissing the first of these, which tries to prove that all crafts serve the interests of their subject matter: no, pronounces Thrasymachus, rulers only appear to care for those they rule so that they can better exploit them, just as a shepherd fattens his sheep to get a better price for them at market. In reply, Socrates makes an unconvincing case for separating the skill of ruling from that of wage-earning. Equally unpersuasive is his next claim that the just are skilled and the unjust unskilled, and that this is shown by the fact that the just do not compete with each other, but only with the unjust, in the same way that skilled doctors or musicians do not compete with each other, but only with the layman. There are a number of problems with this argument,[18] but the fundamental difficulty applies to all three of these responses which appeal to justice as a *technē*: Socrates has in fact given us no good reason to suppose that justice *is* in fact analogous to the expertise of, for example, the doctor or musician, and without such a reason he cannot deal with Thrasymachus' assertion that the just man is not skilled at all, but a gullible fool.

The next two arguments of Socrates are more promising, but incomplete. Injustice, he claims, leads to disunity and the inability to carry out a plan of action, in both the individual and in any group. It is suggestive, but clearly requires the psychology of *Republic* Book 4 to give it substance. So, too, does Socrates' final attempt (which we have briefly mentioned in chapter 2),[19] in which he claims that everything has its own particular function and corresponding excellence (*aretē*), and that the function of the *psychē* is to live, and its excellence is justice. As it stands, it is unpersuasive, as it plays on two meanings of 'good' and 'well' (namely, good *qua* beneficial and good *qua* morally good), but it does at least point to the need for a proper discussion of the *psychē* and what it might mean for it to flourish (and, to be fair, Socrates does admit that as he and his interlocutors have yet to define justice, they are not yet in a position to say whether it really is an excellence, or whether it really does make its possessor *eudaimōn*).

GLAUCON

Nevertheless, although by this point Thrasymachus is sulking and sarcastically pretending to believe that Socrates has 'won', Plato's brothers, Glaucon and Adeimantus, know better, and enter the debate with a great deal more rigour and perseverance, claiming to restate Thrasymachus' position as forcibly as possible (although they do not claim to subscribe to it themselves). For Glaucon, conventional justice is simply a hard-headed compromise. The natural ideal would be to be able to harm others to get what you want without being wronged in return, while the naturally worst option is to be wronged without any means of redress. As the disadvantages of being wronged exceed the advantages of doing wrong, however, people make a social compact to avoid both extremes and agree to set up a system of 'justice'. Yet such a compromise only serves us if we think wronging others will actually bring us retribution: if the usually 'just' person believes that they can do wrong and not be found out, then they too will act according to greed, *pleonexia*, the motive which in nature (*physis*) drives all of us if we are not compelled by laws and conventions (*nomoi*) to respect each other's claims.

To support this, Glaucon tells the tale of Gyges' ring. Gyges was a shepherd in Lydia (in modern Turkey) and during a great storm an earthquake opened up a chasm before him. Descending, he saw many marvels, including a bronze horse, hollow and fitted with doors, and containing the corpse of a giant man. On this man's finger there was a gold ring which Gyges took, and he soon discovered that if he twisted the bezel of the ring towards the inside of his hand, he became invisible; twisting the ring outwards again, he would become visible once more. Within one month he had exploited this magical power to kill the king, marry the queen, and was lording it over Lydia.

Two points immediately strike us. Firstly, Glaucon lays bare the distinction between *nomos* and *physis* that he feels underlies Thrasymachus' position (even though, as we have seen, for Thrasymachus justice itself can only be a matter of convention). Secondly, although Glaucon claims simply to be restating Thrasymachus' real position, in one respect his view differs significantly. He does not subscribe to Thrasymachus' confused (and unacknowledged) ambivalence about the usefulness of justice as an institution: for Glaucon, given the absence of magical rings of invisibility, the institution of justice is openly stated to be a second-best compromise for everyone.

Glaucon, however, has not finished: if this cynical view of human nature and conduct is so prevalent, Socrates, can you *prove* to us that justice really does pay the individual better than injustice, in itself and irrespective of any consequences, and despite all appearances to the contrary? Can Socrates show that the just man leads a more flourishing life *even if* he is wrongly accused of being unjust and horribly tortured (Glaucon goes into gruesome detail) and killed? And even if the unjust man is wrongly perceived to be just and heaped with public honours and financial rewards, some of which he uses to make magnificent sacrifices to the gods?

ADEIMANTUS

Adeimantus picks up the theme with gusto. People, he says, *only* act justly if they can benefit from having a just reputation and reaping the social honours and rewards it brings; the ideal is therefore cunningly to cultivate a reputation for justice while still behaving unjustly in secret. This cynical behaviour will win you the favour not only of your fellow men but also of the gods, whom he portrays as being readily bought off with prayers, sacrifices and the incantatory interventions of charlatan priests who pretend to have magical powers. The poets, indeed, depict these venal gods as being quite happy endlessly to shower banquets on those humans who went to heaven with only a reputation for justice, 'as if they thought the supreme reward of virtue was to be drunk for eternity'. Given all this, the pithy (devil's advocate) advice of Adeimantus is: 'sin first and sacrifice later from the proceeds' (2.365e).

So, he continues, what Glaucon and I want to hear from you, Socrates, is a defence of justice that demonstrates that it is in the class of goods that are worth having not only for their consequences but also, much more importantly, for themselves. Can Socrates show what are the effects of both justice and injustice on the *psychē* of their possessor? And it is at this point that Socrates says that in order to consider justice in the individual it will be advisable first to look at it on the larger canvas of the state.

A WARNING FROM HISTORY

Callicles, Thrasymachus, Glaucon and Adeimantus are all hugely important characters for three main reasons. Firstly, they show the need for Plato to move beyond the historic Socrates and develop a more sophisticated psychology and concomitant theory of action and conception of human flourishing for the individual if he wants to argue that it really is in my best interest to treat others decently and fairly. Secondly, they demonstrate the serious challenges Plato faces if he wants to extend his ethics of flourishing to a *politics* of flourishing: they all voice (albeit in the cases of Glaucon and Adeimantus as devil's advocates) views that Plato not only felt to be widespread amongst individuals in Athens, but believed to be driving forces in Athenian domestic politics and foreign policy – a view of Athenian politics which, as we have seen, was shared by the historian Thucydides. And thirdly, of course, because these are not just challenges and questions faced by Plato in the fourth century BCE, but by all of us right now. Witness, for example, the current debate in the U.K. and elsewhere about who should receive state honours and on what grounds? Are we able to see further than the outward reputation?[20] What actually does ground our moral conventions? If we cannot answer these questions then, as Plato saw, we will be in no position to deal with the threats to democracy that can breed in conditions of moral confusion, indifference and cynicism. In these early decades of the twenty-first century, democracy is under threat all over the world as authoritarian and aspiring authoritarian leaders and their enablers employ all the devices in the modern rhetorician's arsenal to beguile, flatter and frighten with assorted toxic concoctions of lies, fantasies and false promises of freedom. As we have seen, although Plato was no great fan of direct democracy (the only kind he knew), he did think tyranny was a great deal worse, and with uncompromising clarity he shows us how the main threats to democracy may come from within a state at least as often as from without: he shows how the abuse of the freedom of speech and corruption of language that may arise in democracies without careful vigilance provide the perfect breeding ground for tyranny.

In the next chapter we will see how Plato seeks to meet the challenges to individual and communal flourishing that he perceives through the imaginary creation of an ideally just city. We will find, as so often, that even if we consider some of the solutions offered by Socrates to be too extreme, Plato almost always has his characters raising the right questions – questions that we still need urgently to address today. Furthermore, the incisive analysis that Plato offers of his society's ills only too often still rings uncomfortably true.

4

The Ideal City and its Decline

It is of course in response to the challenge of Thrasymachus – picked up and augmented by Glaucon and Adeimantus – that Socrates says that the best way to check whether justice benefits the *individual* is first to examine it on the larger canvas of the ideally just city (*kallipolis*, city of beauty) and sets about constructing such a city on the lines we saw in chapter 2.[1] It is now time to explore this city in more detail, and we should note immediately that the title originally ascribed to this dialogue, *politeia*, refers not just to a formal constitution but to the entire political and social arrangements of the city.

We have seen how by *Republic* 3.414b, Socrates has divided the city into three classes (almost certainly supported by non-Greek slaves),[2] based on the principle that each person should only concentrate on the job for which they are naturally suited. The Rulers are to plan and care for the good of the city as a whole, and they are to be assisted by the Auxiliaries, a combined military, police and executive force; the Rulers and the Auxiliaries together are the Guardians of the city. The Producer class produces and trades the goods: farmers, artisans, merchants. The virtues of the city are located in the functions of these three classes and the relations between them: the city as a whole will be wise due to the wisdom of its Rulers, and courageous due to the courage of its Auxiliaries; moderation will come about in the city if all three classes agree that the Rulers should rule, and abide by the Rulers' rational desires and wisdom. And finally we saw how justice is the condition that makes all the other virtues of the city possible, namely the condition that each class perform its own function, which in turn can only come about if each individual performs their own allotted function.

MAGNIFICENT MYTHS OR DECEPTIVE PROPAGANDA?

Socrates glosses over the obvious query about why he should suppose that the natural distribution of skills happily accords with what the city requires. However, he does try to support his construction with two stories or myths (*pseudos* [3.414b] and *mythos* [3.415a] on which more shortly) in one of the most controversial passages in the entire *Republic*, and indeed in the whole Platonic corpus. Later in this chapter, and throughout chapter 7, we shall be exploring powerful and resonant myths and images in Plato, stories that he tells to make profound points about the human condition. *Republic* 3.414–15, however, is rather different. In the first 'noble' or 'magnificent' (*gennaion*) story (often called the Foundation Myth in the secondary literature), Socrates says that he wants first to attempt to persuade the two Guardian classes, and then the rest of the community, that their upbringing and education have been a dream and that in fact they were all moulded and raised in the same mother earth and only brought into the light when they – and their weapons – were fully formed. Their native earth is thus to be defended as their mother, and they should regard each other as brothers.

The second *mythos* (the so-called Myth of the Metals) elaborates on this. Although all the citizens are brothers, when god fashioned them he put gold into some, silver into others, and iron and bronze into the rest, and these metallic differences are the foundation of the three classes in the city. In general, gold parents will give birth to gold children, and similarly with the rest, but if the Rulers spot that any child has traces of a different metal from that of their parents, they should be promoted or demoted accordingly.

What are we to make of these tales? The clearly stated possibility of both promotion and demotion between classes largely rebuts accusations of racism; nevertheless, serious problems remain. Even within their own terms, are the two stories compatible? Is not the supposed unificatory purpose of the first undermined by the class divisions of the second? Even more problematically, is Socrates guilty here of that very abuse of language with which he has charged the sophists? Are these tales simply crude propaganda and an attempt at brainwashing?

There has always been, and doubtless will continue to be, keen debate about this, and one of the chief reasons is the ambivalence of the noun *pseudos* and verb *pseudomai* that Socrates employs. *Pseudos* can indeed mean an outright and deliberate lie, but it can also refer to something that is simply untrue, or at least untrue at a literal level, and several pieces of evidence suggest that this more neutral meaning is preferable here. Firstly, Socrates calls the first tale 'Phoenician', a clear reference to the mythical tale of Cadmus, Prince of Phoenician Tyre, who sowed the teeth of a dragon he had slain and from which rose fully armed men, the founders of the city of Thebes. This mythical allusion is explicitly highlighted by Socrates when introducing the second tale: 'listen to the rest of the myth', he exhorts a sceptical Glaucon, 'we shall address our citizens in mythical language' (*muthologountes*).

Glaucon's scepticism is, of course, a further clue about how we should interpret this passage, as is Socrates' own professed diffidence, when he says that poets like to tell such stories about things which they claim used to happen, but do not occur now and are not likely to, and that it would take a lot of persuasion to induce people to believe them. He openly hesitates to say more and admits that if he does they will understand his hesitation. Even when he agrees to continue he says he does not know how he will find the boldness or words to do so. When Glaucon scoffs that it is no wonder Socrates was ashamed to tell the story of the earth-born brothers-in-arms, Socrates readily agrees.

My own sense is that Plato is not intending these *mythoi* to be taken entirely literally even *within* the ideally just city – and of course not by readers of the dialogue – but that he still hopes they will serve their purposes in helping the citizens both to unite and to accept their class roles. The function of the *mythoi* is that of the myths and legends of any community or nation about its origins and development: they can provide a sense of identity even when they are not understood as conveying literal historical fact.

THE GUARDIANS' WAY OF LIFE

There follows more description about the way of life of the Guardians – the Rulers and Auxiliaries – every detail of which is designed to ensure that they work for the good of the city as a whole, and not of any one class. They are to live and eat together in camp communes, and all their basic material needs of food, clothing and shelter are to be provided by the Producers, though no luxuries are allowed. Apart from a few small personal items (no examples are given, but perhaps Socrates has things such as combs and sponges in mind), they are not permitted to own any personal property whatsoever: they are not even allowed to touch gold and silver. This simple and austere way of life (doubtless influenced by the Pythagorean communities Plato had visited and been impressed by in southern Italy, as well as by certain features of Spartan culture)[3] is partly intended to prevent any temptation to lord it over the Producers and mistreat them: if you are entirely dependent on the people you rule for your physical survival then that is an excellent incentive to treat your subjects well. It is also designed to prevent personal distractions: the Rulers and Auxiliaries can focus exclusively on their jobs, without the distractions of running homes, looking after property or earning a living. The Producers are allowed personal property and to own land, but extremes of both wealth and poverty amongst them are prevented by city intervention (though precise details are not given).

As so often with Plato (and particularly in the *Republic*), we may feel his proposals regarding the camp communes are too extreme; nevertheless, the strict division of wealth and power may give us food for thought, and accords well with the comment in Book 1 at 347 that good men (later extended to include women) will not consent to rule in return for money or worldly honours, but only out of fear that others would be worse rulers.[4]

In the initial discussion of the communal way of life of the Guardians, there is a passing reference (4.423e) to a 'community of women and children' (disquietingly said to be implied by the phrase 'all things in common between friends'). However, when Socrates is urged by those present to return to the subject in 5.449, it is clear that the roles and status of women in the two Guardian classes are to be far more significant than this phrase suggests. The historic Socrates had thought women could and did display the same virtues as men, and in the same way, but had not appeared to advocate for different roles within society (*Meno* 73a–c and *Gorgias* 470e may offer fair indications of the position held by the historic Socrates).[5] Yet more radical ideas were in the air, enough for the comic playwright Aristophanes to treat them as a subject for mockery: witness his *Assemblywomen*, in which women not only assume political power but also use it to abolish private property and the family. In the *Republic*, Socrates takes such views seriously. Guardian women are to perform the same jobs as Guardian men, and are thus to serve alongside them as both Rulers and Auxiliaries. This is because the only difference between the sexes is that 'the man begets and the woman bears' children, and this one biological difference (as it was generally understood at the time) does not affect what jobs women can do – or indeed, following the historic Socrates, what virtues they can display. Socrates does say at 5.455d that men will usually perform the tasks better – a qualification which his argument does not support;[6] however, despite this annoying caveat, since they are still to perform the same tasks, Guardian women should thus receive precisely the same education and training as men. Whether an individual woman should be a Ruler or an Auxiliary (or anything else) will depend on her natural ability: women differ in their natural talents and aptitudes just as much as men do.[7]

There is every reason to think that Plato intends us to consider these proposals in all seriousness. We have seen in the Introduction that women were allowed to attend his lectures,[8] and in chapter

6 we shall see one of the most profound speeches in the whole of Plato being given to a (fictional) woman, the (apparent) priestess Diotima. And in the *Menexenus*, if it is indeed by Plato,[9] the mistress of Pericles, Aspasia, is credited not only with instructing Pericles in rhetoric but even with composing the famous Funeral Speech he gave in 431/430 during the Peloponnesian War, and which forms one of the most famous passages in Thucydides (2.34–46);[10] however, we should note that, although presented as highly influential and oratorically gifted, Aspasia is hardly depicted as an exemplar of strict truthfulness. Nevertheless, there seems absolutely no doubt that Plato thought that, if properly educated, women could contribute greatly to the city and that their talents were currently being wasted. In this respect too he may well have been influenced by his visits to the Pythagorean communities in Magna Graecia, as women appear to have enjoyed a considerably higher status in such communities than in contemporary Athens, and played more active roles.[11] Another influence may have been his experience of being initiated into the cult of Demeter at Eleusis, as the cult admitted both women and slaves.

The Guardian women have sometimes been criticized for being 'masculine', but this may reveal more about the prejudices of the commentator than about Socrates or Plato. However, it is true that Socrates does not appear to be interested in the rights of women (or indeed the rights of men): his aim is to realize and harness the potential of Guardian women for the overall good of the city. Furthermore, we should note that this realization and harnessing of Guardian women is only possible with the support of Producer women (and almost certainly female slaves). Nor should we gloss over the fact that there are a number of disparaging remarks made about women throughout the dialogue (and elsewhere in Plato): it would appear that Plato perceives a marked difference between women as they might be if properly educated and trained, and women as he sees them in contemporary Athens.

The communal way of life for the two Guardian classes has already freed Guardian women from the domestic responsibilities of running an individual home. Nevertheless, how are they to serve

THE IDEAL CITY AND ITS DECLINE

as Rulers and Auxiliaries if they are preoccupied with raising their children? The solution of Socrates is simple and brutal (though he does express doubts about it): amongst the Guardians, the nuclear family is to be abolished, though it will continue in the Producer class. In a carefully organized programme of eugenics, Guardian men and women are to be brought together at city mating festivals (the stock-breeding terms in this passage are particularly disturbing), with the finest amongst them given the most alluring opportunities to reproduce. Guardian babies are to be removed from their mothers at birth and raised in city nurseries, with the aim that all the Guardians regard each other as possible family members and are not distracted by divided loyalties (Socrates does recognize the dangerous potential for incest here, although the provisions he offers to prevent it are sketchy to say the least).

The proposal to abolish the nuclear family in the two Guardian classes, and the language of eugenics and stock-breeding in which it is presented, have not surprisingly been found profoundly troubling and distasteful, and I would certainly agree. But here again the extreme solution nevertheless highlights real problems, and ones with which we are still grappling. How can women achieve their full potential if they are in sole charge of childcare and housework? And if the childcare and housework are shared by both parents, how can men achieve their full potential as well? A possible response might of course be to say that raising children and creating a welcoming home can be *part* of that potential – but this too will require the kind of considered reflection on different ways of living a fully human life that we discussed in chapter 2.

Nor is Socrates' concern with the proper divisions of 'public' and 'private' only in respect of childcare and the running of the home. At 3.412d he says that their proposed city will need Guardians who really care for the whole community, and that the deepest affection is founded on community of interest, when we feel that our doing well is bound up with the doing well of the community as a whole. This key point is developed in 5.462. The chief good for a city is social cohesion and unity, and the chief evil is disunity and fragmentation. Cohesion comes about when all members of a society feel pleasure and pain at the same things, and this in turn occurs when those members use the words 'mine' and 'not mine' in the same sense, and in respect of the same things. Such a city resembles an individual: if an individual feels pain or pleasure in any particular part of himself, he says that he has, for example, a pain in *his* finger. Each member of such a society is a part of a greater whole, and if any member feels pain or pleasure, the whole city will share in it.

This position gives rise to tensions within Plato's view of the ethical subject: in *Republic* Book 4 the focus was mostly on the ethical subject as an independent entity in their own right; now the focus is on the individual as a part of a bigger whole. It is a political ideal that clearly can seem simultaneously both beautiful and decidedly disturbing, and it is plausible to imagine that it is partly influenced by the faction-torn Athens of Plato's childhood and youth. Nevertheless, the submersion of individual identity within a totalitarian city will and has troubled many.[12]

Nevertheless, the 'communism' and 'totalitarianism' of these sections of the dialogue raise really interesting questions about the proper divisions between public and private, or even whether there should be any private sphere or spheres at all, and they are questions with which we are still wrestling. Should housework and parental childcare (or other family care), for example, be paid? The advent of the Internet and World Wide Web have seen such issues multiply and intensify. What regulations should exist for data protection? How much of our lives is it advisable to post on social media? In general, is some degree of privacy necessary, or desirable, or even possible anymore?

PHILOSOPHER-RULERS

How is this ideally just city to come into being and not simply remain a fantasy? The answer, says Socrates, lies in rule by *philosophers*:

> The society we have described can never grow into a reality or see the light of day, and there will be no end to the troubles of cities,

or indeed ... of humanity itself, till philosophers become kings in this world, or till those we now call kings and rulers really and truly become philosophers. (*Republic* 5.473c–d)

We should note immediately that although 5.473c–d just talks of 'kings', Socrates makes it absolutely clear that there are to be Philosopher-Queens too (7.540c). But, whether kings or queens, who are the philosophers, the lovers of wisdom? Plato may well have been alerted to the possibility of a philosopher taking a leading role in a city by his friend the Pythagorean Archytas in Tarentum, and very possibly by Melissus too, a disciple of Parmenides who was also the leader of Samos and successfully fought against the Athenians in 441.[13] However, the Philosopher-Rulers of the *Republic* have very specific qualifications, and those qualifications depend on Plato's conviction that reality and truth lie apart from the phenomenal world that we perceive with our senses. Philosophers are those who have apprehended and love what he terms the perfect, eternal, unchanging, non-sensible *Forms* of Goodness and Beauty and Justice and so on, and – as Book 10 will make clear – of animate and inanimate objects as well. It is the Form of Beauty, for example, that connects all the beautiful things and people and actions in this world of the senses, and which allows us to arrive at a concept of beauty. The Form itself, however, is more than the concept; the Form would still exist even if there were no humans to apprehend it.[14] The world we perceive through our senses is a shadowy *copy* of reality; it is only the intelligible realm of the Forms that is truly real. The Rulers are the only people who have full access to this realm, and who are experts in what is truly beautiful, good and just.

Forms are undeniably mysterious entities, and when Glaucon at 6.509c remarks sardonically to general amusement that the Form of the Good appears to be 'miraculously transcendent' he is doubtless speaking for many of Plato's circle and students (including, later, Aristotle, who dismisses the notion of separate Forms, though he does propose forms which are not separated from the sensible world, but immanent in material objects).[15] The main argument Socrates offers for their existence is epistemological, based on the conditions he believes to be necessary for knowledge to exist at all. He argues that the world of sense-experience cannot be *known* because it is fluctuating and changing, and subject to different individual perspectives, whereas knowledge (*epistēmē*) requires stable objects. This changing and subjective world can therefore only be the object of opinion (*doxa*), not of knowledge. It follows that if knowledge is to exist at all, it must be of a different realm, separate from this world. This realm is the intelligible realm of the perfect, eternal, unchanging Forms.

What is immediately apparent is the degree to which Plato is also influenced by two mighty Presocratic philosophers, Heraclitus and Parmenides. Heraclitus held that everything in the sensible world is in a state of becoming, that 'everything flows' like a river, and that you therefore cannot step into the same river twice, as the waters are constantly flowing (the banks and riverbed will also be constantly changing).[16] According to Aristotle,[17] the young Plato adopted this view from a radical student of Heraclitus called Cratylus, and never abandoned it. Indeed, Cratylus held that you could not step into the same river even *once*, as in a constantly fluctuating world, identities could not even form.[18] Such a view, Plato thinks, precludes the very possibility of knowledge:

> We cannot even say that there is any knowledge,[19] if all things are changing and nothing remains fixed . . . there will be neither anyone to know nor anything to be known.[20]

Parmenides, in contrast, held that contrary to appearances there is only one thing: unchanging, eternal Being.[21] Plato's solution is to develop a theory which contains elements of both. The world we see around us is a Heraclitean one of many different objects that are constantly changing, and which appear differently to different people at different times, or from different perspectives. However, the world we see around us is not all there is; to discover what is eternal and unchanging we need to turn to the intelligible realm of the Forms, which individually possess the stable qualities of Parmenidean Being.[22]

Plato's attempt to save the possibility of knowledge is powerful, but it can certainly be challenged: perhaps knowledge and opinion should be distinguished not in respect of different objects, but in respect of *reliability*. Knowledge is by definition always true; opinion may be true or false. The fundamental issue, however, is why is Plato so determined that knowledge should exist at all? Why is he so determined to prove that knowledge exists and that humans can access it? The answer again lies partly in his strong desire to separate philosophers from sophists (and the teachers of rhetoric and orators who are influenced by them). We have repeatedly seen his rejection of the sophists' tricks to make the weaker argument appear the stronger, in an attempt simply to win the argument and defeat their opponent rather than engage in the honest and collaborative search for truth which Plato sees as the enterprise of the genuine philosopher. We also saw in chapter 1 how he believes the Man/Measure argument of Protagoras – the argument that each human decides on what is or is not true for them – would swiftly lead to solipsism and the utter impossibility of dialogue or indeed any shared reality. Although Plato thinks philosophers should always question and examine claimed 'facts', he also holds that doing away with any possibility of an agreed reality is both wrong and highly dangerous. It was precisely this confusion between philosophy and sophistry that in part led to Socrates' death.

THE SUN, LINE AND CAVE

The contrast between the phenomenal world of sense-perceptions and the intelligible realm of the Forms is vividly illustrated in three key images from the *Republic*. In the first, the Simile of the Sun, Socrates claims that just as the sun is the source of both light and growth in the phenomenal world, and gives visibility to the objects of sense and the power of seeing to the eye, so the Form of the Good is the source of reality and truth and gives intelligibility to the objects of thought and the power of knowing to the mind. The Divided Line makes further distinctions between the two realms, particularly with reference to the degrees of clarity and understanding with which the mind apprehends objects within the two basic orders. Knowledge (*epistēme*) apprehends the intelligible realm overall, but knowledge is itself now divided into two: intelligence (*noēsis*) or dialectic fully apprehends the Forms, arguing from assumptions to first principles and then back to a complete testing and understanding of the assumptions; whereas mathematical reasoning (*dianoia*) seems to apprehend the Forms in a less complete way, simply starting from untested assumptions and making deductions from them.[23] Opinion (*doxa*), which deals with the physical world, is also now divided into two: belief (*pistis*) apprehends physical objects, both animate and manufactured; while illusion (*eikasia*) apprehends shadows, reflections and images of these physical objects – including, as we will see in chapter 7, works of art.

Most powerful and haunting of all is the Allegory of the Cave, an image which has resonated ever since with writers, artists and filmmakers[24] (and a resonance which raises important questions for the status and power of images in general, relegated to fourth place in the Divided Line). We are to imagine a dark cave with a tunnel leading up to the light. In the cave are prisoners who have been bound by the legs and neck since childhood; they cannot turn their heads and all they can see is the wall in front of them; they cannot see the tunnel or the light world above and have no idea that they exist. Behind them is a fire and between the fire and their backs runs a curtain-wall above which puppets are moved by puppeteers, who sometimes talk amongst themselves. All the prisoners can see on the wall in front of them are the shadows of the puppets, which they mistake for real objects, both animate and inanimate; all they can hear are echoes of sounds, which they mistake for the sounds of real objects: this world of shadows and echoes is for them their only reality. When Glaucon observes that it is a strange picture, and they are strange prisoners, Socrates replies simply that they are 'like us'. We live in a prison and we do not even know that we are in chains.

Escape, however, is possible. Socrates next asks us to imagine what would happen if any of the prisoners were to be painfully released from their shackles and forced up the tunnel into the bright world above. Although at first they will be dazzled by the light, they will in time adjust to the true objects in the upper world and eventually will even be able to gaze at the sun itself, and realize that before they were prisoners in a world of deceptive shadows and echoes. These few who do manage to look upon the sun naturally desire to stay permanently in this glorious realm, but they are not permitted to satisfy this desire: they are compelled to return to the cave and use their arduously acquired knowledge to improve the lives of those who still dwell there, still trapped in a world where all they can do is compete with each other over who can best remember the order of the passing shadows (which they do not realize are shadows) and predict their future appearances.

We can now understand more fully the opening scene of the *Republic*. Socrates' physical descent from Athens to the harbour of Piraeus anticipates the intellectual descent of the Philosopher-Ruler from the sunlit realm of the Forms to the shadowy and echoing cave; the very first word of the dialogue, *katebēn* ('I went down'), looks forward to the philosopher *katabas*, 'going down', in 7.516e.

The implications of the analogy for education in general are profound, and are explicitly drawn out by Socrates in 7.518b–d. We must reject those who say they can simply put knowledge into an empty mind, as if they were putting sight into blind eyes. Each of us[25] has an innate capacity for knowledge, but our *psychē* requires assistance in being directed towards reality and actualizing this capacity. The task of the educator is to turn the mind's eye of the pupil in the direction of the light, but the pupil still has to make the effort required to reach the light. The acquisition of knowledge is, once again, shown to be an active and internal process which the pupil, with proper guidance, has to undertake for himself or herself.

EDUCATION OF THE FUTURE PHILOSOPHERS

Whether or not Socrates really does think that we can all achieve knowledge, his immediate task is the education of future Philosopher-Rulers in particular. After the primary education of all the Guardian children in the arts and gymnastics, and two to three years of additional physical training, some young Guardians are assigned to Auxiliary duties alone, whereas others are selected for a further ten years of military service combined with a rigorous higher education in the mathematical sciences: these studies comprise, in order, arithmetic, plane geometry, geometry of solids, astronomy and harmonics. At the age of 30 they undergo yet further tests and those who pass then receive five years of training in dialectic, the only route to a true understanding of first principles and their interconnection, and reasoned argument based on such principles, as opposed to deductions based on the untested assumptions of mathematics. However, although dialectic is superior to mathematics in this way, it still cannot be properly undertaken without prior mathematical training. Whether or not the later story about the inscription over the entrance to the Academy is true,[26] it certainly reflects Plato's profound belief in the importance of mathematics, which was impressed on him during his sojourn with the Pythagoreans: 'Let no one enter here who has not studied geometry.'

Finally, after an additional 15 years of practical military and administrative experience, a few aged 50 will be guided (we are frustratingly not told how) to a revelation of the Form of the Good, which they will use as a pattern (*paradeigma* 7.540a) both for their own lives and for society as a whole.

UTOPIA OR DYSTOPIA?

Does Socrates think that the supposedly ideally just community he is describing can ever be achieved in practice? The textual evidence is almost entirely positive: Socrates almost always claims that although the realization of the community will be very difficult, it is nevertheless possible (*Republic* 5.473c; 6.502c; 7.540d).[27] Socrates, however, is not the only participant in the dialogue, and Adeimantus expresses doubts about the public acceptability of the proposals at 6.501e. Adeimantus, quite rightly, always wants to know about the practical details of Socrates' schemes: what specific

THE IDEAL CITY AND ITS DECLINE

steps does Socrates suggest? The answer is vague. At 7.541a, Socrates suggests that the Philosopher-Rulers should remove all those over ten from the city, so that the remaining children may receive the requisite city training without competing ties and distractions. Although this proposal would have appeared a little less extreme to Plato's audience than it does to us – mass relocations of citizens were not uncommon at the time, and in the regime of the Thirty Tyrants in 404–3, Plato's relative Critias had expelled all but 30,000 sympathizers from Athens[28] – it nevertheless raises a fundamental chicken-and-egg question. How are the Philosopher-Rulers who are to take these initial actions supposed to have been created in the first place?

Whatever the answer (if indeed one exists), there is no doubt that Socrates' proposals have hugely influenced utopian (and dystopian) writing ever since, not least the *Utopia* of Thomas More.[29] But perhaps even more pressing is the question of how much it matters whether the city can actually be realized. Can it not still function as an ideal to work towards, whether or not it can ever be achieved in practice? This is certainly Socrates' position at 5.472d–473b. Quite apart from the particular community imagined in the *Republic*, the general issue of whether there is ever any point in striving towards a perhaps unattainable ideal has always divided opinion. For the record, I personally think that there is often much to be gained from simply setting a direction of travel.

That, however, is as a general principle. Many, including myself, will of course baulk at the notion that the city outlined by Socrates *is* an ideal. As we have seen, it is certainly a totalitarian vision, in which the individual is part of a greater whole, as a finger is part of the body. We have also seen that, in addition to the tripartite division of Producers, Auxiliaries and Rulers, there are almost certainly slaves.[30] What, too, of the Producers? Can they be persuaded to accept their materially comfortable but politically powerless roles or do they have to be repressed? The evidence is sketchy, and tricky to interpret, just as it was with the appetites, their counterpart in the tripartite *psychē*.[31] The fundamental question is: do the Producers (and the appetites) possess sufficient reasoning ability to allow persuasion to take place? Socrates wants to argue for both a harmonious *psychē* and a harmonious city in which each 'part' understands their function and tasks and contentedly agrees, but if persuasion and understanding are not possible in any particular case, then control will be the only option. Nor does the issue of persuasion versus repression just apply to the Producers: for different reasons, it also applies to the Rulers themselves. They of course clearly have the intellectual ability to understand their role and the reasons for it, but in their case it is precisely this intellectual ability that might make them reluctant to leave the bright, sunlit uplands of the realm of the Forms and descend into the murky, echoing cave to assist those still there. With all three classes, Producers, Auxiliaries and Rulers, the evidence is vague: 7.520a simply talks of the need to use 'persuasion or compulsion' to unite all the citizens by ensuring that they fulfil their allotted roles.

Given all these concerns, is there still any point in reflecting on the supposedly ideal community envisaged by Socrates in the *Republic*? Does it still matter? I strongly believe that it does. As we have seen so often, although Socrates' solutions may appear too extreme for many of us, the questions raised are with us still. We have already noted how his imagined city prompts us to think hard about profound and vexed issues: relations between money and power; the proper boundaries of public and private; how women can actualize their full potential; the uses (and abuses) of identity-forming and sustaining myths. We are now in a position to consider whether there are also fruitful lessons to be learned about the nature of good leadership, even if we do not want to go so far as endorsing Philosopher-Rulers. Again, I believe that there are.

LESSONS FOR LEADERSHIP

Plainly, the chief objection to democracy voiced by Socrates is that the *dēmos* does not generally make well-informed decisions, and this in turn results in leaders being appointed who do not necessarily (or even usually) know either what would be best for the city overall or how to implement it. His view of the situation is vividly conjured up in *Republic* 6.488a–489a in a powerful analogy comparing the democratic city to a ship in which violent, fractious and ignorant sailors compete with each other to persuade the short-sighted and rather deaf captain (who is also the owner) to give them control of the wheel, and have no respect at all for the one person actually qualified to steer the vessel, dismissing him as a useless stargazer. The expertise required does in fact exist, but is ignored by those who need it most.

Although Plato is here writing about the direct democracy of contemporary Athens, Socrates' critique in the *Republic* still raises really interesting questions for our own representative democracies. Do we want our leaders to be experts at anything, and, if so, what? This in turn invites consideration of what in any case we understand is meant by the representation element of representative democracy. Do we want our representatives simply to argue for the interests of those who elected them (or their wishes)? Or do we want them to be representative of their electorates in other ways – representative (taken as a collective) in terms of gender; ethnicity; sexual orientation; religious belief; expertise and education or lack of it? Do we want our leaders to be better informed than us or to be representative of us in all ways, including our ignorance?

Plato, clearly, does not want ignorant leaders. In the *Republic*, Socrates repeatedly emphasizes the utterly vital importance of a leader (or leaders) possessing combined intellectual and ethical excellence, and the *knowledge* to which the combination can lead: 7.535a–c, to take just one example, lists steadfastness; courage, moral nobility; mental acuteness; a good memory and a capacity for hard work.[32] It is not simply that good leaders need to be of sound character and mind: the necessary intellectual studies can *only* be undertaken by those of a well-ordered and stable disposition (7.539d). The moral character, intellectual abilities and educational attainments of the leader (or leaders), in short, profoundly affect the whole city, and the implication is that this would be true of any organization. This in turn has radical implications for the attitude of leaders to their power. It is not just that the ideal city should be so structured as to prevent its leaders from making money out of their power (as we have seen); the ideal city should select leaders who do not love power at all (7.521b).

DEGENERATE CITIES

Timarchy and Oligarchy
Socrates now returns to the subject he postponed at 5.449a to discuss the way of life of the Guardians and rule by philosophers, namely the four main degenerate types of city (as he sees it) and corresponding characters: timarchy, oligarchy, democracy and tyranny. In this chapter we will focus mainly on the imperfect cities; we shall be considering the imperfect characters further in the following chapter on heroes and role models.

The four imperfect cities are presented as a historical decline, but in fact Socrates makes it clear that the slide from, say, oligarchy to democracy, does not *inevitably* happen; indeed it might be possible historically for the change to go the other way, and a democracy become an oligarchy (as had indeed happened in Athens in both 411 and 404). It is more helpful to view the narrative as one depicting *moral* decline, picturing cities and characters in which reason holds less and less sway: the aim, as Socrates makes explicit at 8.544a, is to compare them with the ideally just city and philosopher and see which has the most flourishing (*eudaimonestatos*) life. The enquiry will thus finally answer Thrasymachus' challenge that the conventionally unjust man usually fares much better. The vivid, perceptive and often witty portraits of both cities and individuals that follow have been widely celebrated as some of the most penetrating – and entertaining – passages in the *Republic*.

Socrates begins by declaring that decline starts when rulers begin to disagree amongst (and, as we shall see, within) themselves. This decline is inevitable, furthermore, because decay is inevitable in all created things, and, should their ideal city ever in fact be realized in practice, this rule will apply to it too: the degeneration will be initiated, specifically, by mistakes in the timing of the city mating festivals for the Guardians and the ill-conceived children who will be born as a result; iron and bronze will be mixed into the gold and silver of their *psychai*, and the seeds of material greed will be sown. These offspring will disregard the strict moral principles and austere and communal way of life laid down for them and seek to own private property: wealth and power will be disastrously united and corrupt them further. No longer solely reliant on the goodwill of the Producers for their housing and food, they will start to mistreat them, regarding them as mere serfs rather than as fellow citizens united by a common goal. They are driven not by love of knowledge and virtue but by a love of honour (*timē*) and ambition, which manifests in war against external states and harsh subjection of the former Producers. In all this, Socrates is explicit that he has Sparta and Crete in mind, and deftly highlights a critique that was often made against contemporary Sparta in particular: namely that although it claimed to be devoted to military honour supported by a communal way of life amongst its warriors, in fact increasing materialism was setting in and creating divisions amongst its ruling class.

It is this secret acquisitiveness that proves the undoing of the timarchic society. The warrior rulers make the critical mistake of not just introducing greed into the mix of values, but of *equating* honour with the acquisition, consumption and display of material wealth, and the city declines further into an oligarchy where money and possessions hold sway. This is a key insight on Plato's part. The equation of honour and respect with wealth has proved hugely damaging – morally, politically and socially – at many points, including in our own times: as we will explore in more detail in the next chapter, in the UK alone we have seen the confusion play a central role in driving the parliamentary expenses scandal in 2009 and the England riots of 2011; although in the two cases the socio-economic groups differed to some extent, the motivations behind the behaviours were largely the same.

In this oligarchic city, offices are distributed – by armed force or the threat of it if necessary – on the sole basis of a property qualification rather than competence. The oligarchic leaders abandon all pretence of caring for the city as a whole, and focus exclusively on their own class interests. Their neglect of the rest of the population, and in particular their neglect of providing a general system of education, give rise to the emergence of two groups of malcontents, beggars and criminals, who serve no useful social function whatsoever; Socrates calls them 'drones' and is explicit that such groups arise through 'lack of education, bad upbringing and a bad form of government' (8.552e). One of Socrates' proposed remedies is perhaps especially pertinent to the financial upheavals of the twenty-first century: loans should be made at the risk of the lender rather than the borrower. Be that as it may, the city becomes increasingly divided into the rich and the poor, and in this unhealthy condition it is no surprise that the ignored and materially and culturally impoverished populace rises up and democracy is born.

From Democracy to Tyranny

As we have seen, Plato is only talking of the direct democracy of contemporary Athens, in which adult male Athenian-born citizens vote directly on laws and policies, and take turns (usually decided by lot) at holding the great offices of the *polis*. Nevertheless, his brilliant satire of the Athens of his day in the *Republic* still offers us much food for thought. It is a more nuanced and sympathetic portrait than the scathing image of the ship (6.488a–489a), in which the fractious crew ignore the advice of the one person who can help steer them to safety – an image followed by the still more hostile depiction of the *dēmos* as a large and dangerous animal (6.493a–b). In Book 8, Socrates allows that democracy certainly has its charms: it is varied, colourful, exuberant and tolerant, and its focus on individual freedom and equality of political opportunity clearly have their attractions, particularly as the kind of 'freedom' on offer here is the freedom to do what you individually feel like (which we have seen contrasted in the *Gorgias* with what Socrates views there as the genuine freedom that stems from reasoned choice).[33] In the short run, it can appear the most enticing option.

There is, however, definitely a darker underbelly to the surface charms: it is claimed that when the poor win power, they begin by killing or exiling their opponents, and Socrates also emphasizes the weaknesses of the democratic city that ensues. It is utterly disrespectful of authority and chaotic to the point of anarchy – in a playful mood, Plato even has animals in a democracy doing their own thing and sauntering about the streets as they please. Moods and allegiancies are fickle and change on a whim. The description of the democratic individual that follows also suggests that language is corrupted in a democracy in ways which strongly echo Thucydides' account of the subversion of moral terms in the Corcyran civil war:[34] licence is called liberty and shamelessness courage, while shame is disparaged as foolishness and temperance dismissed as cowardice. All of this results in extreme fragility: the democratic city is highly vulnerable to attacks from without and, above all, from within, when a cynical and opportunistic demagogue sees a way to manipulate a path towards absolute power, pretending to be the people's champion.

Socrates delineates the overturning of democracy with care, and we should do well to take note; as he comments, any extreme is liable to produce a violent reaction, and this holds just as true of cities, extreme anarchy yielding to ferocious oppression. The criminal group of parasites (termed 'drones' by Socrates) seeks to sow division through lies, turning the mass of the people against the wealthy and the elite. The most successful of these parasites, with a sharp eye to the main chance, manages to get himself elected as a single popular leader, making extravagant promises and intoxicating his supporters with the neat spirit of offers of still greater freedom. Using his demagogic rhetorical skills he creates a cult around himself where his followers believe he can do no wrong. At some point, heady with his own power, he corrupts the legal system by bringing baseless charges against his enemies and commits murder (the verb Socrates uses, *miaiphoneō*, unequivocally means 'murder', even though the courts are nominally involved); this first taste of blood initiates his transition 'from man to wolf' and from demagogue to tyrant. If the wealthy whose property he is confiscating succeed in these early days in having him exiled, he returns thirsting for revenge, demanding a personal bodyguard to protect him from his enemies (both real and, increasingly, imagined) and to enable him to continue his alleged championing of the people. Indeed, he now identifies himself entirely with 'the people': anyone who still tries to oppose him is labelled, precisely, 'a hater of the people' (8.566c), and he holds total sway, now the finished tyrant and in the grip of culpable mania.

However, although at the start he smilingly distributes land to the cult followers who raised him to power, their lives very quickly deteriorate under his despotic rule. He continually stirs up wars in order to keep his people fearful and feeling in need of a strong leader; the high levels of war taxation also make them still poorer, and less able to rise up against him. For all these reasons, says Socrates, 'a tyrant must always be provoking war'. As his popularity wanes, and the bolder openly complain, he starts to purge all those possessed of the courage, intelligence and vision (and indeed wealth) to pose a threat. His effect on the city is precisely the opposite of the doctor: instead of cleansing the body politic of poisons, he cuts out all that is healthy and lets the poison remain. As discontent grows, his bodyguard increases as its morality declines, and when the people protest that this is not why they voted him in, and belatedly start to realize what sort of a creature they have bred, he turns on them completely and enslaves them all.

THE *GORGIAS* AND THE *REPUBLIC*

Plato's incisive analysis in the *Republic* of how (direct) democracy provides fertile ground for the emergence of tyranny is a more detailed elaboration of what he has Socrates say in the *Gorgias*, and in general the critique of democracy in the *Republic* is similar to that of the *Gorgias* (even though the *Republic* is more balanced in its acknowledgement of democracy's seductive charms). However, although we have concentrated on the *Republic* because it is so rich and has proved so influential, it is far from Plato's final word on democracy, or on imagined cities, and in the *Statesman* and the *Laws* we find him developing and adjusting his political views in important respects. Although for reasons of space it is not possible to examine either dialogue in any detail here, it is worth concluding this chapter with a few of the modifications they make in respect of the political ideas put forward in the *Republic*, not least because one of the many reasons Plato matters is because his thought never ossifies: he always has the honesty and dedication to keep scrutinizing his own views and developing and altering them as he sees fit.

STATESMAN AND LAWS

In both works there is more consideration of all the citizens in the *polis* and how they are to be educated and interact – although it is not spelled out, one may plausibly suppose that Plato has come to realize that careful attention paid to the education of all citizens is the best way of reducing the chances of a demagogue and future tyrant emerging. In *Statesman* 308–11 the chief task of the ideal ruler is to 'weave' together naturally courageous characters (the warp) with naturally restrained and modest characters (the woof) into a fine and harmonious citizen body, partly through an education which aims at instilling shared beliefs and values, and partly through intermarriage. The *Laws*, too, devotes much attention to the education and acculturation of the citizen body as a whole (more, indeed, than to the actual framing of laws).[35] The vital role of *mousikē*, of poetry and music, is highlighted, and there is scathing criticism of the excessive militarism of Spartan training: the ultimate aim of a *polis* should be to achieve peace, not continual war.[36] There is also more respect paid to the rational capacity of all the citizens and others who make up the *polis*, and the need at least to offer the opportunity to understand, and agree to, the laws and customs that are to guide their lives: each law is to be preceded by a lengthy preamble, explaining why it is necessary and exhorting obedience. In consequence, although the inhabitants of the semi-ideal city envisaged in the *Laws* have little 'negative' freedom, little freedom to follow their individual whims, the 'positive' freedom of rational choice and agency that we explored in chapter 2[37] is a goal for all. And it is made clear that women are in these respects to be afforded the same citizen rights, and the same education, as the men. Although there is no longer any talk of communal living arrangements, and although the main focus is still on the good of the city rather than on individual fulfilment, the commitment to the education of women is something that Plato holds unwaveringly until the end of his life.

5

Heroism, Celebrity and Money

ROLE MODELS, EDUCATION AND THE *THUMOEIDES*

We have seen how an ethics of flourishing considers a whole person, living a whole life, and that this leads one to consider the structure, shape and narrative of a well-lived life, which in turn invites one to consider which historical, fictional and mythical characters might serve as appropriate models of flourishing – and, indeed, which characters serve rather as models to avoid.[1] I intend the term 'model' to embrace a broad range, from trying to emulate a life or character in some detail to using a character simply for inspiration or motivation, or as a guide ('what would x do?'). Such models can exert a powerful emotional appeal on even quite young children, before their reason has fully developed, which as we shall see is one of the reasons Socrates in the *Republic* is so keen to censor the literary and mythical models available to Guardian offspring in their primary education (and even before, in the stories they hear in the nursery). Models can also be used by the adult educator to help impart shape and structure to malleable young *psychai*. And they can, in addition, be used by adults to help them perceive structure and shape in their own lives, or even create them – one of the main reasons why Plato employs the dialogue form, displaying a wide variety of characters for our consideration. Would we want to live a life as chaotic as Alcibiades'?[2]

WHY PLATO MATTERS NOW

This close connection between an ethics (and politics) of flourishing and historical, fictional and mythical exemplars shows that it is an ethical approach which can offer more concrete practical guidance than is sometimes supposed, a point emphasized by the character of the sophist Protagoras in the Platonic dialogue named after him. In his so-called Great Speech he says that children are made to learn the works of 'good poets' by heart, since in these writings exist:

> many admonitions, but also many descriptions and praises and encomia of good men in times past, so that the boy may, through envy, imitate them and long to become such as they (*Protagoras* 326a).

The historic Protagoras may have anticipated some of Plato's thinking on the importance of models, but we have also seen how Plato builds on this through the faculty of the *thumoeides* in his tripartite psychology: the faculty that longs for honour, success and respect will naturally be attracted by the characters – whether historical or fictional – who are already honoured and praised in the community.[3]

HOMER AND HEROISM: TWO KINDS OF HERO

Which characters, then, are particularly admired in the culture in which Plato grows up? Even at the turn of the fifth and fourth centuries, they are still the heroic warriors of the Trojan War and its aftermath, especially as depicted in Homer's[4] *Iliad* and *Odyssey*, and Achilles and Odysseus above all. Yet despite the fact that both Achilles and Odysseus are courageous and skilled fighters, they are very different, and largely admired for contrasting reasons: Achilles is praised for knowingly choosing a glorious early death over return to Phthia and a long life, whereas Odysseus is lauded for precisely the opposite reason, for deploying all his resourcefulness and wiles not only to help the Greeks defeat the Trojans through the stratagem of the Trojan horse, but also to survive all the challenges (and admittedly some enjoyable opportunities) of the following ten years of being buffeted around the Mediterranean, and finally making it home to Ithaca and his long-suffering wife Penelope. It is my aim in this chapter to show how a careful consideration of Plato's treatment of the Homeric heroes, and particularly of Achilles and Odysseus, can assist us with a number of contemporary debates concerning heroism and fame – both general concerns about the corruption of the concepts of 'heroism' and 'hero', and specific questions about statues, memorials and state honours. First, however, we need briefly to remind ourselves of how Homer himself depicts them.

ACHILLES IN THE *ILIAD*

Of all the characters who fight at Troy, Achilles is the most complex. The bravest, swiftest and most devastating warrior in battle, the entire plot of the *Iliad* nevertheless revolves around his capacity for extreme wrath and withdrawal from the fray for much of the poem. In Book 1 he reacts in fury when his commander, King Agamemnon, high-handedly seizes the captured Trojan woman, Briseis, who had been given to Achilles as a reward and mark of honour for the risks he daily takes and the battles he has won. Why, he protests, should he endure such risks and battles if he does not receive the honour he deserves? In fury he withdraws into his tent, refusing to fight and assist his comrades. However, in Book 16, without Achilles to defend him, his beloved companion[5] Patroclus is killed by the Trojan Hector, son of King Priam. Achilles' grief is extreme, and in Book 18 he resolves to return to the fighting to avenge Patroclus and rescue his body, despite knowing full well that if he does so he is destined to die soon:

> For my mother Thetis the goddess of the silver feet tells me
> I carry two sorts of destiny toward the day of my death. Either,
> If I stay here and fight beside the city of the Trojans,
> My return home is gone, but my glory shall be everlasting;
> But if I return home to the beloved land of my fathers,
> The excellence of my glory is gone, but there will be a long life
> Left for me, and my end in death will not come quickly.[6]

When Achilles does re-enter the battle his grief, rage and guilt drive him to acts of savagery which both other Greek warriors and the gods deplore: he slaughters 12 young Trojans on Patroclus' pyre and desecrates Hector's corpse by dragging it round Patroclus' tomb (*Iliad* 23.175 and 24.14 and 24.416–17). Of the latter act, Apollo says that:

> So Achilles has destroyed pity, and there is not in him
> Any shame . . .
> . . . he does dishonour to the dumb earth in his fury. (24.39–54)

Nevertheless, throughout the entire poem Achilles is also the hero most capable of reflection, at times questioning the heroic code itself; in the final book he and the suppliant Priam – for whom

Achilles is explicitly said to feel pity, despite Apollo's view of him – share a moving few moments of grief, Priam weeping for his son Hector, and Achilles for both Patroclus and his aged father Peleus, whom he knows he will never see again:

> . . . far from the land of my fathers
> I sit here in Troy, and bring nothing but sorrow to you and your children. (24.507–42)

Achilles, then, is a very different character from Odysseus. In *Posterior Analytics* 97b, Aristotle says that there are two distinct kinds of *megalopsychia*, greatness of soul. One is a refusal to submit to dishonourable treatment, and one of the examples he gives is Achilles. The other is being unmoved by misfortune, and although Odysseus is not mentioned (we shall shortly be considering one of those who is), he would clearly be a prime candidate.

HEROES AND GODS

Nevertheless, the Homeric heroes do share certain features, and one of these is the fact that several of them have heroes and models of their own: Achilles himself looks up to Heracles (*Iliad* 18.117), and in Book 9 the embassy tasked with trying to persuade him to return to the fighting discover him singing of the 'illustrious deeds of men' (9.189). In the *Odyssey* both the goddess Athena and the aged Nestor separately urge Odysseus' son, the youthful and impressionable Telemachus, to take Orestes as a role model: just as Orestes slew his mother Clytemnestra's lover Aegisthus, who had usurped his father Agamemnon's place during the Trojan War, so Telemachus should also protect his father's interests and slay the suitors who have usurped Odysseus' home in his absence.[7] It is clear that in highlighting the usefulness of role models in moral and intellectual development, Plato is only harnessing and providing psychological backing to practices that were already deeply embedded in Greek culture and educational practice.

Another key general feature of the Homeric heroes is their special connection to the gods. Some, like Achilles, have one divine parent (the sea-goddess Thetis) and one mortal one (Peleus); others, like Odysseus, claim some divine ancestry (his father Laertes, although human, is a descendant of Zeus). All are supported by individual gods or goddesses (both Achilles and Odysseus by Athena) and infused with divine strength at critical moments of the fighting. After Homer, this divine element became more formalized: in the fifth-century lyric poet Pindar, for example, it becomes part of the definition of a hero that he[8] always has one divine and one mortal parent, and, although mortal himself, the hero is thus entitled to a – usually localized – religious cult after his death.[9] Between Homer and Pindar came Hesiod, who in *Works and Days* 109–201 outlines what he terms the 'Five Ages of Man': the Heroic Age – 'a divine race of demi-gods' – comes fourth, after Gold, Silver and Bronze and before the, in Hesiod's eyes, current dismal Iron Age.

What is the impact of the Homeric heroes' semi-divinity on their status as models? While ordinary humans cannot of course emulate a hero's semi-divinity, his divine links generally appear not only to enhance his gleaming allure but also to make his particular qualities, actions and words all the more attractive and inspiring to those searching for an example to follow, especially as the divine backing seems to guarantee immunity from normal civic censure, as Socrates emphasizes at *Republic* 3.391e. In effect, the divine links give us permission to act immorally and be our worst selves; the implication is that the cult around the Homeric heroes has at least partly been created precisely *because* they sometimes behave disgracefully. Although there are exceptions, such as Hippias,[10] Socrates' view of the attractiveness of Homeric heroes as models seems to have been the prevalent one.[11]

PLATO AND HOMER

Plato is fully aware of the continuing power and influence of Homer: at *Republic* 10.606e, Socrates says that Homer is admired as the 'educator of Greece' and, crucially for our discussion, that some say we should model our whole lives on his poetry. He does not, however, think this influence is a wholesome one. Very reluctantly – Socrates adds at 10.607a that Homer is the 'best of poets and the first of tragedians' – Homer is to be courteously escorted from their ideal city. We shall be considering Plato's views on art in general and Homer's art in particular in chapter 7; our task here is to look at what Plato has to say, specifically, about employing the Homeric heroes as role models, and it is abundantly clear that in his view the damaging examples Homeric heroes set to impressionable young minds are one of the chief problems with Homer (even though at *Republic* 10.595b Socrates – and in this case we may comfortably assume Plato too – admits he has loved Homer since he was a boy). Throughout all his works, Plato interrogates the Homeric heroes, particularly Achilles and Odysseus, and seeks to amend or even replace them.[12] This interrogation is not only of historical interest, rich though that is: Plato helps us understand the abiding problems of uncritical hero-worship, whether the worshipper is seeking to emulate the hero's life and achievements in any detail or not. And, as indicated above, his exploration can illuminate current debates about whom we should honour and how, and the danger of cheapening heroism and conflating it with celebrity, particularly if the celebrated behaviour is the consumption and display of material goods.

PLATO AND HOMER: THE *APOLOGY*

Initially Plato seems to view Achilles in a positive light. At *Apology* 28b, Socrates compares Achilles' behaviour to his own: his willingness to die rather than compromise his dedication to philosophy is comparable to Achilles' willingness to sacrifice his life to avenge Patroclus. Socrates imagines a hypothetical critic asking whether he is not ashamed for following a pursuit which has put him in immediate danger of being put to death? Absolutely not, replies Socrates: no one of any worth should consider whether his actions carry any physical risk; the only thing that matters is to consider whether one's actions are those of a good or a bad man.

Achilles, for example, utterly despised danger in comparison with enduring disgrace. He was fully aware that if he re-entered the fighting then he was destined to die soon, but the only thing that he feared was to live as a coward.

At first glance this comparison seems straightforward enough, and clearly well-chosen to appeal to the jury. Nevertheless, a second glance raises questions. Socrates continues:

> Wherever a man stations himself, considering that it is best for him to be there, or wherever he is stationed by his commander, there he must – so it seems to me – remain and take the risks.

Obeying the orders of Agamemnon and remaining at his post – essential to the civic *andreia* of the Auxiliaries in the *Republic* – are scarcely amongst Achilles' strengths. Furthermore, it is very odd that Socrates appears here to be endorsing personal revenge, and indeed describing it in the language of justice:[13] at *Crito* 49c and *Republic* 335d, Socrates unequivocally rejects the law of revenge and we have noted that this was also the view of the historic Socrates.[14] We should also note that in the *Iliad* Achilles says he is returning to battle not only to avenge Patroclus, but also to win 'excellent glory' (18.121); yet at *Apology* 23d and 29d–e, Socrates criticizes his accusers for putting their desire for honour before the truth. Even this is complicated, however, as to achieve glory and honour one must first at least be thought to deserve them, so the desire for them could in itself be considered an honourable thing, a point to which we shall be returning at the end of this chapter.[15]

The more one considers Socrates' comparison between himself and Achilles in the *Apology*, then, the more complicated it becomes. Socrates himself appears to realize this: at 41a–c he says that if Hades exists – he does not commit himself – he is looking forward to meeting Odysseus and Agamemnon and all the other heroes there, and to examining and investigating them. It would seem that the unexamined death is not worth experiencing either.[16]

PLATO AND HOMER: HIPPIAS MAJOR AND HIPPIAS MINOR

Socrates again speaks approvingly of Achilles' fine (*kalon*) choice of a glorious early death at *Hippias Major*: it is precisely this example that we saw caused Hippias to distinguish between what is *kalon* for the offspring of gods (and indeed the gods themselves) and what is *kalon* for ordinary mortals.[17] The *Hippias Major* also recounts how Achilles' son, Neoptolemus, asks wise old Nestor after the fall of Troy (and his father's death) what fine practices a young man should pursue in order to become renowned – the hero's son is eager to know how to become a hero himself.

Yet in the *Hippias Minor*, which follows the *Hippias Major* in its dramatic setting, the *Hippias Major*'s general approval of Homeric heroes is subject to explicit scrutiny. As the dialogue opens we learn that Hippias has just been giving a discourse on Homer, and this reminds Socrates that he once heard a certain Apeimantus claim that the *Iliad* is a finer (*kallion*) poem than the *Odyssey* in as much as Achilles is finer than Odysseus. What, asks Socrates, is Hippias' opinion? Which of the two heroes is better? Hippias replies that Achilles is the best of those who went to Troy, Nestor the wisest, and Odysseus the wiliest. Achilles is not only courageous, but also true and straightforward: he speaks what he thinks, and does what he says;[18] whereas Odysseus is wily and false.

This prompts Socrates to investigate the notions of the true and the false, and the voluntary and the involuntary, in the course of which he makes clearly mischievous assertions – and equally clearly intended to be understood as such – about Achilles being just as false as Odysseus. This investigation, although intriguing in itself, need not detain us here; what matters for our present inquiry into heroism is the reason Socrates gives at 370d–e for asking about Achilles and Odysseus in the first place:

> Now I, Hippias, originally asked my question because I was at a loss as to which of the two men is depicted as better by the poet, since I considered both of them to be excellent, and it was hard to decide which was better . . .

Socrates' dilemma may be clarified if we consider again Aristotle's distinction (*Posterior Analytics* 97b) between two different *kinds* of greatness of soul. We saw above that the first is a refusal to submit to dishonourable treatment, and that Aristotle cites Achilles as a prime example (Alcibiades is also cited). We also saw that the second kind, being unmoved by misfortune, could clearly apply to Odysseus, although Aristotle does not mention him. In the *Hippias Minor*, Socrates appears to be anticipating Aristotle and inviting us to consider that there may be at least two kinds of heroism. And Plato's motivation for making Socrates do this is not hard to find, because one of the examples of being unmoved by misfortune that Aristotle *does* give is the historic Socrates himself.

Aristotle's choice is spot on. Not only was the historic Socrates willing to endure execution by the city rather than compromise his commitment to philosophy, but he was also capable of great feats of physical stamina in the city's service. At *Symposium* 219e–220d, for instance, Alcibiades says that when on campaign at Potidaea, Socrates surpassed them all in his endurance of physical hardships, while his courage and resilience in the retreat from Delium is highlighted at *Symposium* 220e–221a and *Laches* 181a–b. Socrates may have compared himself to Achilles in the *Apology*, but Odysseus would appear to be the more obvious comparison. Indeed, at *Protagoras* 315b, Socrates *does* obliquely compare himself to Odysseus, likening his sighting of Hippias and the other sophists holding court to Odysseus' sighting of the shade of Achilles in Hades (*Odyssey* 11.601). As Odysseus is the only one still alive in this scene, the implication is that he – and hence Socrates – is the more modern hero.

However, Odysseus is clearly not without his problems as an exemplar either: his capacity to deceive is the main reason that Apeimantus thinks the truthful Achilles is the nobler of the two. The most notorious instance of Odysseus' wiliness is his tricking Philoctetes into handing over the bow required for the capture of Troy.[19] In short, each of the two main Homeric protagonists will require considerable purification if they are to be helpful models in Plato's educational project, as the questioning ending to the

Hippias Minor indicates. In the *Republic*, we find precisely such purification and, in Achilles' case, eventual elimination.

PLATO AND HOMER: THE *REPUBLIC*

Although Plato's critique of the Homeric heroes runs throughout the *Republic*, many of the key passages are in Books 2 and 3, in the account of the primary education of the future Auxiliaries in the ideal *polis* (the selection of some Auxiliaries for training to be Philosopher-Rulers happens when they are older). Although Odysseus is chastized for being prone to physical indulgence, Socrates' chief target is Achilles, whose undoubted glamour is more likely to appeal to future fighters (as indeed it did to Alexander the Great, who not only hero-worshipped Homer's Achilles but modelled many of his actions on him, including some of his most repellent).[20] Within *Republic* 2.379–3.391 there are 16 references to Homer's Achilles or his speeches, and 14 of these are critical: Achilles misrepresents Zeus as capricious, whereas God can only be all-good; he disobeys and furiously attacks Agamemnon, his commander-in-chief ('you wine-sack, with the eyes of a dog and the courage of a doe');[21] he launches a verbal assault on Apollo and not only refuses to obey the river-god Scamander but is actually willing to fight him. He is also at times capable of real, uncontrolled savagery. Socrates has no interest in presenting a well-rounded or fair portrayal of Achilles; his concern is to emphasize the dangers of adopting him as a model.

It is notable that Socrates distinguishes the Achilles of the *Iliad* from any possible historical source: Socrates says that he simply cannot believe that the real Achilles would have done or said such things. In Books 2 and 3, therefore, the sections of the poem involving Achilles are to be heavily censored; when we come to the Myth of Er in Book 10, however (which Plato partly invents), Achilles seems to be banished altogether. Er was a soldier killed in battle in Pamphylia (in modern-day Turkey) and his body was put on the funeral pyre; but before the fire was lit he came to life again and told of all that he had seen in Hades, including how various famous figures from legend and myth chose the pattern of life for their next reincarnation. The soul of Odysseus, for instance, now 'cured of all ambition' by the memory of his former hardships, selected 'the uneventful life of an ordinary man'. Achilles, however, does not appear in the Myth of Er at all. A suitably purified Odysseus may be acceptable as a model in the ideal city, but Achilles is beyond redemption.

SOLDIERS AND WARRIORS

What accounts for this dramatic change in attitude towards Achilles? The answer lies in the development of Plato's tripartite psychology, and its analogy in the tripartite city; although Socrates does not formally introduce the tripartite psychic division until *Republic* Book 4, it is clearly anticipated in Books 2 and 3.[22] Achilles is undoubtedly thumoeidic – he is courageous, prone to anger, and driven by the desires for glory and success – but Plato has come to see him as the prime exemplar of the *thumoeides* gone wild, a terrible warning of what can happen if someone is not just characterized by their *thumoeides* but actually dominated by it. This is why Homer's Achilles is so problematic in the primary education of the future Auxiliaries, as they are certainly characterized by their *thumoeides* – and need to be – but must submit to the rational rule of the Philosopher-Rulers. In 4.429c–e, Socrates defines civic courage as holding fast in all circumstances to correct beliefs about what is and is not to be feared, and Achilles' undoubted bravery clearly differs markedly from this kind of steadfast fortitude. Fighting practices have also changed since the *Iliad* was composed (probably in the eighth century BCE): in hoplite formation it is vital that each man holds his place in the line and does not go charging off on some individual quest for personal glory. The city that Socrates is proposing, in other words, needs obedient and disciplined soldiers, not overmighty and egoistic warriors.

AN UNQUIET SOUL

Given the tripartite psychology infusing the selective portrayal of Achilles, it is significant that Socrates emphasizes at 3.391c that the problems with Achilles' behaviour stem from his internal disorder (*tarachē*). It is also highly significant that Socrates makes clear that this internal disorder results not only in insubordinate and at times savage behaviour, but also in wretchedness: he both cites and deplores Achilles' terrible grief on hearing of the death of Patroclus, for instance, and his lament on seeing Patroclus' ghost. Socrates in the *Republic* is uncompromising in his view that nothing in this phenomenal world merits extreme sorrow (10.604b–c): Achilles' emotional responses are disproportionate and another sign that his reason is not in control. Socrates is concerned that Achilles' laments may foster an inappropriate fear of death or excessive emotionalism in general in the young Auxiliaries, and he wants above all to present Achilles as a deeply disturbed man whom no sensible person would want to emulate.

This disturbed behaviour arises in part from the problematic nature of honour and glory as objects of desire. In the *Iliad* honour is a finite commodity to be parcelled out to the various heroes: more for one means less for another;[23] adherents of the life of honour will thus often have to fight over it as well as for it. This is particularly clear in the cases where the honour is symbolized by a material reward (1.171; 6.48), such as the enslaved girl Briseis (a dangerous merging of timocratic and appetitive objects of desire to which we shall be returning). This particular form of vulnerability is part of a greater problem with honour, namely that a life devoted to honour and honours is lacking in self-sufficiency. As Aristotle notes, honour 'appears to depend more on those who confer it than on the recipient'.[24] We may think we have behaved honourably – and we may be right – but whether we actually receive any honours is ultimately not up to us. 'Beware of the desire for glory,' warns Cicero in *de Officiis* (*On Duties*) 1.68, 'because it takes away freedom.'

Another problem arises from the fact that honours and glory are often sought, as they are by Achilles, due to a hatred of death (or indeed fear of it, though fear is not a major motivating factor in Achilles' case), and a desire to seek a lasting name as compensation. But this desire for glory can of course drive one to actions which risk or result in the very death that one loathes, as Lucretius remarks in *de Rerum Natura* (*On the Nature of Things*) 3.59–82, drily observing that some men's fear of death is so great that they 'die for the sake of statues and a name'.

Plato's exploration of the Homeric heroes illuminates how dangerous it is, for both the individual and their society, to aim for worldly honours as one's main goal, unguided by reason; yet it also illustrates how the concept of heroism, and the associated concepts of glory and honour, still remain important for both individuals and society. As Plato sees it, the question is not 'How can we get rid of heroes?', but rather 'How can we harness our longing to be or look up to heroes by reworking heroism, thereby channelling the desires for glory and honour onto the right people and actions?' If Achilles is no longer acceptable, and Odysseus at the very least needs to be purified, then who should the new heroes be?

SOCRATES A NEW HERO?

One answer is clearly Socrates, whom as we have seen is presented by Plato throughout the dialogues in a heroic light, an improved Odysseus willing to endure mockery, abuse and ultimately death in the service of philosophy. The narrative of the accusations made against him, his trial, imprisonment and death by city-administered hemlock, is compellingly told in the *Euthyphro*, *Apology*, *Crito* and *Phaedo*, and it has gripped and moved readers ever since. And we saw above[25] how Alcibiades in the *Symposium* relates instances of Socrates' physical courage and endurance on campaign.

However – and this is really important – in his powerful speech recounting his unrequited love for Socrates (which we shall be examining more fully in the next chapter), Alcibiades also emphasizes at 221c–d that Socrates is *unique*: there has never been anyone like him (and the strong suggestion is that there never will be). It follows that it is very unlikely that Socrates can be emulated in any literal sense; if he is to be a new kind of role model, it must be in a more subtle way, serving as an inspiration to people to follow the Delphic Oracle as Socrates did and to 'know thyself', to take responsibility for cultivating their own intellectual and ethical virtues to help tackle whatever challenges they face. No individual or community can simply hope to rely on Socrates, or a Socrates replica, as a crutch: he will not appear as even a semi-divine *deus ex machina*.

Plato is fully aware of this. Given Socrates' literal inimitability, therefore, it becomes fundamental to Plato's lifelong project to present the philosopher *in general* as a new kind of hero, requiring courage (*andreia*) to persevere with difficult questions and tell people what they do not want to hear, and to endure ridicule, scorn, and even physical attacks and trial as a result.[26] Courage and heroism do not need a battlefield in order to be displayed,[27] though Socrates is also at pains to point out that in his ideal city the Philosopher-Rulers will all have gone through the requisite military training and had to show themselves to be hardy and brave in war. It is in this light of the expanding of the fields of courage and heroism that we should view Socrates' claim at *Republic* 7.540b–c that after their death the Philosopher-Rulers will go to the Isles of the Blessed – the legendary destination (albeit not in Homer) of the Homeric heroes. Furthermore, dead Philosopher-Rulers are now to be awarded public memorials and sacrifices 'as *daimones*, or at any rate as blessed with a good *daimōn* and godlike'. They are, in short, to be the objects of a hero cult, although it is not clear whether they are to be individually named. As such worldly honours are not likely to appeal to the philosophers themselves – who as we have seen in the Allegory of the Cave are said to despise such baubles[28] – Plato's intention must be to attract and encourage *trainee* philosophers, those in whom the *thumoeides* still yearns for some worldly acclaim.

Given that there are to be Philosopher-Queens as well as Philosopher-Kings in the ideal city, and given that both men and women are explicitly said to be able to exhibit *andreia*, this hero cult of wise, courageous, temperate and just Philosopher-Rulers inevitably allows for the notion of a female hero. Admittedly Plato does not make much of this, in part perhaps due to the need to direct the appeal of his teachings to the young males who studied at the Academy,[29] but nevertheless the consequence is there. The field of heroism is being broadened in terms of gender as well as activity. He *is* absolutely explicit about the consequences for education, not only in the *Republic* but also in his final work, the *Laws*, where as we have seen the narrowly militaristic education system for young males in Sparta is heavily criticized in Book 1.[30]

A HERO FOR OUR TIMES?

Such insights will always be valuable. Are there in addition any particular implications for specific contemporary issues? I think there are indeed areas where reflections both by and on Plato can be of profound assistance.

Despite the dangers of wanting to be a hero oneself, or admiring a perceived hero uncritically, I agree with Plato that the term 'hero' has value. There is admittedly always likely to be debate about how much time, energy and material resources we should spend on fostering heroism, and how much on fixing the problems that require it in the first place. There is also always the danger that people will pin their hopes on a hero emerging, instead of taking responsibility for developing their own inner resources to meet current challenges. Nevertheless, it is also true that unforeseen situations may arise which genuinely do require a heroic response. Heroism will always have currency, and the term will always have potency. There is still a need for genuine heroes and heroism: true heroes can inspire us to be our best selves, just as inappropriate heroes can give us licence to be our worst. So the immediate question is: how do you define them?

An initial working definition of a hero might be someone who does or creates something reasonably perceived to be of outstanding benefit to their community, or some sub-section of it, which most people would find impossible to do or create. This suggests that being a hero goes beyond what is ordinarily thought to be one's duty (even though heroes themselves may not see their actions in that light at all, and may well say that they were simply doing what anyone would have done in that situation). It also shows that to be a hero at least one other person must see you as

HEROISM, CELEBRITY AND MONEY

such: it is partly a subjective notion. You can of course be a hero-in-waiting, but the notion of an 'unsung hero' makes no strict sense: at least one person must be doing the singing. It follows, as Plato recognized, that finding out who are the heroes of a person or a community tells you a great deal about them and their values and aspirations: for better or worse, ideals of heroism play a crucial role in the forging of personal and communal identity. They help us understand not only ourselves, but also others, including those with whom we may be in conflict. This understanding is deepened whether or not a particular individual actually wants to emulate their hero, or whether they simply admire them (or even worship them).

STATUES AND MEMORIALS

Plato's perceptive insights into the desires for recognition, honour and glory, and the honours a city bestows, can help inform our current, sometimes heated, debates about statues, memorials and other community and state accolades. Plato understood the depths of feeling involved, and the fact that such accolades both endorse and strengthen individual and communal values and sense of identity. He can thus also help us to think through what we should do if changes in those values over time mean that the subject of a statue, for instance, is now regarded as morally questionable, or even utterly disgraced. Two recent examples are the slave trader and philanthropist Edward Colston in Bristol in the UK, and Confederate generals, leaders and soldiers in the US, such as General Robert E. Lee, quite literally fighting to uphold slavery. In both cases, statues to them were the subject of unauthorized physical attacks in 2020, after the murder of George Floyd in Minneapolis and the Black Lives Matter movement that erupted thereafter. Are unauthorized assaults ever acceptable and, if not, what should happen to such statues? A more detailed plaque, refacing (e.g. with light projections which do not damage the statue itself), or removal to a museum? Such debates – and they also of course arise in connection with military medals and Government Honours Lists – are natural and healthy in a democracy, but at the moment they can tend to generate more heat than light. We need clarity. Few have thought as deeply as Plato about honour, honours and honouring, and their potential for both benefit and harm, and we would do well to reflect on what he has to say. He can help us be more thoughtful and aware of whom we are honouring, and why.[31]

HEROISM DEBASED AND THE TRIPARTITE *PSYCHĒ*

This is why it matters so much if the term 'hero' becomes confused with mere 'celebrity', and the currency of heroism is defaced. Plato can again help us here. As we have seen, he not only understood about our desires for honour, respect and fame as supposed indicators of self-worth; he also understood how corrosive such desires can be if they take control of the *psychē*, and are not guided by reason. In this scenario the *thumoeides* will seek to gain honour and success simply by doing and acquiring the things that the society already values; and given that Plato thinks that all societies short of the ideal are degenerate, this plainly poses a real problem: the celebrity may not in fact have done or created anything genuinely worth celebrating.

The problem is particularly acute if the corrupt society especially values material goods, and in consequence the desires of the *thumoeides* converge disastrously with the materialistic desires of the appetites, and the person seeking affirmation thinks it can be achieved through the acquisition, consumption and display of money and material goods. This is precisely the narrative we have seen Plato depict in *Republic* Book 8 where Socrates recounts the degeneration of the philosophic man first to the timocratic (honour-loving) man, and then to the oligarchic man (543a–555b).[32]

In addition to this general warning about the debasing of heroic ideals, and the notions of glory and success with which they are intricately entwined, the vivid portraits of individual and social decline outlined by Socrates in *Republic* Book 8 (and Book 9) can also illuminate specific recent events. In chapter 4 we touched on two notable examples in the UK: the Parliamentary expenses scandal of 2009[33] and the England riots of 2011, in which shops were looted. Plato's tripartite psychology not only reveals the connections between the two but also makes us uncomfortably aware that we are all to some extent implicated. He would point out that both events were motivated not only by a strong appetite for material goods, but also by the belief that goods bestow status and self-worth; he would also point out that, in the UK at the times in question, these beliefs unfortunately had some specious support: they arose precisely because people could see that this was indeed a way to acquire status in that particular society. And Plato would add that, in respect of basic motivation (though not in law), there was little difference between the looting and the greed manifested by some politicians – greed which also caused great damage to the country as a whole.

What might a Platonic response be? His dialogues in general, and perhaps the *Republic* in particular, suggest a twofold approach. Individuals must certainly take individual responsibility and be held to moral as well as legal account for their choices: this is precisely the message of the Myth of Er at the end of the *Republic*. However, there must also be a willingness by society as a whole to consider its values and the actions and possessions to which it accords status. Each of us needs to ask whether we have, even if unwittingly, helped to create and foster the warped conceptions of value and status that currently obtain: we need to reflect on what we buy, read and write, the music and lyrics that we create and consume, the programmes that we make and watch. We do not need to agree with all or even most of the proposals in the *Republic* for the radical reformation of society to recognize the brilliance of Plato's analysis of social ills in Books 8 and 9, and his diagnosis that the material greed which fuels such activities as looting, or the abuse of expense accounts, does not simply result from the unnecessary appetites having run amok; it results from an unguided *thumoeides* as well, a *thumoeides* which values and seeks glory and success in the wrong places because it is in precisely those places that the degenerate surrounding society locates them. If we want to diminish instances of looting and political abuse of our taxes then we need to pay far less attention, and accord far less status, to the supposed 'goods' that such activities seek (I do not know, but I would bet that in the 2011 England riots no one looted a work of Plato). As long as rewards and status are given, and can so clearly be seen to be given, to selfishness and greed, we cannot pretend that such behaviour has nothing to do with us.

HEROISM REMADE

One of the main ways in which Plato still matters, then, stems from his profound reflections on the concept of heroism and the associated notions of honour, glory and fame. Yet although he is fully aware of the dangers of misplaced heroic aspirations and hero-worship, and seeking glory in the wrong places, he never abandons the notions but seeks rather always to rework them and channel our thumoeidic desires towards rationally approved ends. He understood that the notion of a hero, and the longing for glory, can still have real potency and value: properly formed and guided, these concepts can enlarge our moral ambition and offer us a vision of what the best version of ourselves might be. Improperly formed, they give licence to realizing the worst version of ourselves. It follows that we abuse and debase heroic ideals at our peril: in the present age, as in all ages, there are urgent threats to face and surmount. Here be dragons, and to find the heroes to conquer them we first need to look within; for that strategy to work, however, we have to make sure that what we find within is true.

6

Love and Friendship

Plato's dialogues contain some of the richest explorations ever composed of erotic love (*erōs*) and friendship and affection (*philia*) – explorations again brought to vivid life through being articulated and embodied by a diverse and memorable cast of characters. His powerful, witty and at times moving discussions can help us think through a number of our own current confusions about different forms of relationship and their role in a good life, and his innovative treatments of issues concerning sex and gender can also inform current debates. The treatments of *philia* throughout the dialogues prompt us to ask not only about its role in our private lives, but also about its place in civic associations, and even whether it should guide policymaking as a civic goal.

We have seen throughout how Plato quite often depicts Socrates debating with uncooperative or even hostile interlocutors – debates from which we, the readers, can nevertheless still learn much.[1] However, we have also seen how the actual *participants* in the dialogues make more progress if they engage in debate in a friendly and cooperative spirit: Cleinias in the *Euthydemus*, Theaetetus and Theodorus in the *Theaetetus*, Megillus and Clinias in the *Laws* (with the Athenian Stranger), and Glaucon and Adeimantus in the *Republic* (even though the two last often serve as decidedly critical friends at times). Furthermore, as we shall see in this chapter, in some dialogues such as the *Symposium* almost all the characters are friends to some degree.² Nor did Plato simply compose such amicable settings for constructive discussion through his words: he also created just such a productive setting in the Academy he established, influenced in part by his positive experiences staying with the Pythagorean communities in southern Italy.

The very term *philosophia* of course involves the *phil*-stem, so a deeper appreciation of Plato's thoughts on *philia* will help us better understand his conception of philosophy too. And, as we shall see when we come to the *Symposium*, *erōs* is fundamental to Plato's conception of philosophy as well.

PHILIA: THE *LYSIS*

Although *philia* usually refers to friendship or family affection, it can sometimes mean 'love' in a more general sense – which can make the boundaries between *philia* and *erōs* particularly porous. The relationships that *philia* embraces would have been of special prominence in the relatively small Greek *polis*, in which adult and teenage males would have encountered each other all the time.³ In the *Lysis*, Socrates recounts a conversation about the nature of *philia* and *philos* (both the noun and the adjective) he had in a wrestling-school with a group of young men and boys, especially the beautiful young Lysis and his close friend Menexenus. As ever, Plato makes sure that readers have a lot of interpretive work to do and problems to solve for themselves; and, as also so often, the issue of *philia* is not simply discussed, but also enacted through the relationships between the various characters. In the early sections various problematic arguments and positions are set up, which seem designed to prompt us to try to disentangle *philia* from *erōs*, and to consider to what extent such disentanglement is even possible; the erotically charged atmosphere of the wrestling-school, in which males wrestled naked, is emphasized, including the fact that one of the others present is Hippothales, the older lover (*erastēs*)[4] of Lysis; at 211e, Socrates also says that he is 'passionate' (*erōtikōs*) about possessing friends. These early positions (which Socrates quickly dismisses) also appear intended to invite us to distinguish friendship from affectionate family ties, and to clarify when *philos* is being used in an active or passive sense – whether it refers to the person feeling affection or the person for whom it is felt. The main arguments concerning *philia* as friendship begin at 213d when Socrates engages in elenchus with Lysis: why do individuals form the friendships that they do?

The first model considered is that of like being attracted to like – but this is rejected on the grounds that bad people do not become friends with bad people, as their badness would lead them to injure each other, and hence to hatred rather than friendship. It is suggested that perhaps people alike in goodness become friends, but at this stage of the *Lysis* doubts are raised about this: if someone is good they are surely self-sufficient and have no need of the goodness of another? The next theory considered is that opposites attract – a popular saying in ancient Greece, just as it is now – but this too is rejected, as it would mean that good people are attracted to bad people, and the just to the unjust, and they agree that this cannot be the case. The model to which they seem most sympathetic is that friendship arises between two good people who are drawn to each other not on the grounds of their *likeness* but their *goodness*; there is also the suggestion that this form of true friendship is not based on lack or need either, although that is not clearly spelled out. Indeed, nothing is clearly spelled out and the dialogue ends in apparent perplexity, although it has given us many fruitful trails to pursue. It also ends with Socrates declaring that although they have not yet defined *philia*, he is sure that he, Lysis and Menexenus are all friends. True friendship matters in a flourishing life, including for philosophic discussion and our moral and intellectual development. And it is of necessity a reciprocated relationship, which raises questions regarding the possibility of online friendships, a subject we will return to at the end of this chapter.

PHILIA IN THE CITY

Plato's consistently held ideal of social and political harmony is hardly surprising given his early years in an Athens – and a family

– bitterly divided between democratic and oligarchic (and in many cases also Sparta-leaning) factions. At *Republic* 3.412d, Socrates says it is very important to select as Guardians those who really care for and love (*philein*) the city, feeling that they all share a common interest. These Guardians will work to promote the flourishing of the whole city (4.420b–421c), a city which will be temperate because all three classes are in natural agreement about who should rule and who be ruled (4.432a). Furthermore, Socrates declares triumphantly (and optimistically) at 9.590c–d, this harmony will not only exist between the classes: if we are all ruled by reason, whether our own or that of the Philosopher-Rulers, then in that respect we will all be equal and all be friends (*philoi*).

The rulers' desired aim of promoting friendship between classes and citizens is stated even more clearly in the *Statesman* and *Laws*. We have seen in chapter 4[5] that in the *Statesman* the chief task of the ruler is to weave together opposing dispositions in the community, partly through an education system which instils shared values and beliefs, and partly through intermarriage. At 311b–c the resulting cloth is said to be one in which the disparate characters, both courageous and gentle, are drawn together in friendship (*philia*) and concord and share a common life. (It is even claimed that this common life will be shared by slaves as well as the freeborn, though no plan is proposed for checking on whether the slaves would agree.) In the *Laws* the main protagonist, the Athenian Stranger, declares at 1.628c that a lawgiver should always aim at the highest good, namely to create peace and friendly feeling (*philophrosunē*) amongst the members of the community – a point reinforced many times throughout the dialogue: at 3.693b–c, for example, we are told that the lawgiver should legislate with a view to creating a *polis* that is free, wise and 'in friendship with itself'; while at 5.743c it is boldly claimed that the fundamental purpose of all the laws they are proposing is that the citizens should flourish as much as possible, and to the greatest degree be united in mutual friendship.

It may be protested that such aims all sound very lovely, but that they are hopelessly unrealistic. Others may object that even if the goal sounds appealing, the various practical means to achieving it are not appealing at all – and that this charge applies to the means put forward by Socrates in the *Republic*, the Eleatic Stranger in the *Statesman*, and the Athenian Stranger in the *Laws*: no end is worth the means of the various applications of invented origin stories, censorship of the arts, abolition of the nuclear family and private property, arranged marriages and so on.[6] Furthermore, even within the ideal *polis* of the *Republic* and the semi-ideal *poleis* of the *Statesman* and *Laws*, there are still slaves, and it is not clear whether or how the promotion of friendly relations could apply to them too (despite the optimistic language of *Statesman* 311c noted above).

It is even less clear how the recommendations of legislating for harmony and friendship could be put into practice in Plato's Athens: quite apart from the fact that Plato does not think that any rulers to date (apart, perhaps, from Solon) have exhibited the requisite reasoning ability, how might not only the slaves of Athens but also its women and resident foreigners (metics) be integrated into a harmonious whole, when they are currently so radically excluded from civic life? And, it might well be thought, it is just absurdly naïve to suppose that any contemporary ruler or rulers could succeed in creating anything like friendly harmony amongst the much larger and more diverse communities with which they usually have to deal, and if they cannot hope to succeed, it is a waste of time even trying. Some might add too that friendship can also at times be a dangerous political force, in that leaders can give unwarranted favours and unmerited offices to particularly intimate friends.

My response is twofold. Firstly, a distinction is needed between generally amicable relations and close personal friends: seeking to promote the first does not, and should not, have to involve nepotistic or corrupt favours to intimate friends or relatives. Secondly, as I suggested in chapter 4, the fact that an ideal cannot be fully implemented does not mean it has no value in setting the direction of travel: indeed, in the case of simply aiming at social harmony between groups and individuals, this goal seems far less problematic than that of the supposedly ideally just city as a whole, about which we rightly raised a number of concerns. It has of course always been true that some leaders and prospective leaders have quite deliberately tried to create suspicion, fear and disunity, in the hope that they can exploit such divisions to entice the larger group to support them (and although this applies most obviously to those in democracies, it is relevant to autocracies too: autocrats also want to avoid coups and revolution); nevertheless, although this is doubtless always true, there are perhaps certain periods when such tactics are deployed with particular brazenness, and in an especially large number of countries. The early 2020s appears to be just such a period. However, the fact that it is happening does not mean that it has to happen, or continue to happen (at least to such a degree) in the future. It is not hard to think of issues about which our individual well-being is clearly interdependent with the well-being of those around us – pandemics; air and water pollution; climate change – and unifying narratives around such things could truthfully be told without any resort to dubious mythology or propaganda, if the political will and courage were there. It is notable that although Plato became increasingly despondent about a genuine Philosopher-Ruler ever emerging (hence the need for a 'second-best' system of laws in his final work), he became even *more* committed to the need for leaders to aim for harmony and friendship in the laws they made. The world badly needs leaders of such ambition right now, and we should resist the temptation to give in to cynicism, exhaustion and a sense of futility; we should continue to look for, vote for (if we have a vote), and, if in the position to do so, even be leaders who genuinely seek unity.

PHILIA IN THE PSYCHĒ

Given the analogy drawn in the *Republic* between city and *psychē*, it is not surprising that the language of friendship is applied not only to relations between the classes, but also to relations between the three faculties of the *psychē*, and at 4.442c the *psychē* is said to be moderate (*sōphrōn*) when all three faculties are in 'friendly and harmonious agreement' that reason should rule; while at 4.443d–e the just person is the person who has united his psychic faculties into a harmonious whole and consequently lives on good terms with himself (literally: 'is a friend to himself').[7] We have already noted the possible influence on Freud of this conception of a healthy, integrated *psychē*.[8] Interestingly, in the accounts in *Republic* Books 8 and 9 of degenerate *psychai*, Socrates makes it clear that those whose *psychai* are in a state of internal fragmentation and conflict can also lack actual friends. At 9.576a the tyrant is said to possess no real friends at all, fawned on by parasites but also tormented by suspicion and fear.

ERŌS: THE *SYMPOSIUM*

What of the relationship between *philia* and *erōs*? For this we need to return to the *Symposium*,[9] a sparkling dialogue which tells of a drinking-party in Athens at which a wide variety of characters – including a tragic poet, comic poet, doctor, philosopher and general-cum-statesman – meet to celebrate the tragedian Agathon's victory on the previous day in a dramatic contest. Feeling decidedly fragile after over-imbibing the night before, they decide to forgo the usual sensuous entertainments and heavy drinking associated with symposia and give speeches instead on *Erōs*, the god of erotic love (throughout the dialogue the speakers move fluidly between *Erōs* the god and *erōs* the human experience). Through both their formal speeches and their lively personal interactions, Plato explores profound questions about the origins, definition, aims, objects and effects of *erōs*, vividly showing us what sort of life and moral character a particular view of *erōs* might promote and reflect. Are some kinds of love more beneficial than others – and to whom? Do we love people for their unique individuality, or because they manifest, to varying degrees, certain qualities of goodness and beauty? Is the rechannelling of erotic energy onto artistic, intellectual or devotional objects either possible or desirable?

Furthermore, the distance between the date of composition (c.384–378 BCE) and the dramatic dates of the symposium itself and the framework conversation (416 and c.404 BCE respectively) allows Plato to make ironic references to future events known to his readers: in chapter 1, for instance, we saw how he adroitly foreshadows both the downfall of Alcibiades and the death of Socrates, and the uncomfortable connection between their two fates. The choice of a relaxed symposium setting also enables Plato to reveal different facets of Socrates' complex personality, such as his ability to remain self-controlled at all times, physically and psychologically unaffected by external conditions (and even by alcohol). The occasion also allows the beautiful Alcibiades to recount how Socrates resisted all his youthful attempts to seduce him; in this respect at any rate, Plato implies, Socrates did not corrupt the young. The entire work is part of Plato's lifelong defence of his mentor.

The tale of the drinking-party is intricately nested: Apollodorus, a follower of Socrates, recounts it to a group of unnamed businessmen, having heard it himself from Aristodemus, another Socratic acolyte who was actually present; one of the central speeches, that of Socrates, relates Socrates' purported conversations with a priestess-like figure named Diotima. Furthermore, Aristodemus cannot remember all the details clearly (*Symposium* 180c) and admits to having fallen asleep towards the end. Plato is thus creating even more distance than usual between himself as author and the content of the speeches – we have no option but to engage in active interpretation. He is also inviting us to reflect on the crucial but unreliable nature of intermediaries, which will be a central theme of the dialogue (especially in Diotima's speech). All this storytelling and myth-making in turn compels us to wonder how best to get at the truth of different kinds of subject matter: in particular, what is the relation between *mythos* and *logos*? Can there even be a *logos* of love?

Considerable emphasis is placed on the order of the speeches, which anticipates the importance of an orderly, rational and emotional progression up the rungs of the ladder of love in Diotima's speech; in general, order, not disorder, is seen as the more creative force in the dialogue (in addition to moderating their drinking, the female pipe-player is banished at 176e – Plato always felt the *aulos* was too conducive to licentious and rowdy behaviour [and that the musicians did not necessarily restrict themselves to musical entertainment]). However, before we examine the speeches and interchanges, we need to put them briefly in a general framework of Greek conceptions of *erōs*, and in particular conceptions of its sexual component.

The *Erastēs* and the *Erōmenos*

In theory, at least, Greeks of the classical period (at least amongst the upper-class Athenians who provide much of our evidence) articulated sexual intercourse in terms of active and passive roles: in heterosexual sex, in terms of an active male penetrator and a passive female penetrated. They also articulated male homoerotic sex in terms of these active and passive roles (there is very little evidence for female homoerotic sex, although we shall see a reference to it in Aristophanes' speech in the *Symposium*). Amongst upper-class Greeks in particular, there was a cultural practice of *paiderastia*: a (slightly) older male, usually in his twenties, would court a teenage male (as Hippothales courts Lysis). The older male was viewed as the active lover, the *erastēs*, and the younger male was viewed as the passive beloved, the *erōmenos*.[10]

In addition to romantic and erotic elements (just how much physical eroticism was acceptable was much disputed, as we shall shortly see), these *erastēs*/*erōmenos* relationships were supposed to have a social and cultural angle. The older male was supposed to educate the teenager about various social practices and cultural norms, and initiate him into elite and influential society.[11] Both lover and beloved were expected to go on to marry and have children for the *polis*, and most did. Male homoerotic relationships between two adults were rare, but not unknown (Pausanias and Agathon in the *Symposium* are a case in point, as we shall also see).

Despite the prevalence of the convention of *paiderastia*, attitudes to it were highly complex. Outside the upper classes it was mainly viewed with suspicion or mockery. Within the upper classes, it was permissible for the active older lover to pursue, but the chosen younger beloved was not supposed to appear too keen. There was also ambivalence about what physical and sexual acts were permissible: hand-holding and embraces were fine, but there were very mixed views on the acceptability of penetration, as this would involve the teenager taking on the (perceived) passive, 'female' role. The key point is not involvement with someone of the same sex, but the perception of passivity.[12]

THE EARLY SPEECHES: PHAEDRUS, PAUSANIAS AND ERYXIMACHUS

The first speaker in the *Symposium* is Phaedrus, an ardent student of rhetoric who will later be given his own eponymous dialogue. He gives a lush encomium to love of a particular individual, and it is a conception of *erōs* that is very close in some respects to modern notions of romantic love, although (as all the speeches do, at least formally) it speaks of erotic relationships mainly in terms of an older lover and a younger beloved. He also depicts *erōs* as a powerful moral educator: we long for our beloved or our lover to admire us and accordingly we behave at our very best in their presence, if necessary sacrificing our lives for their sake – a sacrifice that will be rewarded by the gods after death. Phaedrus recommends forming an army of lovers and beloveds, saying that their wish to impress each other would result in the most courageous and effective fighting force – an interesting reflection to include, perhaps, in contemporary discussions of homosexuality in the military.[13] Phaedrus believes he is portraying love as entirely desirable and beneficial; the reader, however, may feel that his lovers and beloveds do tend to die rather young.

A more pragmatic view is taken by Pausanias, a follower of the sophist Prodicus, who distinguishes between 'heavenly' and 'popular' *erōs*, and anticipates Diotima in arguing that the quality of *erōs* depends on the nature of its object, and the manner in which it is performed. 'Popular' love is concerned with the body and can be directed by the male lover (Pausanias talks only of a male subject) towards either women or boys; 'heavenly' *erōs* occurs when a man is attracted to a boy's intellect, and is concerned to further his cultural and political education. Pausanias depicts this heavenly love as perfect, but as with Phaedrus' speech we may have our concerns: as we have seen, the *erastēs/erōmenos* relationship was not generally supposed to continue when the teenager reached adulthood, and this usual time-limit plus the double-standards noted above means that it is a relationship which contains inherent tensions. The fact that Pausanias ignores all such tensions in his rosy depiction of 'heavenly' love may well involve some special pleading given that his relationship with the teenage Agathon did indeed continue into adulthood: at the time of the symposium they have been together for at least 16 years.[14]

The doctor, Eryximachus, continues the distinction between good and bad *erōs*, but, in a further anticipation of Diotima, the concept of *erōs* is widened. It is now a cosmic force, the attraction of one element for another, and has both physical and moral dimensions: deploying features of two Presocratic[15] philosophers, Empedocles and Heraclitus, he claims that the right kind of attraction leads to harmony and health, the wrong kind to conflict and disease, and it is well worth reflecting on his speech in the light of our discussion of mental and physical health viewed in normative terms of harmony in chapter 2.[16] For Eryximachus, the good *erōs* reconciles opposites in fields as diverse as medicine, music and the climate and is, critically, the force that mediates between humans and gods – a key point on which Plato will elaborate in Diotima's speech.

ARISTOPHANES

Eryximachus assumes that erotic love, properly conducted, is essential for our physical and mental well-being. The comic playwright Aristophanes expands on this, claiming that to understand love we need to know first about the nature of human beings, which the previous speakers have failed to explain (189d) – Plato is challenging us to consider which speaker (and which kind of expertise) gives the most accurate account of our human needs.

Erōs, claims Aristophanes, is a god who gives succour to humanity and our most perfect flourishing lies in the healing he provides. There follows one of the most powerful, moving, witty and ultimately disturbing accounts of *erōs* that I know, told in the form of a myth (which Plato makes Aristophanes call a *logos* [193d]). Originally humans were not as we are now but were spherical, with two faces on one head, four arms, four legs and two sets of genitals; when they ran they whirled over and over, like acrobats. Some of these proto-humans were all-male, some all-female. and some half-male and half-female. These forceful circular beings challenged the gods and in punishment Zeus split them in two, aiming thereby both to weaken them but also double the number of sacrifices and libations; he then ordered the god Apollo to sew them up. Wounded and bereft, they searched the world for their missing half, and this desire for and pursuit of the whole, says Aristophanes, is what we call *erōs* (192e); the lost half does not have to be good or beautiful, as suggested by Phaedrus, Pausanias and Eryximachus, but simply one's own.

There was no guarantee that the search would be successful, but even if it was, the positioning of their genitalia apparently made it impossible for them to make love; they just clung to each other and yearned to be grafted together again, and began to perish through hunger and idleness, as they refused to let each other go and get on with the business of staying alive. So Zeus moved their genitalia to make intercourse possible, and after making love the pair would then return to their daily tasks (though ideally in each other's company), and life would continue. It is this splitting in two which explains why some humans now desire the opposite sex and some desire their own sex (female homoeroticism is mentioned explicitly at 191e; we should note, however, that Aristophanes' myth cannot accommodate bisexuality, nor indeed asexuality): your sexual orientation depends on the sex of your missing half. *Erōs* arises from lack. If two halves do chance upon each other, they are:

> amazed and overcome by *philia* and a sense of belonging and *erōs* – not even wanting to be apart for a single moment. And these

are the ones who go on to be together throughout their lives, though they would be unable to say what they want to have from each other. For no one could imagine this to be simply sexual intercourse (*ta aphrodisia*), or that it is only on account of this that each so eagerly delights in the other's company – clearly the soul of each wants something else that it cannot express, but only dimly divines and obscurely hints at what it wishes. (192b–d)

It is a profoundly affecting description of what it feels like to be passionately in love. Plato, however, then compels us to interrogate what the lovers really desire. Aristophanes continues:

And suppose [the blacksmith god] Hephaistos were to come and stand over them as they lay together, holding his tools,[17] and were to ask: 'What is it, mortals, that you want to have from each other?' And suppose they were at a loss and he were to ask them again: 'So do you desire this, to be together, in the same place as far as possible, so as not to be separated from each other either by night or by day? If this is what you desire I am willing to fuse and smelt you together into the same piece, so that from being two you may become one, and as long as you live, the pair of you, being as one, may both live a single life, and when you die, there also in Hades you will be one instead of two, having died a single death. But see if this is what you are in love with and if it would satisfy you if this were your lot.' We know that not a single person on hearing such things would hold out in denying it, nor would he be found wishing for anything else, but he would think that he had heard what it was after all that he had been yearning for for so long, namely to be joined and fused with his beloved that the two might become one. The cause is this, that our original nature was as I have described and we were whole. *Erōs* is the name that we give to the desire and pursuit of the whole'.

In Aristophanes' myth, the lovers readily and enthusiastically agree to Hephaistos' offer. But should we? Does Plato think we should?

Note how Plato makes Hephaistos say '*if* this is what you desire' and 'see *if* this is what you are in love with and *if* it would satisfy you'. He clearly wants us to think very hard about this.

And there is much to ponder. It would appear that accepting Hephaistos' offer would entail the loss of separate physical identities, and the subsequent loss of most forms of sex. The suggestion is also that we are being offered psychic as well as physical fusion – a *complete* loss of a discrete identity. It is therefore not clear what sort of love could continue apart from self-love. This point receives formal clarity when we are told that *erōs* is the desire for and pursuit of the whole: if you define something in terms of a lack, and a quest to fill that lack, then that thing must disappear if the quest is successfully completed. So the key question is: does the consummation of erotic love cancel out the conditions that make erotic love possible? Does erotic love, thus conceived, work towards its own annihilation? And if the transformative power of *erōs* is simply a stepping-stone towards a further, different state, what is this state? What becomes of the transformed lovers?

There is a further troubling concern. Note the extreme egoism of Aristophanes' pairs of lovers: each views the other not as a whole, separate person in their own right, but as their missing 'half', to be absorbed back into them. This situation is both ethically highly disturbing and metaphysically highly questionable. Even if one decides to treat the language of the missing 'half' as merely metaphorical, and treats each of the pair as a whole, we are still left with the conclusion that two wholes are being reduced to one, which will worry many. I suggest that while Plato is vividly alive to the powerful appeal of this conception of erotic love (which as we have seen includes many of the features that we would also associate with romantic love), he is also scrutinizing it with a clear and steady gaze, and his analysis should at least give us pause for thought. Perhaps the message we are meant to take away is that erotic love is only healthy, and indeed can only properly continue at all, if we continue to see, respect and love our beloved *as other*, as a whole person in their own right, with their own needs and desires and goals, and not just there to fill gaps in our own needy and appropriative selves.

However one interprets Aristophanes' fabulous story (and of course Plato has deliberately written it to invite discussion), it has been hugely influential in Western thought and art: direct and indirect references to it appear in philosophy, poetry, novels, psychology and film; as far as I am aware, it is the first time in Western literature that the notion of one's 'other half' is articulated. Freud refers approvingly to the speech[18] and the stage (1998) and film (2001) versions of the musical comedy-drama *Hedwig and the Angry Inch* both make direct references to the myth. As Plato has of course deliberately written it in such a way as to spark discussion and re-imagining, and as it speaks to so many of our deepest longings, its influence is set to continue for as long as there are humans entranced and bewildered by love.

AGATHON

After Aristophanes comes the speech of the host Agathon, the man of the hour. He depicts the god *Erōs* in his own image as a beautiful, winsome and perfectly good youth, and the likeness to himself is not lost on the other symposiasts; apart from *Erōs*' youthfulness, however, in most other respects his portrayal is very similar to that of Phaedrus, as Agathon himself notes. Nevertheless, Plato's intentions in including Agathon's anodyne and sentimental poetics become clear when Socrates immediately subjects them to a searching elenchus, arguing that Agathon has unwittingly described the beloved rather than the lover: as *erōs* is of the beautiful and good things that it lacks (and not simply of what belongs to it, in marked and deliberate contrast to Aristophanes' account), *erōs* itself cannot be beautiful or good. Socrates' argument depends on beauty being both homogeneous and also co-extensive with equally homogeneous goodness, and both assumptions can of course be questioned; we may also wonder why, even if beauty is homogeneous, one could not desire more of what one already has. For present purposes, however, we need to focus on their points of agreement concerning *erōs* and its lack of beauty and goodness, as they are explicitly said (*Symposium* 201d) to form the basis of Socrates' account of Diotima's teachings on *erōs*. In addition, despite the fact that Aristophanes and Socrates claim that *erōs* lacks different things, the very fact that Socrates conceives of it in terms of lack at all is critically important, as it again raises the question: what happens to *erōs* if it fulfils this lack?

SOCRATES

Socrates is usually adamant that the only thing he knows is that he knows nothing. However, in the *Symposium* when the topic of the god *Erōs* is first proposed he welcomes it, saying that he knows nothing *except ta erōtica*, matters pertaining to E/*erōs*.[19] When it is his turn to speak he tells us how he gained this knowledge: as a young man he had many conversations with a woman from Mantineia named Diotima, and he learned everything about erotics from her. Instead of giving a speech in his own voice, therefore, he will summarize their conversations from long ago.

Diotima is almost certainly a fictional character, and in the dialogue structure she performs many functions. Her introduction allows for the elenchus to continue, and Socrates can thereby tactfully claim that he used to make the same mistakes about love that Agathon has just done; he can offer us a model of how he himself moved from confusion to enlightenment. She appears to be some kind of priestess: her name means either 'honouring Zeus' or 'honoured by Zeus' and Mantineia seems intended to invoke the word '*mantis*', 'seer'.[20] We are told that she delayed the plague coming to Athens by ten years, and the language she uses connects her strongly to the Eleusinian Mysteries (of which as we have seen Plato was almost certainly an initiate);[21] there may be connections too with the mystery Orphic cults of the Greek settlements in Magna Graecia. The fact that Plato here introduces a female voice is also significant, after the earlier banishment of the female aulos-player (albeit she is voiced by Socrates). It is tempting to see a link with the Philosopher-Queens of the *Republic*, and perhaps also Aspasia, Pericles' highly cultured and influential mistress. Plato may also have thought it appropriate to give to a woman the startling claim at 206c (which we shall be discussing below) that all humans are pregnant in both body and soul (*psychē*), although this is complex: as some sort of priestess she may not have had children of her own, and she also seems to privilege male homosexual paiderastic relationships.[22] To add to the complexity there are hints in the text that she may not be entirely trustworthy: in addition to the fact that she only delays the plague rather than averting it altogether, she later shamelessly rewrites Phaedrus' speech (which of course she is not supposed to have heard – another clue from Plato that she is fictional), and Socrates even says that in doing so she spoke 'like a perfect sophist' (208c). As ever, Plato is ensuring that we engage in active interpretation for ourselves.

DIOTIMA

However, whether or not she is entirely trustworthy, her status in the *Symposium* as an intermediary between the human and divine worlds is of critical importance, and Plato gives to her one of the most profound speeches in his entire works, of which we will only be able to touch on some of the main points here. Diotima claims that *Erōs* is not in fact a god at all, but a great *daimōn*, and that:

> everything daimonic lies between the divine and mortal realms . . . its power being that of interpreting and conveying things from humans to gods and gods to humans . . . Being in the middle, it fills in the space between them, so that the whole is bound together into one continuum. It is through this that the whole skill of the seer operates, and that of priests, and of those concerned with sacrifices, rites and incantations, and everything to do with the seer and with magic. God does not mix with humanity, but it is through the daimonic that all association and converse exists between gods and humans, whether awake or asleep. (202d–203a)

She goes on to say that *Erōs* 'philosophizes throughout his life, a clever magician, wizard and sophist' (203d).

This linking of *Erōs* (and *erōs* the experience that *Erōs* represents) with both philosophy and magic is intriguing, and exploring it can tell us more about the conceptions of both erotic love and philosophy itself. It may be that *E/erōs* can help reveal usually hidden truths in a way that at least initially appears to us to be magical; it may also be that philosophy is most effective when it works on the non-rational as well as the rational faculties of the *psychē*, something of course that Plato does through his skilful deployment of the dialogue form and its use of characterization and imagery. These are issues that I have discussed in detail elsewhere,[23] although we shall be returning to them briefly when we look at Diotima's Ladder of Love. The key point for now is the function of *Erōs* (and hence also *erōs*) as an intermediary connecting the entire cosmos, and building on Eryximachus' portrayal of *Erōs* as a cosmic force. We should also note the links between *E/erōs* and *philia*: *Erōs* is a *phil*osopher, feels *philia* for wisdom. In itself, it is neither wise nor ignorant, but it is aware of its lack of wisdom, and desires it. The same applies to its intermediary status between beauty and ugliness, and goodness and badness.

Diotima continues by telling a story about the birth of this *daimōn Erōs* from the seduction of its father, Resource, by its mother Poverty, and there are marked similarities between her description of *Erōs* and the portrayal of Socrates in the dialogue: both spend time in doorways and on thresholds, both usually go barefoot; both are poor but resourceful; and both, of course, are lovers of wisdom.[24] And as we saw in chapter 1, at 219c, Alcibiades will say that Socrates is daimonic. It is starting to make sense why Socrates claims he knows about nothing except erotics.

At this point the young Socrates asks Diotima what *use E/erōs* is to humanity, and Diotima moves from describing the *daimōn* to exploring the human emotion. *Erōs*, lacking beauty, pursues beautiful people and things in order to possess them (note the language of possession and appropriation again, as in

Aristophanes' speech) – but *why* does the lover of beautiful things want to possess them? What does he think he will gain? The young Socrates cannot answer this, so Diotima asks him to substitute 'good things' (*agatha*) for 'beautiful things' (*kala*): what does the lover of good things achieve if he gets them? It is, on the face of it, a highly questionable substitution, and depends on the fact that we have already been told that the younger Socrates and Diotima had come to the same conclusions about beautiful and good things that the older Socrates has just assumed in his elenchus with Agathon, namely that they are both homogeneous and co-extensive. The intricacies of the argument need not detain us here: what matters for present purposes is that the young Socrates says he *can* answer this rephrased question: the person who possesses good things will flourish, and flourishing (*eudaimonia*) is the final goal of all our desires. Diotima sums up this stage of their discussion at *Symposium* 206a with a definition: *erōs* is of permanent possession of the good. In what appears to be a direct reference back to Aristophanes' speech (which of course Diotima is not supposed to have heard either), she emphasizes that the story that we seek our other half simply because it belongs to us is wrong: love loves only what is good.

This definition, however, does not usefully distinguish the species, or aspect,[25] of *erōs* that we normally *call erōs*: to say that erotic love is the desire to possess the good for ever is hardly a vivid description of how *erōs feels*. So Diotima goes on to distinguish this species or aspect of *erōs* as a 'giving birth in or by means of the beautiful, in relation to both body and soul (*psychē*)'. The young Socrates is unsurprisingly baffled by this statement too, and it is at this point that Diotima makes her startling announcement that 'all humans are pregnant both in body and in soul'. Plato often uses gendered imagery in deliberately surprising ways, and the *Symposium* is no exception: males can be pregnant too, and in their bodies as well as their souls. It is an image which has proved highly controversial: does it show disrespect to biological women by appropriating the specifically female functions of pregnancy and giving birth, or does it enhance the status of women by linking their activities to divine philosophic activity? Or does it rather show how cavalier Plato is about sex and gender altogether, given that they are both for him only features of the transient physical body and our embodied lives on this earth?[26]

Whatever our response to the image, Diotima proceeds to explain her deployment of it. If we ultimately desire 'permanent possession of the good' then we must also desire immortality – but personal immortality is not available to us so we seek various forms of 'giving birth' as substitutes: our various creations will live on after us.[27] Very possibly utilizing the tripartite psychic division that we have seen in the *Republic* (though it is not explicitly mentioned in the *Symposium*), Diotima claims that there are three different grades of creation, and three corresponding grades of substitute 'immortality' (though as we shall shortly see, there are subdivisions within the top grade): physical offspring are the lowest grade; then comes the fame and (hopefully) everlasting name that results from having performed noble deeds; at the top are the durable creations of reason, such as poetry, or making laws, or educating the young. But all these different types of creation require the assistance of a fine and beautiful body or soul – either to beget in, or as inspiration in general, or as the inspiring recipient of the education in particular; as we have seen throughout, beauty plays a central role in Plato's thought as a motivating and creative force. Finally, those who are already capable of rational creations may be ready to 'approach the rites and revelations to which these, for the correctly instructed, are only the avenue' (*Symposium* 210a). They may be ready to ascend the Ladder of Love.

THE LADDER OF LOVE

For those who think of Plato as a straightforwardly austere rationalist, it might be a surprise to learn that the starting-point of the ascent is to fall in love with a beautiful (*kalon*) body, and being inspired by it to bring forth fine and beautiful (*kala*) words which serve to educate the beautiful body's possessor (the *erōmenos*). Then the lover (the *erastēs*) realizes that in fact the beauty of one body is no different to that of any beautiful body, and that it would be sheer foolishness not to love all beautiful bodies. And so he slackens the intensity of his feeling for the original beloved and becomes a lover of all beautiful bodies, generating ever more beautiful, fine and educational words. However, he next realizes that the beauty of souls (*psychai*) is even more beautiful than that of bodies and so he turns his attention and love to beautiful souls, still continuing to generate ever finer educational words. And so he progresses, as if up the steps of a ladder (*Symposium* 211c), focusing his love (*erōs*) on ever more abstract and more beautiful objects – laws and practices; branches of knowledge; at each step he brings forth still finer and more virtuous words, and at each stage, too, he increases his disregard for physical bodies and individual people. At the zenith of his ascent he is able to behold the entire sea of beauty and in this blessed state is set free from the slavery of intense attachments to individuals, and in contemplation brings forth a generous outpouring of philosophy. And finally there is revealed to him the Form of Beauty itself, perfect, pure, unchanging, eternal and wondrous, and it is here that his life becomes 'truly liveable'.

It is an extraordinarily powerful exhortation: the widening of *erōs* that we saw in Eryximachus' speech is here hugely expanded. At its conclusion the suggestion made above about why Diotima called the *daimōn Erōs* a 'clever magician' is confirmed: *El erōs* creates profound transformations not only in our understanding of the different love objects but of the cosmos as a whole and indeed transforms the lover himself or herself, and initially these transformations are so startling as to appear magical. It is as if curtains are being drawn aside and luminous reality is being revealed for the first time. Later on, of course, when the lover has a better understanding of what underlies these newly revealed connections and harmonies, the appearance of magic may start to fade. That would not, however, take anything away from the wonder of the expanding cosmic vision on the initial ascent.

It is a vision, furthermore, which also claims to offer more enduring attractions. Diotima is trying to make love, and life, safe. There is to be no risky dependence on one individual viewed as irreplaceable: all beautiful and fine individuals are, *qua* beautiful and fine, simply tokens of a type – and in any case, our desires soon appear to move beyond individuals altogether. She is also claiming that reason and desire will go hand in hand as we ascend the ladder and that there will be no painful mental conflicts.

However, while these features will attract some, for others they will raise profound questions and concerns. Is such security and freedom from pain really worth the price? At the top of the ladder we will apparently come to despise our former individual beloveds as 'mortal trash' (211e): is this what we really want? Yet despite the disturbing talk of 'trash', it is not in fact entirely clear what exactly we *are* being asked to give up. Do we really have to give up our beloveds completely as we ascend? Or, even if we do have to move beyond the *erastēs/erōmenos* relationship, could we not transform it into friendship, into *philia*? After all, the (former) lover still needs to be inspired by the inner and outer beauty of his (former) beloved in order to bring forth the fine and beautiful words that will educate him; he still needs contact with his (former) beloved in order to produce the educational creation that will bring him the highest grade of substitute 'immortality'. If this is so, then perhaps the most beneficial and truly loving thing he could do is to try to turn his former *erōmenos* into an active *erastēs*, capable of climbing the ladder for himself.

And what, we may ask, happens if we reach the top of the ladder – as in Aristophanes' speech, if *erōs* is a quest, what happens if that quest is fulfilled? Does *erōs* again work towards its own annihilation? If it does, does it transform into something else – perhaps something that later Christian writers will call *agapē*, the love of humans for God and God for humans (Plato does use the verb in the ladder of love,[28] although not in this sense)? Yet we should note that the Form of Beauty is unlike the Christian God in that it is not going to love us back; and in any case, for the ladder to work, does not *erōs* need to be viewed as a single stream, a single motivating force which takes on different forms according to its objects and the resulting creations? Or is it permissible for there to be one final transformation of itself at the very top of the ladder?

The questions continue, particularly with respect to what exactly being with and contemplating the Form of Beauty involves. Does it have to be a solitary experience which then *results* in the educational and other creative practices by which the best form of substitute immortality is achieved, or could the actual contemplation take place within a context of human friendships – for example at a symposium? Similarly, is not Diotima's account at the least put into question by the fact that it is being relayed by Socrates to a group of friends and lovers? Is what Socrates is doing compatible with contemplating the Form of Beauty or not? And what of Plato's activity in addressing his readers? Surely both the character of Socrates and Plato are showing by their actions that they still care deeply about the world of 'mortal trash' (although perhaps Plato might say that that is because neither he nor Socrates has yet reached the top rung)?

I shall leave addressing such questions concerning the Form of Beauty (and there are many more) for another occasion, although we shall shortly be considering whether Plato actually wants us to ascend the ladder at the end of our discussion of the *Symposium*. Before turning to Alcibiades' speech, however, we should note how deeply and widely influential the image of the ladder of love has been – in theology, the arts and psychology as well as in philosophy, many have found in Diotima's speech rich sustenance on how we could or should love. To take just one example, Freud says he was profoundly influenced by Plato's notion of *erōs* as a single stream of erotic energy which could be channelled onto different objects, and claims that his theory of the libido is basically a reworking of Platonic *erōs* and that his notion of sublimation is a reworking of Platonic channelling and rechannelling. In addition to referencing the *Symposium* with regard to these points, he also highlights *Republic* 6.485d, where Socrates says that it is very dangerous simply to block the desires (*epithumiai*): one must divert them, not dam them.[29]

ALCIBIADES

We might think that the climax of Diotima's ladder would be the climax of the dialogue, but we would be wrong, because at this point in bursts the beautiful and dissipated general and statesman Alcibiades[30] – haphazardly crowned with a wreath of ivy and violets and with ribbons entwined in his hair (ribbons which he partially presents to Agathon but then takes some back for Socrates), and so raucously drunk that he has to be held up by a female pipe player and other carousers. His explosive entry injects glamour, disruption and, of course, a female presence into the relatively restrained and until now exclusively male setting. The ivy connects him to Dionysus, god of wine, disorder and ecstatic revelry, and we may remember that earlier Agathon had called on Dionysus to adjudicate between himself and Socrates.[31] Violets are linked to Aphrodite (e.g. in *Homeric Hymns* 5.18), and they may also be meant to represent Athens: a fragment of Pindar calls Athens 'violet-crowned'.[32] While the Form of Beauty exists in a purely intelligible realm, Alcibiades' allure is unequivocally located in the sensory and sensuous world.

Alcibiades says he is too drunk to give a formal speech in praise of *Erōs* – and he is certainly too drunk to climb Diotima's ladder, which in any case he arrived too late to hear about – so he announces that instead he will give a speech in praise of Socrates, offering in the process a passionate, witty and moving account of his love for the older man, and his repeated and comically unsuccessful attempts to seduce him. These attempts culminate in a self-deprecating tale of a night when he finally contrived to get Socrates alone with him under their cloaks on a couch, and put his arms around him – only to meet with Socrates' steadfast refusal to touch him. Alcibiades is explicit that although Socrates had pretended to be the conventional older *erastēs* in their relationship, in reality he played the role of the younger *erōmenos*, and it was Alcibiades who did the (fruitless) pursuing.

Alcibiades' vivid narrative exudes his passionate love for Socrates in every detail (a love which clearly still burns in him all these years later, as the other symposiasts realize). As we saw in chapter 5,[33] he emphasizes Socrates' courage and feats of endurance while on military campaign; tellingly, and as we also saw in the same chapter,[34] he builds on these details to make a claim that Socrates is utterly *unique* – there has never been anyone like him. In marked contrast to the account of Diotima's teaching which he has missed, Alcibiades does not view his beloved Socrates as a replaceable token of Beauty, but values him for his individuality. While profoundly moving, however, Alcibiades' speech, and his barbed interchanges with Socrates and Agathon at the symposium, are also disturbing: he represents the destructive as well as the creative potential of intense personal erotic attachment. He says he hated it when Socrates used to admonish him and urge him to improve – Socrates is the only person who has ever made him feel ashamed – and admits that there were many times when he wished him gone from this world; rather than deal with Socrates' criticisms, he would run back to the adoring crowd.[35] These complicated feelings are clearly still sharp: on his arrival at the party, Alcibiades jealously accuses Socrates of contriving to sit next to the beautiful Agathon, and Socrates urges Agathon to protect him, saying that Alcibiades has often threatened violence towards him in jealous rages.

How serious a challenge to Socrates (Diotima) is Alcibiades supposed to be? Plato allows him to be glamorous, sexy and charismatic, and to give the final speech; he also repeatedly has Alcibiades say that he both will and is telling the truth, challenging the other symposiasts to interrupt him if he does not – and no one does. At the very least Plato is showing us that he understands the power and attraction of passionate love for an individual (an understanding to which his elegiac verses for his beloved Dion bear witness);[36] he understands what we are being asked to give up if we are to try to ascend Diotima's ladder. And the challenge may go even deeper: we may be being asked whether it is really worth climbing the ladder at all?

Yet at the conclusion of his speech another rowdy group of revellers bursts in, 'having found the door just opened for someone who was going out'. As Alcibiades is not mentioned again, we are left to assume that the person leaving is him, but the fact that Plato deliberately does not name him is significant: he is disappearing drunkenly into the night and his uncertain future, having finally rejected the moderating influence of Socrates, perhaps even to effect that very night the damage on the herms which the Athenians thought precipitated their downfall in the Sicilian expedition.[37] After his departure, all semblance of order breaks down until eventually most of the revellers depart or fall asleep, including Aristodemus, the follower of Socrates who recounts the tale of the symposium to Apollodorus. When Aristodemus wakes towards dawn, he finds Socrates debating with Agathon and Aristophanes whether the same person can write both tragedy and comedy – perhaps Plato believes that in the *Symposium* he has combined both, particularly in the example of Alcibiades; and when Agathon and Aristophanes also fall asleep, Socrates simply gets up and goes to the Lyceum to wash and begin a new day of philosophical conversations. He is, literally, the only one left standing.

Yet even if the contribution and murky exit of Alcibiades is supposed to represent some kind of warning, Plato is still not telling us exactly what to think: he is still requiring us to interpret and think for ourselves. Is his chaotic career a warning about what might befall us if we do not try to climb the ladder? Or is

Plato showing us just how difficult climbing the ladder will be? Alcibiades and Socrates/Diotima, furthermore, are of course not the only accounts of *erōs* on offer. What does Plato want us to make of the dialogue as a whole? Are we meant to choose just one approach, or are we meant to select elements from more than one speech and create our own philosophy of love? My own view is that Plato at the time of writing the *Symposium* is deeply attracted to the rechannelling of *erōs* depicted by Diotima, but is fully aware of the sacrifices it will entail and just how difficult it will be to leave individual human loves behind. But we do not have to follow Plato in this. Whatever his intention, it remains true that this beautiful, witty and profound exploration of *erōs* compels us to think hard about our own past, present and hoped-for future relationships. What is really motivating us, and is that motivation healthy or unhealthy? What form or forms might a truly healthy *erōs* take, one(s) that would make our lives truly liveable?

ERŌS: THE *PHAEDRUS*

The *Symposium* is not Plato's final discussion of *erōs*, and in the *Phaedrus*, the overall theme of which is rhetoric, his position on whether lovers need to give up their earthly beloveds in the course of their philosophic quest appears in Socrates' second speech to soften – a position described in some of the most powerfully affecting passages on love ever composed. The dialogue begins with Socrates, very unusually for him, going for a walk outside the walls of Athens with the charming and ardent young Phaedrus, enjoying the lush countryside, paddling in the Ilisos stream, and eventually lying down together on soft grass in the shade of a suggestively soaring plane tree. It is a secluded and seductive spot, and they remark appreciatively on the gentle breeze, fragrant blossoms and sound of the cicadas, dangling their feet in the cool stream. Plato is in playful mood and the play continues when Socrates asks Phaedrus what he is holding in his left hand under his cloak. It turns out to be a speech by the orator Lysias[38] on the subject of *erōs*, and claiming that a beautiful youth should grant his favours to a non-lover (such as Lysias?) rather than a lover: the non-lover is more rational and of a steadier and more loyal disposition; lovers themselves agree that *erōs* is a sickness and that lovers are not in their right mind.

When Phaedrus invites Socrates to elaborate on the superiority of the non-lover, Socrates drily exposes the disingenuousness of Lysias' speech and the craftiness of the lover who pretends to be a non-lover; nevertheless, in his first speech he acquiesces to Phaedrus' request and belittles *erōs* as a merely sexual desire to possess beauties which overcomes reason and in its controlling jealousy seeks to keep both lover and beloved away from what is best and would strengthen them in both mind and body. Lovers are ultimately fickle and at 241a *erōs* is portrayed as damaging because it is linked to madness.

At this point, however, Socrates pulls up. His *daimonion*, his private spirit guide, has forbidden him to proceed until he recants this blasphemous speech against the divinity that is *Erōs*[39] and has purified himself by making a second speech. And it is in this speech that Plato gives us one of the most compelling accounts of the power of love, and what it feels like to be in love. Socrates says yes, the lover *is* mad, but there are beneficial kinds of madness too and in fact the greatest of blessings come to us through madness, when it is sent as a gift of the gods. To understand this, however, we need to understand the human *psychē*. Our *psychē* is immortal and can most easily be described through the figure of a winged charioteer[40] driving two winged horses, one noble and obedient and the other bad and unruly: the charioteer represents reason, the good horse represents the spirited faculty, the *thumoeides*, and the bad horse represents the appetites. Before incarnation these *psychai* circle the heavens, straining to catch sight of the eternal Forms of Beauty and the Good and all the rest which exist in a still higher region; they are usually only able to catch brief glimpses because the bad horse keeps pulling them down and in the confusion some of their wings get broken. The damaged soul then falls to earth and enters a body – which body depends on how clear a vision of the Forms has been attained. Souls which have witnessed the most enter the body of a lover of wisdom (*philosophos*), or a lover of beauty (*philokalos*), or one devoted to the muses (*mousikos*), or an erotic lover (*erōtikos*); the harmony between *philia* and *erōs* in this passage is important, and something to which we shall be returning.

When these lovers of wisdom and beauty see an instance of beauty in this phenomenal world, particularly in the form of a beautiful youth, it reminds them of their glimpse of the Form of Beauty, and the lover, the *erastēs*, experiences the most profound physical and emotional symptoms: in the presence of his beloved he shudders and sweats and his whole soul palpitates and itches, and his wings start to grow again, nourished and moistened by the sight of the beautiful youth. When his beloved is absent, the outlets for the feathers start to dry up and close again. This condition is a kind of madness, but a beneficent kind: the lover not only reveres his beautiful beloved but finds in him the healer of his greatest pains. And it is this condition which is called *erōs* by humans.

Crucially, it does not appear that the lover has to give up his beloved, and furthermore, although the language of the *erastēs* and *erōmenos* continues to be used, it is clear that the relationship becomes reciprocal. Streams of beauty from the beloved enter the eyes of the lover and inspire desire, and these streams of beauty are then reflected back and enter the eyes of the beloved, inspiring desire in him too, and his soul also starts to regrow its wings: the beloved is becoming a lover in turn. The two lovers may embrace and hold hands (although full sex is strongly discouraged), and they can continue their philosophic quests together in both friendship and love, enabling the wings of the other to regrow. The paddling philosopher is learning to fly once more.

It is certainly true that the *Phaedrus* raises many questions in its treatment of *erōs*: is its profoundly affecting account of the power of love supposed to be applicable outside the *erastēs*/*erōmenos* relationship, for instance? However, as with the *Symposium*, we do not need to endorse the *erastēs/erōmenos* relationship, nor believe in the Forms, nor in the Greek gods, to gain a great deal of sustenance from Plato's explorations of love and friendship, of *erōs* and *philia*: as so often with Plato, his discussions can highlight the most pressing questions, and help us think through them for ourselves. What motivations are really behind the different kinds of relationships we make, and which forms of *erōs* and *philia* will benefit us, and which harm? And which kinds of *philia* contribute to wider social harmony? Would Plato think that either *erōs* or *philia* could exist solely in the online world? How much should we focus on issues of sex and gender, or should the degree of, particularly, inner beauty of the beloved be our most important concern? In short, what are love and friendship, and what could they be? Through reflecting on these questions we increase our chances of being better friends and lovers, and contributing more effectively to better relations in our various communities. We may even, both individually and collectively, start to grow wings.

7

Art, Censorship and Myth

THE IMPORTANCE OF BEAUTY

We have seen (particularly in chapters 2 and 6) that beauty plays an utterly central role in Plato's thought, so long as it is what he regards as true, objective beauty, derived ultimately from the Form of Beauty. Let us briefly remind ourselves of *Republic* 3.401c–d, where Socrates sums up the aim of the primary education of the Guardians:

> We must look for artists and craftsmen capable of perceiving the real nature of what is beautiful (*kalon*), and then our young men, living as it were in a healthy climate, will benefit because all the works they see and hear influence them for good, like the healthy breezes from wholesome places . . .

Artistic and aesthetic influences can be absorbed and emulated not only through formal education, but also informally through immersion in both the human-made and the natural environment. The key term here is the Greek *kalon*, which as we have seen can mean both aesthetically beautiful and also morally fine and honourable. For Plato, true, objective outer beauty arises from true, objective inner moral beauty – a moral beauty which is the internalization of reason (*logos*), but which exerts a strong power of attraction to young people even *before* their reason has fully developed. It is this attraction that motivates the ascent up the Ladder of Love.

THE DANGERS OF ART

Given this, it is perhaps easier to understand Plato's criticisms of works of art which he feels are not objectively beautiful, and which do not originate in the inner beauty of the artist's *psychē*: such degenerate works will have precisely the opposite effect on the impressionable young citizens, and cumulatively pollute their *psychai*. There is a general view amongst those who have not read much Plato that he is straightforwardly hostile to art. As we will see in this chapter, the full picture is much more complex and interesting than this, but it is certainly true that in the *Republic* the character of Socrates raises some profound challenges. In Books 2 and 3, as we saw in chapter 5, he begins by heavily censoring much existing art, for intertwined religious, ethical and political reasons. Homer, Hesiod, Aeschylus and other poets may be deeply revered, but they misrepresent the gods as deceitful, lustful, cruel and capricious, indiscriminately handing out good and bad fortunes to hapless humans, entirely indifferent to moral worth and desert (2.376c–3.392c). In fact, says Socrates, god – and we should note the switch from the plural gods of Greek mythology to a single god in 2.379a[1] – is entirely good, and hence the cause only of good. All evil in the world has some other origin: god is all-good but not all-powerful. Secondly, as we saw in detail in chapter 5, poetry frequently describes and represents in its heroes both immoral desires and disproportionate emotional responses, and in consequence fosters similarly intemperate behaviour in the humans who may be tempted to emulate them. Representation (*mimēsis*) is particularly dangerous in that it involves direct speech, and thus direct identification amongst the audience or readers, particularly if they are – as was common – reciting the lines out loud with accompanying gestures.

In *Republic* Book 10 the censorship is even more extreme, and most art is to be banned altogether. This is due to the fact that in the intervening books Socrates has outlined the Theory of Forms and the different metaphysical and epistemological levels that flow from it. All the objects of our phenomenal world – the world we perceive through our senses – are simply imperfect representations of the perfect, intelligible, eternal Forms, the only entities which are truly real and which can be truly known. At *Republic* 10.596b, Socrates takes the example of a couch. First, the craftsman copies the ideal Form of the couch which he apprehends – doubtless imperfectly, as he is not a philosopher – in his mind's eye; then the artist copies – also imperfectly – the craftsman's copy. Works of art are therefore far removed from true reality, on a par with the shadows and reflections which we saw illustrated in chapter 4 by the Simile of the Divided Line. Artists have no real knowledge or understanding of what they represent, and should not be considered as reliable guides or teachers. This claim of Socrates would have been regarded as profoundly shocking at the time, as many people did indeed look to artists for all kinds of guidance. As we saw in chapter 5, this was especially so in the case of Homer (regarded as one person in classical Greece, with no thought of modern controversies): the *Iliad* and the *Odyssey* were considered by the majority of Greeks to be near-sacred repositories of moral, technical and practical knowledge. Socrates himself calls Homer the educator of Greece at *Republic* 10.606e.

Republic Book 10 also takes up the argument first broached in Books 2 and 3, namely that the arts represent, appeal to and feed dangerous and irrational emotions which should be left to wither and die, and Socrates is now in a position to bolster this charge by referring to the tripartite psychology of Book 4: art specifically targets and emboldens our spirited (thumoeidic) and appetitive elements. The result is that almost all art is to be banished unless and until a truly philosophic art emerges; there has been 'an ancient disagreement between philosophy and poetry', and philosophy must emerge the victor. Socrates admits that he finds this conclusion difficult: he says that he has loved the poems of Homer in particular since he was a boy (10.595c–d), but nevertheless Homer is to be graciously escorted out of their ideal city (3.398a). Until a truly philosophic art is created, all that is to be allowed is a meagre and grim-sounding diet of hymns to the gods and paeans to good men.

Why should this attack on art still be of interest to us, particularly as we are unlikely to believe in the Theory of Forms which underpins it? It should matter because, irrespective of the specific metaphysics and epistemology, Plato is raising fundamental questions about the nature and effects of art, and about freedom of expression (and its limits), which are both a bracing challenge to liberal views and directly relevant to current debates on censorship and 'cancel culture' and 'no-platforming'. Suppose an artist says something demonstrably false, either through one of the characters they create (clearly very common), or perhaps in their own voice, in their public work as an artist? Do we care if consumers of the art, or fans of the artist, also adopt such false views as a result? And what about moral degeneration? Do we think that a work of art can ever corrupt, and induce copycat atrocities, and, if so, is that sufficient reason to censor or ban the work of art? Does, or should, the quality of the art make a difference?

Supposing the work leads to emotional pain or offence? Salman Rushdie's 1988 novel *The Satanic Verses* was found offensive by some Muslims in particular, and led to Rushdie going into hiding for many years. Should it have been published? And does it alter the debate if we consider that in this case the threats led to actual violence? When Rushdie finally decided to make appearances again, in 2022 he suffered an appalling and life-changing physical attack at a public reading in the United States. We also need to consider our responses to scenarios in which censorship does take place. For example, in 2018 the Manchester Art Gallery removed from view John William Waterhouse's 1896 painting *Hylas and the Nymphs*, arguing that it wanted to start a debate – which indeed it did – about how the bodies of the naked females were here depicted as seductive femmes fatales (after public protest, Manchester City Council replaced the painting one week later). These are just two recent examples from an exceptionally rich field. The debates are hotly contested and, whether one agrees with the views expressed by Socrates in the *Republic* or not, Plato

ART, CENSORSHIP AND MYTH

initiated these debates with clarity and precision. (Indeed, the clarity of the dispute is at the expense of strict historical accuracy, as in fact it was simply not true that there had been an 'ancient disagreement between philosophy and poetry': witness the fact that amongst the Presocratic philosophers, Parmenides' *On Nature* is in epic hexameters, and Empedocles' *On Nature* and *Purifications* are also in verse.)

Plato's student Aristotle took a largely different view, arguing that works of art – such as Sophocles' tragedy *Oedipus Tyrannos* – which caused disturbing emotions of pity and fear in the audience (and perhaps even more so in the actors) could have a cathartic effect. The exact meaning of catharsis in this context is disputed, but the most likely interpretation is that, by enabling us to experience these emotions in a safe environment, the works of art help to cleanse us of them. This would not need to be restricted to pity and fear: by seeing violence enacted and identifying to some extent with the actors (or enacting it ourselves), we could perhaps purge ourselves of darker, violent emotions too. But in the *Republic* Socrates is unequivocal: any indulgence of such dark desires, even at second-hand, will not lead to catharsis but instead to their unhealthy growth.

PLATO THE ARTIST: THE LEGEND OF ATLANTIS

In the *Republic*, therefore, Plato instigates an important debate that still simmers, and occasionally erupts. Even if most of us are unlikely to adopt Socrates' proposals for extreme censorship, his concerns about the power of art – including its power to harm – should certainly be heard and addressed. Yet, as we saw in the Introduction, Plato the author should not be confused with the character of Socrates, and Plato's position on art is in fact considerably more complex than this: the work we call the *Republic* would be *banned* in the ideally just city it purportedly depicts as it does not meet the censorship criteria of that city. One of the infringements is the introduction of the aggressive and unsavoury character of Thrasymachus, whom we have met in chapters 1 and

3. In addition to its vivid characterization, we have also seen how the *Republic* is interwoven with powerful and haunting images and myths, such as Gyges' Ring, the Allegory of the Cave and the Myth of Er, and we have seen similarly vivid characterization, myths and imagery elsewhere.[2] Plato's dialogues are unquestionably great works of art as well as seminal works of philosophy and the artistry does not merely embellish the philosophy: as we have seen throughout, the philosophical ideas and arguments could not be conveyed in any other way.

Indeed, myths and legends feature in so many of the dialogues that it would seem that Plato regards them as fundamental to a vibrant, healthy culture in general and to the educational process in particular, and his use of them is multi-layered and subtle. To explore why and how this is so, let us examine in some detail one of Plato's most famous tales, that of the fabulously powerful and wealthy, but ultimately doomed, maritime empire of Atlantis. The tale is told in the *Timaeus* (20c–26e) and *Critias* (106c–121c – the entirety of this broken-off dialogue); both works were probably composed in the 360s, but they are set dramatically c.429–408 BCE. There are four main characters: Socrates, Timaeus, Critias and Hermocrates. As the *Timaeus* opens, Socrates reminds the others that the previous day they had been discussing certain features of the ideally just city (the features roughly correspond to *Republic* Books 2–5), and he says that he now wants to see this ideal tested *in action* – in particular he wants to see how it withstands the stresses of war and whether the virtues that have been inculcated via its education system will really help it. Critias, a friend of Socrates, replies that, funnily enough, on his way home after the discussion of the previous day it had occurred to him that the ideal *polis* they had been outlining reminded him of a story he had heard as a very young boy, told to him by his grandfather.

The grandfather had heard the tale from his own father, who had heard it from his relative, the great Athenian lawgiver and poet, Solon (c.630–c.560 BCE), who in turn had been told the tale on his travels by Egyptian priests at Saïs in the Nile Delta. Solon had been telling the priests about the Greek legend of Deucalion and Pyrrha and the great flood, but one of the priests had mocked him 'O Solon, Solon, you Greeks are always children; there is no such thing as an old Greek.' Naïve Greeks do not realize that there had been many natural catastrophes before Deucalion and Pyrrha, unknown to contemporary Greeks but preserved by the Egyptians in the hot desert climate in records going back 8,000 years. Yet the key catastrophe the priest cites is said by him to occur even further back – 9,000 years before (a gap to which we shall be returning). At this time a war had taken place between prehistoric Athens and Atlantis, an island kingdom beyond the Pillars of Heracles (the Straits of Gibraltar) and ruler of a vast empire. All on Atlantis prosper so long as the kings care for virtue more than wealth or power; but when their lust for expansion takes control and they attempt to extend their empire into the eastern Mediterranean, including Greece, that is when the gods decide to punish them.

Prehistoric Athens was poor and powerless by comparison, yet 'by some miraculous chance' (*Timaeus* 25e) it matched the ideal city they have been describing in almost every detail, and its courage and self-discipline helped it to see off the aggressor – although later *both* the island of Atlantis *and* prehistoric Athens were destroyed by floods and earthquakes in a single dreadful day and night, the Athenians being swallowed up by the earth and the island of Atlantis disappearing into the sea. Nevertheless, if Socrates wants to see his ideal city in action, he should turn to this tale.

The *Critias* describes Atlantis in luscious and seductive detail. It is fabulously opulent and technologically sophisticated, abundant in flowers, fruits and cultivated crops, and provided with natural hot and cold springs; rich in metals, including gold, silver and the mysterious 'orichalc' ('mountain-copper'), its wealth literally gleams. Animals abound, including bulls and elephants – intricate carvings from their ivory are also a feature. The central citadel is surrounded by concentric circles of land and canals; the bridges crossing them are guarded by towers and gates constructed of white, black and red stones, sometimes in elaborate patterns. The citizens enjoy a life of luxury and considerable leisure: there are beautiful gardens, gymnasia and a track for horse-racing. The island was originally ruled by ten kings, five sets of male twins, offspring of the sea-god Poseidon and the human Cleito; the oldest was chief king. They and their descendants rule according to the precepts of Poseidon, which are inscribed on a pillar of orichalc in an ornate temple dedicated to him in the centre of the citadel. Bulls roam in the temple. Alternately every five and six years the kings assemble in this temple to discuss and adjudicate, first hunting a bull, sacrificing it, and drinking its blood mixed with wine. They then pass judgements in robes of rich dark blue.

MYTHOS OR *LOGOS*?

Before we can examine what Plato wants us to make of this intriguing tale, we first need to consider whether it *is* even a tale – a *mythos* – or whether it is supposed to be factual: after all, Socrates teases us by saying (*Critias* 26e) that the great thing about it is that it is *not* a *mythos*, but an *alēthinos logos*, a true account.

The evidence is ambiguous, and I will argue that this is absolutely deliberate on Plato's part. Let us first consider the evidence for unreliability. The Egyptian priest says that their records go back 8,000 years; yet the alleged war between Atlantis and prehistoric Athens is claimed to have taken place 9,000 years before – so out of reach of written history. But even if we take there to be some kind of genuine origin to the tale, there are still plenty of opportunities for alterations during its transmission from the priests to Solon and eventually to the young Critias. Solon may have misunderstood or misremembered what the priests told him (we do not even know whether they were speaking the same language or whether interpreters were present). The priests themselves may have been confused over some elements of the story.

What about the possibility that the tale is not simply unreliable, but a carefully constructed fiction by Plato? As we have seen, he certainly possessed the creative imagination to invent it: witness the detailed utopian fantasies in the *Republic* and *Laws*, and the intricately embroidered myths of the *Gorgias*, *Phaedo*, *Symposium*, *Republic* and *Statesman*. The occasion on which Critias hears the tale from his grandfather is during the Festival of Apaturia (at the end of October). *Apatē* means 'deception' and although the derivation of Apaturia from *apatē* is not in fact secure, the salient point here is that the ancients thought it was. So warning bells are sounded from the outset. Critias further emphasizes his youth and his grandfather's extreme age at the time (*Timaeus* 21a–c), and at *Critias* 112e he says that he will see *if* he can remember what he was told as a child (and note that it is only Critias who tells us about Atlantis, not Socrates).

Plato may also be alerting us to be on our guard in the account of Solon's conversation with the Egyptian priests. The gap of a thousand years between the alleged war and the start of Egyptian records may be thought a suspiciously convenient way to avoid having to provide firm evidence; it is also suggested that the priests might have deliberately set out to deceive Solon, or simply told him what they thought he wanted to hear, confident that innocent Greeks are easy to dupe ('O Solon, Solon, you Greeks are always children.' And for whom is Plato writing? Greeks!). There is surely also irony in Critias' claim that prehistoric Athens matches their ideal city in almost every respect 'by some miraculous chance' (25e), and irony too – at least at some level, though the full picture is complex, as we shall see – in Socrates' tease that the great thing about the tale is that it is not a *mythos*, but a true *logos*. In the detailed account of Atlantis in the *Critias*, some elements are clearly fantastical, such as the union between the god Poseidon and Cleito. If Plato did not invent these details, someone did.

Yet there are also clear signs that the tale is to be understood as true at least at some level. If the dramatic date is taken to be c.429–408 BCE, then the chronology is certainly possible.[3] And Critias claims (*Timaeus* 20d–e) that Solon, 'the wisest of the seven wise men', once vouched its truth. Solon was almost invariably held in high regard, including by Plato, who counted him as an ancestral relation on his mother's side. Critias also makes a pointed reference (*Critias* 113b) to possessing Solon's actual manuscript. The Egyptian source is interesting: Plato was always fascinated by Egyptian culture (it is very likely that he had travelled there), and generally respectful of it – particularly its emphasis on unvarying constancy in artistic expression and custom once the 'correct' forms have been achieved (*Laws* 656d–657b) – although he did also unfortunately make disparaging remarks about, specifically, the trustworthiness of Egyptians themselves (e.g. *Laws* 747c), a criticism which is clearly pertinent for our assessment of the veracity of the Egyptian priests in the *Timaeus*. And what, after all, of Socrates' mischievous claim that Critias' story is *not* a *mythos* but an *alēthinos logos*, a true account? Is it solely ironic? We shall be returning to this.

ATLANTIS AND THERA

As we shall shortly see, the main 'truth' of the story lies in its ethical, political and theological instruction. But first, is there – could there be – any historical basis for it whatsoever? Could Plato perhaps be incorporating some, perhaps only half-remembered, oral folk tales which do indeed have a historical origin, even though Plato himself is unaware of it? We cannot know for sure, but there are some tantalizing details which may put us in mind of the Minoan civilization on Thera (modern Santorini) and Crete – a civilization which was profoundly damaged by the massive volcanic explosion and subsequent tsunami on Thera around 1610 BCE. The Greeks of Plato's day knew nothing of this in terms of location or date, but it is at least intriguing that in both Atlantis and Minoan Crete and Thera bulls figure prominently (see *Critias* 119d, although Critias only mentions bulls roaming in the Temple of Poseidon; he does not allude to bull-leaping), and furthermore in both Atlantis and Minoan Crete and Thera there are buildings composed of patterns of red, white and black stones (*Critias* 116a–b; as for Minoan culture, one can not only see evidence of this in the wall-paintings at Knossos, but still see piles of stones in these colours by the side of the road in Santorini/Thera). Dolphins are also important in both Atlantis and Minoan culture (*Critias* 116e; Knossos wall-paintings) – hardly surprising, of course, in that both are seafaring civilizations. More generally, both are wealthy, luxurious and technologically sophisticated cultures (both, for instance, have hot and cold water), inhabited by pleasure-loving peoples. So although Plato has no direct knowledge of the Minoans, and although any historical origins are not in any case his main interest here, there could indeed be some indirect links via legends passed down orally, although such legends are not likely to have had one single source. The tale, or tales, which he may have heard could have combined folk memories of Minoan Crete and Thera with the opulent culture of the Mycenaean kings, the maritime daring and expansionism of the Phoenicians, assorted fantasies of a Golden Age – very much in vogue in Plato's lifetime – and, as we shall soon see, the very real wars between Greece and Persia in the early fifth century BCE.

ANCIENT RECEPTION OF THE ATLANTIS TALE

First, however, in assessing whether the tale of Atlantis has any credible historical roots and, crucially, how Plato wanted his audience to receive it, we need to ask whether other ancient writers believed it (as there is no record of any mention of the story before Plato). The evidence is mixed. There is no instance where we can say with absolute certainty that an author believed Atlantis was based on fact. However, Crantor (mid-fourth century–276 BCE), the middle Platonist Posidonius (135–51 BCE) and the geographer Strabo (c.64 BCE–24 CE) all seem to have considered it possible, even probable. Yet Aristotle (384–322 BCE) almost certainly thought that Plato made it up (see Strabo 13.1.6).

Aristotle was taught by Plato himself, and Crantor was an early follower and a head of the Academy. If even they did not agree on the historical status of Atlantis, this suggests that Plato's multi-layered text is difficult – perhaps impossible – to interpret conclusively. I believe that this ambiguity is deliberate. By keeping people guessing about the historical roots – if any – of his Atlantis tale, he compels his readers to engage in close textual interpretation and active philosophizing for themselves (we are after all still discussing the matter over 2,300 years later). As we have seen, Plato does not think that we learn through being passive recipients into whom knowledge can be poured: we have to think and question for ourselves. Furthermore, the *Timaeus* and *Critias* clearly emphasize the need for interpretation. At *Critias* 107b, Critias says that 'all the statements we make are inevitably representations (sing. *mimēsis*) and images (sing. *apeikasia*)', and although this particular passage is discussing the limits of human knowledge concerning the gods, it could very plausibly be read as a strong hint about how to approach all the discussions in the *Timaeus* and *Critias*, including about Atlantis. Even more explicit is *Timaeus* 22c–d. The Egyptian priest claims that although the *mythos* of Phaethon, son of Helios, has the form of a story, in fact it symbolizes a cosmological process and subsequent historical event on earth.

ETHICAL AND POLITICAL PURPOSES OF THE ATLANTIS TALE

Myth, then, may serve a number of purposes (and to keep us even more on our toes, let us again remember Socrates' claim that the Atlantis tale is not a myth, but a true account!). So what are the purposes of the *mythos/logos* of the Atlantis tale? Like many ancient writers, Plato is not usually particularly concerned with a precise factual recovery of the past (the historian Thucydides might be considered an exception, but even Thucydides' primary goal is to shape the events of his narrative to underscore his uncompromising view of human nature and agency). Plato is generally quite content to mix historical and mythological sources (as we might distinguish them) and to embellish them with his own fertile imagination in order to make philosophical points. It is true that in his final work, the *Laws*, and especially in Book 3, he does show signs of an increasing interest in history, but even here his overall aim is to show how historical events demonstrate what he takes to be ethical, political and theological truths.

In the *Timaeus*, as we have seen, the immediate objective is stated explicitly: namely to provide a rich and powerful opponent to prehistoric Athens, to show how the virtues of the latter, which anticipate those of the ideal *polis*, can overcome wealth and martial might – a tale that, as Socrates points out (26e), is admirably well-suited to the Festival of Athena which is currently taking place. Politically, there also appears to be a strong anti-imperialist message: very probably an allusion to the combined Greek cities defeating the expansionist dreams of the sumptuously wealthy Persian Empire in 490 at Marathon, and in 480 at Salamis and at Mycale and Plataea in 479 (historical events vividly relayed by Herodotus and which Plato will himself recount in *Laws* Book 3). After the Greeks saw off the Persians, however, the Athenians then developed imperialist ambitions of their own: the Delian League which Athens led with the ostensible aim of protecting Greece from future Persian aggression swiftly grew into an empire in all but name, and, as Thucydides makes clear (*History of the Peloponnesian War* 1.23), fear of the intentions of Athens provoked the bitter civil war between Sparta and Athens which began in 431 and concluded in 404 with Athens' utter and humiliating defeat. One of the most disastrous episodes from the point of view of Athens was their doomed attempt to invade Sicily in 415–413; Plato may well be reminding his audience of this catastrophic enterprise by making one of the characters in the *Timaeus* and *Critias*, Hermocrates, come from Syracuse. It seems highly likely that by means of the Atlantis story Plato is critiquing not only the imperialism of Persia but the subsequent expansionist hubris of Athens. The *polis* which in 490 at Marathon had exemplified the virtues of courage and discipline – the very virtues that had helped its forebears see off the Atlanteans – had by 431 to a significant degree transformed into its old enemy, the Atlanteans (and in respect of hubris at least into the Persians too).

Plato may even be warning his Athenian contemporaries in the 360s not to abuse their headship of the Second Athenian League (378–355, formed to keep Sparta, and Persia, in check), and develop imperialist ambitions again. At *Critias* 121a, Critias remarks caustically that the over-zealous pursuit and worship of material wealth destroys both virtue and the wealth itself. Wars are very, very expensive.

There may even be a further warning here, a warning about Macedonian expansion. During the 360s most Athenian eyes were still fixed on Sparta and Persia, but Plato may have had particular information about the Macedonian threat from his most illustrious pupil and research associate, Aristotle. Aristotle arrived from Stagira in northern Greece to study with Plato at the Academy around 367. Aristotle's father had been doctor at the court of the Macedonian King Amyntas III, father of Philip II and grandfather of Alexander the Great. Plato might well have heard from Aristotle about the growth of Macedonian power and ambitions, and realized, several years before the anti-Macedonian speeches of the orator Demosthenes, that this was where the new danger lay. However, whether this supposition is true or not, the anti-imperialist message of the Atlantis tale is clear and powerful: imperialism spells trouble, for the aggressor as well as the aggrieved.

CYCLICAL CATASTROPHES AND CIVILIZATIONS REBORN

However, even though gallant little prehistoric Athens defeats hubristic Atlantis, we still need to remember that later *both* civilizations are destroyed by earthquakes and floods, the Athenians being swallowed up by the earth and the island of Atlantis by the sea in one single terrible day and night. Natural cataclysm is a phenomenon of abiding interest to Plato, and in the *Statesman* (268d–274e) and *Laws* (3.676c–683b) he explores the theory that such cataclysms are cyclical: human achievements and hopes, even when supported by virtue, are fragile. Virtue is indeed our best defence against human vice, but even the virtuous are at risk from disasters which are both natural and divinely engineered: we are all, ultimately, at the mercy of the gods. Cyclical cataclysms also allow Plato to examine how civilizations can develop again after disaster and near-extinction. In this rebuilding the virtues are again our best resource, and philosophy too will be needed, both to help us understand the nature of the virtues and how best to implement them, and also because philosophic wisdom is a virtue in its own right.

ART, CENSORSHIP AND MYTH

THE IMPORTANCE OF MYTH

In the case of the Atlantis story, therefore, the acts of interpretation and re-interpretation by successive generations will in turn keep the tale and its multi-layered meanings and questions alive, and one of the most important of these questions is the complex relationship between *mythos* and *logos*, a complexity embedded in the very word 'mythology'. We have seen how Plato deploys myth to stimulate enquiry – and myths of course have the additional pedagogic advantage of being vivid and memorable – and the reason they can take such a deep hold on us lies, for Plato, in our psychology: myths embed themselves deep within our *psychai* because they engage our non-rational as well as our rational elements. This applies whether Plato is working with the bipartite division between reason and the appetites of the *Gorgias* or the tripartite division of the *Republic*, *Phaedrus* and *Timaeus* into reason, a spirited element and the appetites. What is the *logos* of *mythos* itself? And is *mythos* better than *logos* for exploring certain concepts and issues? Or at least needed in addition to *logos*? We have already touched on these questions when we considered the treatment of *erōs* in the *Symposium*.

All this helps explain both why in the *Republic* Socrates deploys myths, legends and imagery to convey his philosophical points (such as Gyges' Ring, the Allegory of the Cave and the Myth of Er), and also why the Philosopher-Rulers themselves create foundation myths (such as the Myth of the Metals)[4] to persuade the citizens to acquiesce in the tripartite class structure. As we saw in chapter 4, the stories told by the Philosopher-Rulers in particular have often been strongly criticized as propaganda and falsehoods – some would say plain lies – and I do not wish to deny their morally problematic nature, though I argued in chapter 4 that Plato does not intend them to be taken entirely literally; the issue is undeniably a complicated one. Nevertheless, the fact that both the Rulers and the character of Socrates (and of course Plato, the creator of both) find it natural to use myths suggests that for Plato myths play an important part in education, and in a healthy culture in general. We may of course disagree about the content and deployment of particular myths — we may indeed want to charge Socrates in the *Republic* with employing propaganda at certain points, particularly in Book 3 — but we should still reflect on the possibility that the underlying implication about the importance of myth may be correct.

Phaedrus 229c–d is interesting here. Socrates and Phaedrus, an ardent young student of rhetoric and philosophy whom we have met in chapter 6, are taking a walk outside the walls of Athens, paddling along the Ilisos stream and near the point where according to legend the god of the north wind, Boreas, abducted an Athenian princess, Oreithyia. Phaedrus asks Socrates if he believes the tale (*muthologēma*), and Socrates says that wise men — *sophoi* — give a rational explanation for it (much as the Egyptian priest does at *Timaeus* 22c–d): according to these *sophoi*, it is a story invented to account for Oreithyia being blown off the rocks by the north wind and dying as a result. But Socrates' *own* response is ambiguous: he says that although such explanations are pleasing enough and the mark of a clever mind, that mind is also a pedantic one — and furthermore those who want to explain away all such myths have let themselves in for a great deal of laborious and pretty futile work.

It is an intriguing passage, and it requires nuanced interpretation in its own right. Socrates appears to suggest that while the old myths are probably rooted in natural and historical events — just as the Egyptian priest says — they nevertheless still cannot be fully explained away. The reason for this may be that the mythical form speaks to the non-rational parts of our *psychē* which the historical or scientific account cannot, and in consequence myths can help shape individuals and communities in different ways than those available to such rational accounts. Individual lives and communities need myths. Myths can live on through the generations and each generation needs to reinterpret them and reapply them.

This brings us to the question of the legend of Atlantis today. We have to consider not only all the multi-layered meanings that Plato wove into it in the 360s, but also why we are still so fascinated by it. Why do there continue to be so many theories about its location, and so many expeditions to try to find it? Would we be

ART, CENSORSHIP AND MYTH

elated or disappointed if it were ever actually found? Do we need it to remain a myth?

And, crucially, why in the recreations of it and in our imagining of it do we so often forget that Atlantis is in fact the *enemy* in Plato's story? What does this tell us about ourselves and our values? The key issue, of course, is how to distinguish nourishing myths from harmful ones, and how to prevent the former from being misused and turned into the latter. The afterlife of Plato's legend of Atlantis is a disturbing case in point.

THE AFTERLIFE OF ATLANTIS

The history of the legend of Atlantis is also important in that it illustrates only too powerfully the darker uses of myth. For 2,000 years its afterlife is innocent enough: the story was enjoyed on its own terms and also served as a stimulus for debates about whether it was fact or fiction or a bit of both. Around 1500 CE it unsurprisingly became linked in Europe with the 'discovery' (from a European perspective) of the Americas. Although Thomas More's *Utopia* (1515) owes most to Plato's *Republic* and *Laws*, there are also echoes of Atlantis in his depiction of Utopia (as well as elements of Amerigo Vespucci's 1503 *Mundus Novus* [*New World*], recording a voyage begun in 1501).[5] Francis Bacon offers his *New Atlantis* (1626) as an express improvement on Plato's maritime power, situating his island in the Pacific ocean off Peru; one of the characters in the work places (the original) Atlantis in America.

In the nineteenth century, however, the use of the Atlantis tale takes a very different turn. Various scholars (and *soi-disant* scholars) of Mesoamerica, such as Charles Etienne Brasseur de Bourbourg, put forward the racist view that fabulously beautiful and technologically advanced cultures such as that of the Maya could not have been created by Mesoamericans: Europeans, and specifically European Atlanteans, somehow managed to reach Mesoamerica and act as the driving creative force behind such sophisticated cultures (theories of continental drift were mooted). In the 1880s the darkness deepens. First, in 1882 the United

States Congressman and self-styled historian Ignatius Donnelly writes *Atlantis: The Antediluvian World*, claiming that *all* ancient civilizations stem from (European) Atlantis. Then, in 1888, the theosophist Madame Blavatsky proposes a theory of racial evolution in *The Secret Doctrine*, in which she pronounces that the Aryan race evolved from the Atlanteans; from circa 1900 a number of German and Austrian writers (such as Guido von List) pick up on this seductively flattering baloney, and by the 1920s Karl Georg Zschaetzsch and Herman Wirth are locating Atlantis in the north Atlantic or the far north of Europe, which they term 'Hyperborea' (referring to the same far northern region in ancient Greek mythology and conveniently forgetting that Blavatsky had in fact stated that the Atlanteans were olive-skinned). They posit a Hyperborean/Atlantean Nordic master race who are the progenitors of the Aryans, and they specifically distinguish the Atlantean Aryans from the Jewish race. In the 1930s the head of the SS, Heinrich Himmler, and the Nazi Party ideologist Alfred Rosenberg make this poisonous nonsense official Nazi doctrine.

It is unclear how many of those who perverted Plato's legend of Atlantis knew that the legend was created by him – whether or not it had any historical roots – in his *Timaeus* and *Critias*; it is also unclear how many of them genuinely believed in the historicity of Atlantis, or simply found it expedient to do so. However, whatever the answers to these questions, this twisted perversion of the story is yet another reason why it is so important that we continue to read and study Plato. It is vital that we are able to spot these misuses and call them out. Plato says that art can be dangerous, and the distortion of his Atlantis myth shows that he is right. However, the solution is not to expunge myths altogether – as we have seen, they have an essential part to play in a vibrant culture – but always to approach them with all our faculties alive, responding to them with our critical intelligence as well as our emotions and aesthetic sensibilities.

Epilogue

According to another legend related by a sixth-century CE anonymous biographer:

> Plato himself, too, shortly before his death, had a dream of himself as a swan, darting from tree to tree and causing great trouble to the fowlers, who were unable to catch him. When Simmias the Socratic heard this dream, he explained that all men would endeavour to grasp Plato's meaning, none however would succeed, but each would interpret him according to his own views, whether in a metaphysical or a physical or any other sense.[1]

As I said in the Preface, I have tried hard not to project my own views onto Plato, but have endeavoured to be true to the texts; however, as I also made clear, of course I accept that there is no view from nowhere, and my selections and emphases, and to some extent my interpretations, will inevitably reflect my own interests, my own sense of why Plato still matters, as they would and will for any individual, or indeed any generation. Plato deliberately writes in a way which requires his readers to engage in active interpretation, to think for themselves and reflect on what we can learn from him and apply to the ever-changing and ever-present 'now'. As Simmias realized, this work of interpretation will never be completed, but engaging in it will always be important. Plato mattered then and he matters now.

Notes

PREFACE

1. Diogenes Laertius 3.5. As Atack notes (2024:62), this story is unlikely to be true, and was probably designed to connect Plato to the god Apollo, to whom the swan was sacred (and to whom Socrates had also dedicated his life, declaring on his final day in prison that the reason swans sing so sweetly just before they die is because they know they are going to an afterlife blessed by Apollo (*Phaedo* 84e–85b).
2. Cicero *De Divinatione* 1.36, 78.
3. The Greek for 'stranger', *xenos*, can also mean visitor. I have translated it 'stranger' to emphasize the fact that Plato chooses not to identify the visitor, and, I believe wishes to create an air of mystery. The same applies to the 'Eleatic Stranger' of the *Sophist* and *Statesman*.
4. 155d.

INTRODUCTION: PLATO'S LIFE AND THE SOCRATIC INHERITANCE

1. *Polis* has variously been translated in English as 'city', 'city-state' and 'state'. I have chosen 'city' (which is the most usual current translation) to distinguish it from the modern concept of the nation-state. In Plato's time, the term refers to an independent community and often also embraces the political and social arrangements of that community (more strictly, its *politeia*); I have in consequence occasionally left *polis* untranslated to remind the reader of this wider frame of reference. Geographically, it includes the surrounding territory, the produce and resources from which are required for independence. It does not refer to the physical

NOTES

buildings of the city, for which there is a different term: *astu*. I use 'state' when referring to contemporary nation-states.

2 Aristoxenus, a pupil of Aristotle and writing in the second half of the fourth century, says Plato served on campaigns during the Corinthian War (395–387/6, fought against Sparta by a coalition of Corinth, Athens, Thebes and Argos).

3 Nails (2002) places this first trip a few years later. In any event, the journey would only have been possible after the King's Peace of 387/6 which ended the Corinthian War, and was guaranteed by the Persian king Artaxerxes II and worked out by the Persians and Spartans.

4 For Plato and Orphism, see Cornelli 2023: 311–13.

5 Diogenes Laertius 3.30.

6 Ancient accounts of Plato's three (or conceivably only two) visits to Sicily vary considerably: see Atack 2024 for a judicious analysis of these accounts. In the light of a newly deciphered section of a carbonized papyrus scroll from the Villa dei Papiri at Herculaneum, it seems possible that Plato was sold into slavery on the island of Aegina much earlier than previously thought, perhaps in 404 BCE, when the Spartans conquered the island. (The scroll, recently re-edited by Fleischer [2023], is *The History of the Academy* by the Epicurean philosopher and poet Philodemus of Gadara, c.110–c.40 BCE.) However, whatever the results of further research concerning when (and indeed whether) Plato was sold into slavery, all the sources agree that his relations with Dionysius I became increasingly difficult, and the whole episode helped inform his coruscating analysis of the evils of tyranny.

7 See Atack 2024:215 n. 4. In this work 'the Academy' will refer to Plato's Academy rather than the general public training ground.

8 The ancient sources are particularly hard to disentangle here, and it is not clear whether this quasi-imprisonment and escape happened on the third trip, or the second, or both (or indeed whether there was only one further trip); see Atack 2024:156–7 and 178–9. In any event, the attempt to turn Dionysius II into a Philosopher-King was an utter failure.

CHAPTER 1: THE DIALOGUE FORM

1 There is debate over whether Gorgias was also a significant philosopher as well as a renowned orator and teacher of rhetoric; I tend to think that he was.

2 In Thucydides' version of the Funeral Oration that the Athenian democratic leader Pericles gives at the end of the first year of the Peloponnesian War, he claims proudly that Athens is 'open to the world' (1.39).

3 There is no rigid distinction between elenchus and dialectic, but there is general agreement that Socrates' question-and-answer technique of elenchus is principally aimed at exposing confusions and contradictions, and that, while never abandoning the elenchus, as Plato developed he wanted to incorporate it into a broader approach to discussion which can yield more positive results: see *Phaedo* 90b; *Republic* 7.533c; *Sophist* 277a. However, according to Xenophon, the destructive elenchus was only the first stage of Socrates' methodology (see Atack 2024:63).

4 See e.g. *Meno* 84e–85a. Socrates is conversing with Meno's young slave-boy, and asking him how to create a square of an area twice the size of a given square. The slave-boy is at a loss until Socrates invites the slave-boy to consider the diagonal line of the square.

5 According to Andocides *On the Mysteries* 16, one of the houses in which Alcibiades profaned the mysteries was that of Charmides, Plato's uncle.

6 Xenophon *Memorabilia* 1.2.12–48.

7 *Apology* 18b appears to be referring explicitly to Aristophanes' hostile portrayal of Socrates in the *Clouds* (423 BCE), where he is depicted as both a natural philosopher obsessed with trivia and a disingenuous sophist.

8 See e.g. *Phaedo* 97b–98b; *Cratylus* 400a; *Philebus* 28d–30e; *Laws* 12.967d–e.

9 E.g. *Republic* 10. 611e; *Timaeus* 90a.

10 *Theaetetus* 176a–c; *Republic* 10.613a–b; *Timaeus* 90a–d; *Laws* 4.716c.

11 *Isthmian Odes* V.16.

12 As expressed, for example, in Hawking and Mlodinow, *The Grand Design* 2010.

13 In highlighting Euthyphro's confusion over the nature of piety and impiety, Plato may well also be commenting on Socrates' trial: how can the Athenians convict Socrates of impiety when they do not even know what it is?

14 Two other worldviews which, if true, would raise serious problems for the possibility of language and dialogue are an extreme version

NOTES

of Heraclitean flux and Parmenides' view that there is only one thing, Being. For the difficulties of expressing extreme flux in language see *Cratylus* 440a–b and *Theaetetus* 179e–183b, and for the problems of articulating monism see *Sophist* 244b–d.

15 There is no evidence, however, that they do.

16 In Aristophanes' *Clouds*, the character of 'Socrates' is portrayed in part as a fraudulent sophist who teaches his students to make the weaker argument the stronger: see particularly 873–1153.

17 The exact nature of Plato's beliefs is not known and much discussed. However, there is clear internal evidence in the dialogues that, at least for a period of his life, he was strongly attracted to the mystery religions of the cult of Demeter at Eleusis and the cult of Orphism (or Pythagorean-Orphism) in the Western Greek world. It is also telling that although Plato often talks of 'the gods', referring to the traditional Greek Olympic pantheon, in some of what appear to be his most personal and profound passages on religion he quite often switches to 'god' in the singular: e.g. *Republic* 2.382a; *Laws* 10.902e, 10.903d. However, the relevant point here is that this 'god' does not refer to any of the current global monotheistic religions: although Judaism was of course in existence in Plato's lifetime, there is no record of any significant engagement between Jewish and Greek philosophers or Jewish and Greek philosophy until the first century BCE, when the Jewish philosopher Philo of Alexandria explored relations between Platonism and Second Temple Judaism.

18 It has long been debated whether Plato transmitted 'unwritten doctrines' (or even secret doctrines) to select students – doctrines which he felt should not be exposed to the possible misinterpretation inherent in publication. See Atack 2024:173 and 220 n. 31.

CHAPTER 2: HARMONY AND THE GOOD LIFE

1 *Daimones* will put in appearances throughout this book, and particularly in the discussion of erotic love, *erōs*, in ch. 6.

2 It should immediately be emphasized that, although we shall explore the links Plato makes between individual and communal flourishing, this 'excellent realization' should not be confused with the 'optimization' beloved of HR departments, which can

sometimes focus on the needs of the organization to the detriment of the individuals concerned.
3 Mill's version of utilitarianism, which (problematically for the arithmetic) introduces quality into the quantitative calculations, in fact owes a lot to Plato: Mill's distinction between 'higher' and 'lower' pleasures (relating to 'higher' and 'lower' faculties) is largely based on *Republic* 9.580d–587b.
4 See Hobbs 2000:173–4.
5 Glaucon's and Adeimantus' challenges are also discussed in more detail in ch. 3.
6 For a detailed study of the analogy see Williams 1973.
7 In the *Republic*, these 'parts' are not necessarily spatially located. The issue is not finally decided in the scholarship, but fortunately for present purposes all we need to acknowledge are the existence of different faculties or motivational sets, whether or not they have separate physical origins within the body. In the *Timaeus*, however, the three motivational sets are located in the head, chest and abdomen respectively (69c–70e); although we should note that this is in the context of a 'likely story' about the natural world told not by Socrates but by Timaeus, so even here there is room for speculation about how Plato wants us to interpret these apparent spatial locations.
8 I discuss them in Hobbs 2000:15–21.
9 It may also have been Philolaus who first proposed that the movement of each celestial body emitted a sound, and that the movements of the planets revolving around the earth produce a series of coherently related pitches, the proportional relations between them creating the 'music of the spheres'.
10 Another major contribution of Archytas was working out how to double the volume of a cube (Atack 2024:138).
11 Although it will later be made clear that there are to be female as well as male Guardians, in this passage Socrates only talks of young males.
12 See Hobbs 2000 ch. 1 and *passim*.
13 See Sedley 2024.
14 The ideas in this section are discussed more fully in Hobbs 2007a.
15 See, for example, the scathing analysis of democracy and its *laissez-faire* interpretation of freedom at *Republic* 8.557b–e and 8.561d–e.

NOTES

The relation between acting according to one's informed wishes and political freedoms will be explored a little further in ch. 4.

16 At *Gorgias* 466b–468e, for example, the distinction between acting on a whim and acting according to one's 'true', informed, rational wish is clearly demarcated by the contrast between *moi dokei* + infinitive and *boulēsis*.
17 See Frankfurt 1971:5–20.
18 See Hobbs 2000:46–9 and 2025.
19 See Price 1990:258–70; Hobbs 2000:46–9.
20 I discuss these issues in more depth in Hobbs 2007a.
21 There is not complete agreement, but most scholars concur that there are to be slaves in the 'ideal' city that the *Republic* describes. See *Republic* 4.433d and Vlastos 1981. For a contrary view see Calvert 1987.
22 See also *Timaeus* 45–7 and *Philebus* 51.
23 There is strong evidence from both the dialogues and other ancient sources that Plato loved what he regarded as the right kind of music, properly played.
24 Beethoven's Ninth Symphony was, for example, played at the 1936 Berlin Olympics, organized by Goebbels.
25 Some of these studies are helpfully listed on the Thoughtful (formerly SAPERE) website: www.thoughtful.org.uk/research
26 This will also help the pupils and students to address the problems caused by damaging *false* narratives – narratives which are not presented as fictional but purport, inaccurately, to give a factual account of historical or contemporary events.
27 https://www.strategyunitwm.nhs.uk/publications/what-are-ethical-challenges-addressing-inequities

CHAPTER 3: DEMOCRACY, DEMAGOGUERY AND TYRANNY

1 A salient example of the misuse of oratorical persuasion is provided by the Athenian demagogue Cleon in the famous Mytilenean Debate recounted by Thucydides (3.37–49). In 428 BCE the city of Mytilene on the island of Lesbos had revolted against Athenian rule. The revolt was ultimately suppressed and the following year Cleon persuaded the Athenian *dēmos* that all the men in Mytilene should be put to death as punishment, and all the women and children enslaved, and a ship was dispatched with the orders.

Fortunately, the following day the Athenians were persuaded by the more moderate Diodotus to revoke their decision and another, better-manned and better-equipped ship set sail which managed to get to Mytilene just in time to stop the massacre.

2 See ch. 2 p.39 n.16.
3 See the discussion of the close links Plato makes between reason and freedom in ch. 2 pp.37–41.
4 Socrates has pointedly emphasized at 470e that he is discussing the *eudaimonia* of both men and women.
5 I discuss Socrates' arguments against Callicles in more detail in Hobbs 2000:142–7.
6 Thucydides makes it clear at the start of his work (1.22) that 'my method has been, while keeping as closely as possible to the words that were actually used, to make the speakers say what, in my opinion, was called for by each situation' (trans. Warner).
7 See Ch . 3 n . 1.
8 The evidence is collected by Dodds in the appendix to his edition of the *Gorgias* (1959:387–91). See also Hobbs 2000:151.
9 Plato rarely introduces fictitious named characters. An exception (and even this is disputed) is the mystical priestess-like figure Diotima in the *Symposium*. There is no historical evidence for Timaeus from Locri in southern Italy (in the *Timaeus*), but it is possible that he is partly modelled on Plato's friend Archytas of Tarentum, whom we have met in the Introduction and ch. 2.
10 Almost certainly the Pythagoreans, as Dodds notes (1959:337–8).
11 See Hobbs 2000:157.
12 The view that we should never return wrong for wrong is one we can attribute with confidence to the historical Socrates. See Introduction p. XXVI.
13 'Rubbish' translates *phluaria* – the same term that Callicles had used to denigrate Socrates' views at *Gorgias* 498b, 490c and 490e.
14 Like Callicles, Thrasymachus conceives of rulers solely as male.
15 Thucydides, *History* 3.82.4.
16 The corruption and subversion of moral terms in the *psychē* of the democratic character and his associates in *Republic* 8.560d–561a appears to be a deliberate allusion to Thucydides 3.82.4.
17 For a more detailed discussion of Socrates' arguments see Hobbs 2000:170–4.

NOTES

18 See Hobbs 2000:171–2.
19 Ch. 2 p. 25.
20 We shall be returning to the question of honours in ch. 5.

CHAPTER 4: THE IDEAL CITY AND ITS DECLINE

1 Ch. 2 pp. 25–7.
2 Although Socrates makes almost no mention of the existence (or non-existence) of slaves in his imagined community, *Republic* 433d provides strong evidence for their existence: see Vlastos 1981. For an argument against, see Calvert 1987: 367–72.
3 As we will see when we consider the *Laws* later in this chapter, Plato is highly critical of the extreme militarism of Sparta and its focus on war rather than peace; nevertheless, he is attracted to other aspects of its culture, such as the communal messes for the ruling warrior class and the official (not always practised) frugality and physical toughness.
4 A point reinforced at 7.520d, where Socrates says that the city in which rulers take up their duties with the least enthusiasm will have the best and most stable government, whereas the city in which rulers are eager to rule will have the worst.
5 At *Politics* 1.13 1260a20–4, Aristotle criticizes the historical Socrates for holding that the temperance, courage and justice of a man and a woman are the same.
6 Glaucon also emphasizes that there will be some individual women who outperform individual men.
7 For a more detailed discussion of the position of women Guardians, see Hobbs 2000:245–8.
8 Both Diogenes Laertius (3.23) and Philodemus (*History of the Academy* vi.26–7) give us the names of two: Lastheneia of Mantineia and Axiothea of Phlius.
9 Its authenticity has been disputed, but Aristotle refers to it as genuine. Whatever the truth of its authorship, however, its precise tone and intention are also much debated.
10 See ch. 1 p. 3 n. 2.
11 In *On the Pythagorean Life*, Iamblichus lists 17 Pythagorean women and 267 Pythagorean men.
12 Zamyatin's dystopian futuristic novel *We*, a satirical critique of the increasingly totalitarian direction of the Bolsheviks after the

October Revolution (and in which the secret police are called the Bureau of Guardians), is just one of many powerful and eloquent examples.
13 For Archytas, see Introduction XXII and ch. 2 p. 31. Plato mentions Melissus at *Theaetetus* 180e.
14 Not all scholars agree on this point. For a judicious discussion, see Sedley 2024.
15 For Aristotle's rejection of Plato's Forms, see *Metaphysics* 1.6.
16 See Plato *Cratylus* 402a.
17 Aristotle *Metaphysics* 1.6 987a31–b7.
18 *Metaphysics* 4.5 1010a10–15.
19 Here 'knowledge' translates *gnōsis*.
20 *Cratylus* 440a–b.
21 Plato writes of a (possibly fictitious) visit to Athens around 450 by Parmenides and his student Zeno in the *Parmenides*, and he would also have discussed Parmenides' philosophy with Euclides and his circle, when he stayed with Euclides in Megara after Socrates' enforced suicide in 399.
22 Plato may well also be influenced by the fact that Heraclitus' changing phenomena are regulated by what Heraclitus terms the *Logos*.
23 Some commentators hold that mathematical reasoning deals with the objects of mathematics alone, and that these mathematical objects are to be distinguished from the Forms. The Divided Line has given rise to a wealth of different interpretations, but the nuances do not need to concern us here. For further discussion see Burnyeat 2012:145–172: 'Platonism and mathematics: a prelude to discussion'.
24 To take just one example from many, the film *The Matrix* adapts the Cave in its disturbing portrayal of humans unwittingly trapped in a fake reality.
25 Whether this 'each of us' is in fact compatible with the tripartite class system will be discussed below.
26 See ch. 3 p. 63.
27 At 7.536c, Socrates does say that they have been amusing themselves with an imaginary sketch, but this in itself does not preclude the possibility of its realization. A helpful discussion of the whole issue can be found in Schofield 2006:234–40.

NOTES

28 See Schofield 2006:238.
29 For More's indebtedness to Plato, see Hobbs 2024:19–35; for the place of the *Republic* in Greek utopian and golden-age writing see Hobbs 2007b:176–94.
30 See n. 2 in this chapter.
31 See ch. 2 p. 28.
32 See also 2.375a and 6.484d.
33 Ch. 2 p. 39 and notes 16 and 17.
34 Thucydides 3.82.4, quoted in ch. 3 p. 71.
35 In the *Laws*, unlike the *Republic*, artisans are not citizens at all, but foreign residents (metics) and foreign slaves (8. 846d–847b). However, the comments made about the importance of creating and protecting appropriate cultural artefacts and practices clearly apply to them too, as both creators and also consumers and practitioners.
36 We shall be returning to the contrast between Athenian and Spartan education and attitudes to war in the next chapter.
37 Ch. 2 pp. 37–41. The distinction between 'negative' and 'positive' liberty was made by Berlin 1969.

CHAPTER 5: HEROISM, CELEBRITY AND MONEY

1 Ch. 2 p. 24. See also ch. 1 pp. 6–10.
2 Ch. 1 pp. 6–9.
3 Ch. 2 pp. 34–5.
4 As we have seen, the keen scholarly debate over whether 'Homer' refers to one, two or more authors does not concern us; the relevant point here is that for Plato and his contemporaries the *Iliad* and the *Odyssey* were written by one man.
5 In Homer, Patroclus and Achilles are not lovers (as they will later be depicted in Greek literature), but nevertheless the powerful romantic bond between them is vividly portrayed.
6 *Iliad* 9.410–16, trans. Lattimore.
7 *Odyssey* 1.296–302 and 3.195–200.
8 We shall be exploring the question of heroism and gender below.
9 See Currie 2005.
10 In Plato's *Hippias Major* 293a–b, for example, the sophist Hippias is reluctant to look to Achilles as a model, precisely because Achilles had a divine mother, Thetis. His self-sacrifice, while

fine (*kalon*) and appropriate for the son of a goddess, is not a suitable example for ordinary mortals, claims Hippias, for whom *eudaimonia* includes providing a beautiful (*kalon*) burial for their parents, and receiving in turn a beautiful burial from their children.
11 Alexander the Great hero-worshipped Achilles and consciously tried to emulate or even surpass him. See Hobbs 2000:175–8.
12 I explore Plato's treatment of the Homeric heroes, and his relation to Homer in general, in much more detail in Hobbs 2000, particularly chs 6, 7 and 8.
13 Hobbs 2000:183.
14 See Introduction p. XXVI.
15 At *Ars Rhetorica* 1367a23–4, Aristotle says that honour is regarded as fine because it is the mark of superior excellence (*aretē*). See also *Nicomachean Ethics* 1095b26–8: people seek honour to convince themselves of their own goodness.
16 See Introduction p. XXIV.
17 Note 10 above.
18 Hippias quotes Achilles' declaration to this effect at *Il.*9.309–13.
19 In Sophocles *Philoctetes*, Achilles' son Neoptolemus initially agrees to Odysseus' trick, but he later repents, and at 902–3 and 908–9 calls it 'shameful' and 'not right'. At *Nicomachean Ethics* 1146a16–21, Aristotle says it is sometimes praiseworthy to give up a fixed opinion, and cites this episode as an example: Neoptolemus is right to abandon the resolution to deceive Philoctetes which Odysseus persuaded him to adopt.
20 See Hobbs 2000:175–8 and 206 n. 26.
21 *Iliad* 1.225, cited by Socrates at 3.389e.
22 See Hobbs 2000:200.
23 See e.g. *Iliad* 9.616 and 16.87–9.
24 *Nicomachean Ethics* 1095b24.
25 Ch. 5 p. 110.
26 See Hobbs 2000:242–4.
27 This rethinking of courage and 'manliness' (*andreia*) is a theme that runs throughout Plato's works. In addition to the *Republic* and the *Laws*, see also the *Protagoras* and the *Laches* and their thoughtful discussions of the relations between courage, risk and different kinds of knowledge: Hobbs 2000 ch. 3.

NOTES

28 *Republic* 7.516d.
29 The two women named by Diogenes Laertius as attending Plato's lectures (See Introduction p. XX and ch. 4 p. 81 n. 8) only appear to have been present at public lectures, rather than enrolled as students.
30 Ch. 4 p. 99.
31 For a more extended discussion of statues and memorials, see Hobbs 2021.
32 Ch. 4 p. 95.
33 Politicians fiddling expenses obviously happens almost everywhere, almost all the time, but the scandal that broke in the UK in 2009 was an especially egregious example.

CHAPTER 6: LOVE AND FRIENDSHIP

1 See in particular ch. 1 pp. 14–17 and ch. 3 pp. 55–62 and 64–70.
2 Although Plato gives hints of the tension between the characters of Aristophanes and Socrates – hardly surprising given the highly unfavourable (and damaging) depiction by Aristophanes of Socrates in the *Clouds*.
3 Estimates vary, but in the fifth and fourth centuries BCE there were perhaps about 40,000 adult male citizens in Athens.
4 We shall be discussing the Greek conventions of the active 'lover' (*erastēs*) and the passive 'beloved' (*erōmenos*) shortly, when we explore the *Symposium*.
5 Ch. 4 p. 99.
6 See ch. 4 pp. 78–80, 83, 94.
7 Although Socrates uses male pronouns in this passage, it is clear that it applies to the just woman too.
8 Ch. 2 pp. 41–2 and n. 19.
9 See ch. 1 pp. 5–10.
10 The practice of *paiderastia* was common in a number of cities as well as Athens, such as Sparta and Thebes.
11 Upper-class men tended to marry rather late, and many then died fairly young; many teenagers would have lost their natural father, and *paiderastia* partly fulfilled the role of guidance into adulthood (which of course makes any sexual component of the relationship even more complicated).

12 Michel Foucault is very perceptive on the ambivalence and double standards in *The History of Sexuality*, vol. 2, 'The Use of Pleasure' (see especially part 4, 'Erotics'): it is just about acceptable to *be* penetrated as a teenager, but far less acceptable for an adult male to be known to *have been* penetrated in his youth, particularly if he is seeking political office.
13 Intriguingly, there was just such a fighting force of lovers and beloveds formed at Thebes, the so-called 'Sacred Band' which was formed in 378 BCE and distinguished itself at Leuctra in 371 BCE. However, as we do not have a definite date for the *Symposium*, we don't know whether the existence of this band might have inspired Plato, or whether the inspiration might have worked the other way.
14 Agathon is described as Pausanias' favourite at *Protagoras* 315e, set in 432 BCE.
15 The philosophers we now term 'Presocratic' would at both the dramatic date of the *Symposium* and its date of composition have been called '*physikoi*', 'those who explore *physis* (nature)'.
16 Ch. 2 pp. 36–7 and 49.
17 There is the same double entendre in the Greek as in the English.
18 See Santas 1988 and Price 1990.
19 As we have seen (p. 127), the speakers move between *Erōs* the god (or *daimōn*, as we shall shortly see) and *erōs* the human experience which the god (or *daimōn*) represents.
20 And we may remember that one of the women named by Diogenes Laertius as attending Plato's lectures was Lastheneia from Mantineia.
21 See, for example, 209e–210a, where she says that she thinks Socrates could be initiated into the matters concerning *erōs* she has described so far, but she doubts whether he could approach the rites and revelations to which they lead (very probably an indication by Plato that from this point in Socrates' speech he is moving beyond anything that the historic Socrates might have said). For Plato and the Eleusinian Mysteries and Orphic cults, see Introduction pp. XVIII–XIX and Cornelli 2023: 311–13.
22 For more on Diotima and the female imagery she uses, see Hobbs 2006.
23 Hobbs 2017.

NOTES

24 As someone who combines religious expertise with philosophy and a knowledge of erotics, Diotima also inhabits this daimonic realm.
25 There are sharply divergent scholarly interpretations of this passage: see Rowe 1998: 181–2 for a helpful discussion of the issues. For our purposes, the main point is that Diotima is here turning to the experience that we call being in love.
26 I discuss all these issues in much more depth in Hobbs 2006.
27 The *Symposium* only denies that the whole human, living in this world and in time, will be immortal; this view does not necessarily conflict with the fact that in the *Republic* Socrates claims that the rational part of the *psychē* will exist eternally in some other realm, separated not only from the body but from the spirited and appetitive faculties which accrue to it. In the *Phaedrus*, as we will see below, the entire tripartite *psychē* is immortal and exists between incarnations in a separate eternal realm.
28 Diotima uses the verb '*agapōn*' at 210d2, but of an *erastēs* loving an individual human or activity.
29 There are in fact marked differences between Plato and Freud regarding *erōs*/eros: in Freud, eros works away from its original state, whereas in the *Symposium*, *erōs* is returning to it (if we think that the view expressed in the *Republic* and the *Phaedrus* that our rational souls [*Republic*] or entire souls [*Phaedrus*] dwelt in the realm of the Forms before incarnation applies to the *Symposium* too). Furthermore, Freud sometimes seems to be sexualizing all love, whereas Diotima appears to be de-sexualizing even originally sexual love.
30 See ch. 1 pp. 6–10.
31 175e; see ch. 1 p. 9.
32 Nussbaum 1986:193.
33 Ch. 5 p. 110.
34 Ch. 5 p. 114.
35 Ch. 1 p. 7.
36 Introduction p. XX.
37 Ch. 1 p. 7.
38 Lysias was another son of Cephalus, in whose house the conversation of the *Republic* takes place, but the speech attributed to him here was almost certainly composed by Plato himself, skilfully imitating Lysias' style.

39 In the *Phaedrus*, Socrates refers to *Erōs* as a god or 'something divine', and not specifically as a *daimōn* (as Diotima had done).
40 When the image is introduced in 246a, only the horses are described as winged, but it is made clear at 251b and 254a that the entire soul is winged, including the charioteer.

CHAPTER 7: ART, CENSORSHIP AND MYTH

1 See ch. 1 n. 17.
2 For Gyges' Ring, the Allegory of the Cave and the Myth of Er, see chs 3, 4 and 5 respectively. The *Gorgias, Symposium, Phaedo, Timaeus, Phaedrus* and *Statesman* are also particularly rich in imagery and myth, but most of Plato's texts contain memorable examples.
3 The Critias of the *Timaeus* is almost certainly not the same Critias as the leader of the Thirty Tyrants of 404–403 BCE but his grandfather, although this is disputed. See Schofield 2006:208 and n. 47.
4 Ch. 4 p. 78.
5 See Hobbs 2024.

EPILOGUE

1 The story appears in Westerink (trans.) (2010), *Anonymous Prolegomena to Platonic Philosophy*, 1.29–35.

References

PRIMARY SOURCES

Barker, E. (trans., rev. R. F. Stalley) (1995), *Aristotle: The Politics*. Oxford: Oxford University Press.

Burnyeat, M. (intro. and trans.) and Levett, M. J. (trans.) (1990), *The Theaetetus of Plato*. Indianapolis, IN: Hackett.

Bury, R. (trans.) (1926), *Plato: Laws*. Cambridge, MA: Harvard University Press.

Cooper, J. and Hutchinson, D. S. (eds) (1997), *Plato: Complete Works*. Indianapolis, IN: Hackett.

Dillon, J. and Hershbell, J. (trans.) (1991), *Iamblichus: On the Pythagorean Way of Life*. Atlanta, GA: Society of Biblical Literature.

Griffin, M. T. and Atkins, E. M. (eds) (1991), *Cicero: On Duties*. Cambridge: Cambridge University Press.

Hammond, M. (trans.) and Atack, C. (intro. and notes) (2023), *Memories of Socrates: Xenophon's 'Memorabilia' and 'Apology'*. Oxford: Oxford University Press.

Henderson, J. (trans.) (2002), *Aristophanes: Frogs/Assemblywomen/Wealth*. Loeb Classical Library. Cambridge, MA: Harvard University Press.

Kennedy, G. A. (2007), *Aristotle, On Rhetoric: A Theory of Civic Discourse* (2nd edn.). New York and Oxford: Oxford University Press.

King, J. E. (trans.) (1989), *Cicero: Tusculan Disputations*. Loeb Classical Library. Cambridge, Mass.: Harvard University Press.

Kirk, G. S., Raven, J. E. and Schofield, M. (1983), *The Presocratic Philosophers* (2nd edn.; includes Heraclitus, Parmenides and Melissus). Cambridge: Cambridge University Press.

Lattimore, R. (trans.) (1967), *The Odyssey of Homer*. New York: Harper and Row.

Lattimore, R. (trans.) (1968), *The Iliad of Homer*. Chicago, IL: Chicago University Press.

Lee, D. (trans.) and Lane, M. (2007), *Plato: Republic*. Harmondsworth: Penguin Classics.

Lee. D. (trans., rev. Johansen, T.) (2008), *Plato: Timaeus*. Harmondsworth: Penguin Classics.

Maidment, K. J. (trans.) (1941), *Andocides, On the Mysteries*, in Loeb Classical Library, *Minor Attic Orators: Antiphon, Andocides*. Cambridge, MA: Harvard University Press.

Mensch, P. (trans.) and Miller, J. (ed.) (2018), *Diogenes Laertius: Lives of the Eminent Philosophers*. Oxford: Oxford University Press.

Morrow, G. R. (1962), *Plato's Epistles: A Translation with Critical Essays and Notes*. Indianapolis, IN: Bobbs-Merrill.

Race, W. H. (trans.) (1997), *Pindar: Nemean Odes, Isthmian Odes, Fragments*. Loeb Classical Library. Cambridge, MA: Harvard University Press.

Raeburn, D. (trans.) and Easterling P. (ed. and intro.) (2008), *Sophocles: Electra and Other Plays: Women of Trachis/Electra/Ajax/Philoctetes*. Harmondsworth: Penguin Classics.

Rowe, C. J. (trans. and ed., with commentary) (1998), *Plato: Symposium*. Warminster, Aris and Phillips.

Schofield, M. (ed.) and Griffith, T. (trans.) (2010), *Plato: Gorgias, Menexenus, Protagoras*. Cambridge: Cambridge University Press.

Sommerstein, A. H. (trans.) (2003), *Aristophanes: Lysistrata and Other Plays: Acharnians/Clouds/Lysistrata*. Harmondsworth: Penguin Classics

Warner, R. (trans.) (1954), *Thucydides: History of the Peloponnesian War*. Harmondsworth: Penguin.

West, M. L. (trans.) (1978), *Hesiod: Works and Days*. Oxford: Clarendon Press.

Westerink, L. G. (trans. and ed.) (2010), *Anonymous Prolegomena to Platonic Philosophy*, 2nd edn. Dilton Marsh: The Prometheus Trust.

Wynne, J. P. F. (2019), *Cicero on the Philosophy of Religion: On the Nature of the Gods and On Divination*. Cambridge: Cambridge University Press.

SECONDARY SOURCES

Atack, C. (2024), *Plato: A Civic Life*. London: Reaktion Books Ltd.

Bacon, F. (1626), *New Atlantis*, in S. Bruce (ed.) (2008).

REFERENCES

Bentham, J. (1996), *An Introduction to the Principles of Morals and Legislation* (eds J. H. Burns and H. L. A. Hart, with a new introduction by F. Rosen). Oxford: Clarendon Press.

Berlin, I. (1969), *Four Essays on Liberty*. Oxford: Oxford University Press.

Betegh, G. and Tsouna, V. (2024), *Conceptualizing Concepts in Greek Philosophy*. Cambridge: Cambridge University Press.

Blavatsky, H. (1888), *The Secret Doctrine: The Synthesis of Science, Religion and Philosophy* (2 vols). London: Theosophical Publishing Co., Ltd.

Bruce, S. (ed.) (2008), *Three Early Modern Utopias. Thomas More: Utopia/Francis Bacon: New Atlantis/Henry Neville: The Isle of Pines*. Oxford: Oxford World's Classics.

Burnyeat, M. F. (2012), *Ancient and Modern Philosophy vol. 2: Philosophy and the Good Life*. Cambridge: Cambridge University Press.

Calvert, B. (1987), 'Slavery in Plato's *Republic*'. *Classical Quarterly*, 37.2: 367–72.

Cornelli, G. (2023) 'Orphism' in G. A. Press and M. Duque (eds) (2023): 311–13.

Currie, B. (2005), *Pindar and the Cult of Heroes*. Oxford: Oxford University Press.

Dewey, J. (1916), *Democracy and Education*. New York: Macmillan.

Dodds, E. R. (1959), *Plato: Gorgias. A Revised Text with Introduction and Commentary*. Oxford: Clarendon Press.

Donnelly, I. (1882), *Atlantis: The Antediluvian World*. New York: Harper and Brothers.

Fleischer, K. J. (ed.) (2023), *Philodem, Geschichte der Akademie*. Boston: Brill.

Foucault, M. (2020), *History of Sexuality vol. 2: The Use of Pleasure* (trans. R. Hurley). Harmondsworth: Penguin Modern Classics.

Frankfurt, H. G. (1971), 'Freedom of the Will and the Concept of a Person', *Journal of Philosophy*, 68: 5–20.

Gill, C. (ed.) (1990), *The Person and the Human Mind: Issues in Ancient and Modern Philosophy*. Oxford: Oxford University Press.

Harte, V. and Woolf, R. (eds) (2017), *Rereading Ancient Philosophy: Old Chestnuts and Sacred Cows*. Cambridge: Cambridge University Press.

Hawking, S. and Mlodinow, L. (2010), *The Grand Design*. New York: Bantam Books.

Hobbs, A. (2000), *Plato and the Hero*. Cambridge: Cambridge University Press.
(2006), 'Female Imagery in Plato', in J. Lesher, D. Nails and F. Sheffield (eds): 252–71.
(2007a), 'Plato and Psychic Harmony: A Recipe for Mental Health or Mental Sickness?', *Philosophical Inquiry*, 29.5: 103–24.
(2007b), 'Plato on War', in D. Scott (ed.): 176–94.
(2017), 'Socrates, Eros and Magic', in V. Harte and R. Woolf: 101–20.
(2021), '*In Memoriam*: the Who, How, Where and When of Statues', *Journal of the Philosophy of Education*, 55.3: 425–9.
(2022), *Ethics Review* of NHS Strategy Unit *Strategies to Reduce Inequalities in Access to Planned Care*: https://t.co/NtRsATpgcC
(2024), 'More and the Republics of Plato', in C. Shrank and P. Withington (eds): 19–35.
(2025), 'Platonic Proportions: Beauty, Harmony and the Good Life', in M. Poltrum, M. Musalek, K. Galvin and Y. Saito (eds): 48–67.
Kant, I. (2019), *Groundwork for the Metaphysics of Morals* (trans. C. Bennett, J. Saunders and R. Stern). Oxford: Oxford World's Classics.
Kesey, K. (1962), *One Flew Over the Cuckoo's Nest*. New York: Viking Press and Signet Books.
Lawson-Tancred, H. (1998), *Aristotle: The Metaphysics*. Harmondsworth: Penguin Classics.
Lee, E. N., Mourelatos, A. P. D. and Rorty, R. (eds) (1973), *Exegesis and Argument: Studies in Greek Philosophy Presented to Gregory Vlastos*. *Phronesis* Supplement 1. Assen: Van Gorcum.
Lesher, J., Nails, D. and Sheffield, F. (eds) (2006), *Plato's Symposium: Issues in Interpretation and Reception*. Washington, DC: Center for Hellenic Studies, Trustees for Harvard University Press.
Mill, J. S. (2015), *On Liberty, Utilitarianism and Other Essays* (2nd edn, eds M. Philp and F. Rosen). Oxford: Oxford World's Classics.
More, T. (2016), *Utopia* (3rd edn, trans. R. M. Adams and ed. G. M. Logan). Cambridge: Cambridge University Press.
Nails, D. (2002), *The People of Plato: A Prosopography of Plato and Other Socratics*. Indianapolis, IN: Hackett.
Nietzsche, F. (1966), *Beyond Good and Evil* (trans. W. Kaufmann). New York: Random House.
Nietzsche, F. (1967), *On the Genealogy of Morals* (trans. W. Kaufmann and R. J. Hollingdale, ed. W. Kaufmann). New York: Vintage.

REFERENCES

Nietzsche, F. (1968), *Will to Power* (trans. W. Kaufmann and R. J. Hollingdale, ed. W. Kaufmann). New York: Vintage.

Nietzsche, F. (2005), *Thus Spoke Zarathustra* (trans. C. Martin). New York: Barnes and Noble Classics.

Northrup, G. T. (trans.) (1916), *Amerigo Vespucci: Mundus Novus: Letter to Lorenzo Pietro di Medici*. Princeton, NJ: Princeton University Press.

Nussbaum, M. (1986), *The Fragility of Goodness*. Cambridge: Cambridge University Press.

Poltrum, M., Musalek, M., Galvin, K. and Saito, Y. (eds) (2025), *The Oxford Handbook of Mental Health and Contemporary Western Aesthetics*. Oxford: Oxford University Press.

Press, G. A. and Duque, M. (eds) (2023), *The Bloomsbury Handbook of Plato*. London: Bloomsbury.

Price, A. W. (1990), 'Plato and Freud', in C. Gill (1990): 258–70.

Rushdie, S. (1988), *The Satanic Verses*. London: Vintage Books.

Santas, G. (1988), *Plato and Freud: Two Theories of Love*. Oxford: Oxford University Press.

Schofield, M. (2006), *Plato: Political Philosophy*. Oxford: Oxford University Press.

Scott, D. (2007), *Maieusis: Essays in Ancient Philosophy in Honour of Myles Burnyeat*. Oxford: Oxford University Press.

Sedley, D. N. S. (2024), 'Are Platonic Forms Concepts', in G. Betegh and V. Tsouna (eds) (2024): 74–95.

Shrank, C. and Withington, P. (eds) (2024), *The Oxford Handbook of Thomas More's Utopia*. Oxford: Oxford University Press.

Vespucci, A. (1504), *Mundus Novus: Letter to Lorenzo Pietro di Medici*, in G. T. Northrup (trans. 1916).

Vlastos, G. (1981), 'Does Slavery Exist in Plato's *Republic*?', in Vlastos, *Platonic Studies* (2nd printing with corrections). Princeton, NJ: Princeton University Press.

Whitehead, A. N. (corrected edition 1978, eds D. R. Griffin and D. W. Sherburne), *Process and Reality: An Essay in Cosmology*. Free Press.

Williams, B. (1973), 'The Analogy of City and Soul in Plato's *Republic*', in E. N. Lee, A. P. D. Mourelatos and R. Rorty (eds), 1973: 196–206.

Zamyatin, Y. (1993), *We* (trans. Clarence Brown). New York: Penguin Books.

Further Reading

Annas, J. (1999), *Platonic Ethics, Old and New*. Ithaca, NY, and London: Cornell University Press.
Annas, J. and Rowe, C. J. (eds) (2002), *New Perspectives on Plato, Modern and Ancient*. Washington, DC: Center for Hellenic Studies, Trustees for Harvard University.
Betegh, G. (2022), 'Plato on Philosophy and the Mysteries' in Ebrey and Kraut (eds) 2022: 233–67.
Burnyeat, M. and Frede, M. (ed. D. Scott) (2015), *The Pseudo-Platonic Seventh Letter*. Oxford: Oxford University Press.
Cartledge, P. (2016), *Democracy: A Life*. Oxford: Oxford University Press.
Dodds, E. R. (1951), *The Greeks and the Irrational*. Berkeley, CA: University of California Press.
Ebrey, D. and Kraut, R. (eds) (2022), *The Cambridge Companion to Plato*. Cambridge: Cambridge University Press.
Ferrari, G. R. F. (1987), *Listening to the Cicadas: A Study of Plato's Phaedrus*. Cambridge: Cambridge University Press.
(ed.) (2007), *The Cambridge Companion to Plato's Republic*. Cambridge: Cambridge University Press.
Gill, C. (1977), 'The Genre of the Atlantis Story', *Classical Philology*, 72: 287–304.
Guthrie, W. K. C. (1975), *A History of Greek Philosophy*, vol. 4: *Plato: The Man and His Dialogues: Earlier Period*. Cambridge: Cambridge University Press.
Hobbs, A. (2023), 'Women', in G. A. Press and M. Duque (eds) (2023): 358–61.

FURTHER READING

McCabe, M. M. (2000), *Plato and his Predecessors*. Cambridge: Cambridge University Press.

Nehamas, A. (1998), *The Art of Living: Socratic Reflections from Plato to Foucault*. Berkeley and Los Angeles, CA: University of California Press.

Press, G. A. and Duque, M. (eds) (2023), *The Bloomsbury Handbook of Plato*. London: Bloomsbury.

Price, A. W. (1989), *Love and Friendship in Plato and Aristotle*. Oxford: Oxford University Press.

Rowe, C. J. (trans.) and Broadie, S. (introduction and commentary) (2002), *Aristotle: Nicomachean Ethics*. Oxford: Oxford University Press.

Sheffield, F. (2006), *Plato's Symposium: The Ethics of Desire*. Oxford: Oxford University Press.

Acknowledgements

It is a great pleasure to express my profound gratitude to all the many people who have made this book possible. I am indebted to my agent, Philip Gwyn Jones, for his support and encouragement and deep love of books. I am very grateful to Robin Baird-Smith, who invited me to write it and gave excellent feedback during its early stages; to Octavia Stocker, who took the project over and guided it through to completion with perfect judgement and good humour; and to all the wonderful Bloomsbury team: Fahmida Ahmed, the project editor, Richard Thomson, the illustrator, Richard Mason, the copy-editor, Guy Holland, the proof-reader, Colin Hynson, the indexer, Rachel Nicholson, the senior head of publicity, and Lizzie Dorney Kingdom, the publicist.

I was very fortunate to be introduced to ancient Greek philosophy at Cambridge by a number of superb scholars and teachers: Mary Margaret McCabe, who first instilled a love of Plato in me; Malcolm Schofield; David Sedley and Geoffrey Lloyd. Many thanks too to my fellow graduates, Sr Margaret Atkins and Dominic Scott and Voula Tsouna, for many enriching discussions of ancient Greek philosophy over the years. My deepest intellectual debt is to Myles Burnyeat, who supervised my PhD thesis on Plato and Homer: inspirational teacher, writer and friend, and the embodiment of the very best kind of expertise. Malcolm Schofield and David Sedley also helped with certain points of scholarship in the writing of this book, as did Carol Atack, Paul Cartledge, P. N. Singer and Mark

ACKNOWLEDGEMENTS

Vernon: my grateful thanks to all of them. I am also indebted to my colleagues past and present at Cambridge, Warwick and Sheffield for their support and invigorating conversations, and to all those who have heard me give papers and talks about Plato and much else, for their penetrating and thought-provoking questions.

I am grateful too to all my students at Cambridge, Warwick and Sheffield for their perceptive questions and lively engagement; their particular concerns and interests have helped me greatly in the very difficult task of deciding what to include and what to leave out from such a massive oeuvre. I have also learnt much from taking part in a number of *In Our Time* programmes on BBC Radio 4, including several specifically on Plato, and I should like to express my deep gratitude to Melvyn Bragg and all the producers with whom I have worked, most recently Simon Tillotson, and also to my fellow guests. I am grateful in addition to all the producers, directors and presenters with whom I have worked on programmes about Socrates and Plato and ancient Greek culture, including James Cook, David Edmonds, Bettany Hughes, Faith Lawrence, Leonidas Liambeys, Anya Leonard, Ian McMillan, Donald Robertson, Sophie Roell, Dixi Stewart, Anna Thompson, Nigel Warburton, 1895 Films and *National Geographic*.

A number of friends have provided various forms of practical support during the writing of this book, and it is a pleasure to thank Olivia Case, Wendy Finke, David Gibbins, Wiebke Roloff Halsey, Suzanne Orsler, Katie Robinson, P. N. Singer, Robert Stern, Crosby Stevens, Marina Tsoulou, Simon van der Borgh, Jordan Erica Webber and Vicky Wetten.

Finally, I should like to express my love and gratitude to my family, who have given me unstinting support and intellectual stimulation: my late parents, Anthony and Rosemary, Mike and Maureen Hobbs, and my daughter Molly, who has always encouraged me to keep exploring and take on new challenges.

Index

abuse, political and psychological 43–4
Academy xx–xxii
Achilles 102–5, 106, 107–13
Adeimantus 12, 25, 27, 30, 40, 65, 74–5, 90–1, 121
Agamemnon, King 104, 105, 108, 111
Agathon 9, 135–6, 146
Al-Farabi 20
Alcibiades 6–9, 101, 144–7
Alexander the Great 164
Allegory of the Cave 88–9, 156
Amyntas III, King 164
Anaxagoras 1
Anniceris xx
Apology
dialogue in 2–3, 10–11, 14, 20
on heroes 107–8
on trial of Socrates xxiii–xxiv
Archytas xxii, 31, 85
Aristodemus 146
Aristophanes 131–5
Ariston xviii
Aristotle 23, 42, 86, 105, 110, 161, 164
art 152–5
Athenian Stranger xiii, xiv, xxv, 12–13, 70, 121, 124, 125
Athens

and Alcibiades 7–8
and Atlantis 157, 158
dialogue in 2–3
invasion of Sicily 163
and Macedonia 163–4
and Peloponnesian War 59–60
political struggles in xvi–xvii
struggle with Sparta xvi, xvii, 163
Atlantis 155–68
Atlantis: The Antediluvian World (Donnelly) 168
Augustine, St xii
Auxiliaries
in flourishing 26, 44
role of 80–4
Averroes 20
Axiothea of Phlius xx

Bacon, Francis 167
beauty, inner and outer 32–3, 35–6, 44–6, 54–5, 151–2
Bentham, Jeremy 24
Berlin, Isaiah xii
Beyond Good and Evil (Nietzsche) 61
Blavatsky, Madame 168
Bourbourg, Charles Etienne Brasseur de 167

Callicles 15–16, 17, 20, 55–64, 69–71
censorship 153–5

INDEX

Cephalus 10, 12, 65
Cicero xii, xxv, 113
Cleinias 11–12, 17–18, 121
Cleon 59
Clinias 121
Colston, Edward 117
of flourishing 46–50
Crantor 161
Cratylus 86
Critias (dialogue) 156, 157–9, 160–1, 162, 163, 168
Critias 91, 156, 158–9, 160, 162, 163
Crito (dialogue)
  dialogue in 2–3, 14
  on flourishing 23
  on justice 68, 69
Crito 23, 68
Ctesippus 18–19

debating styles 10–19
degenerate cities 94–8
Delian League xvi, 163
Demeter cult 82
democracy
  Callicles on 70–1
  in *Gorgias* 70–1, 96, 98–9
  and leadership 92–4
  Socrates on 92–3, 97–7
  in *Statesman* 99–100
  and tyranny 96–8
Demosthenes 164
Dewey, John 21
dialogue
  contemporary applications 19–22
  debating styles 10–19
  definition of 2
  and ethics 6
  form as a whole 5–10
  and friendship 121–2
  and Plato 1–2, 3–17, 19–22
  power relations in 2–3

and Socrates 1, 2–3, 4–9, 10–14, 15–19, 20–1
Dion xix–xx, xxii
Dionysius I xix, xx
Dionysius II xxii
Dionysodorus 11, 17–19
Diotima 82, 130, 136, 137–40, 141, 143, 144–6, 147
Divided Line 87–8, 153
Donnelly, Ignatius 168

education
  and flourishing 3203, 44–6, 47–9
  in the ideal city 89–90
  and role models 101–2
Eleatic Stranger xxiv, 125
Empedocles 131, 155
Er, Myth of 156
erastēs/erōmenos relationships 129–30, 140–1, 142–3, 149–50
Eryximachus 131
erōs 127–9, 130–4, 135–6, 137–9, 141, 142–3, 147–50
ethics
  and dialogue 6
  and flourishing 23–4
  and Socrates xxv–xxvii
eudaimonia see flourishing
Euthydemus (dialogue) xxi, 10, 11–12, 17–19, 121
Euthydemus 17–18
Euthyphro 13–14

Ficino, Marsilio xii
flourishing
  and abuse 43–4
  challenges to 42–6
  contemporary applications 46–50
  education in 32–3, 44–6, 47–9
  ethics of 23–4
  and Forms 35–6, 38–9

195

and healthcare 49
hierarchy of 44
justice in 25–30
inner and outer beauty in 32–3, 35–6, 44–6
mental health in 36–7
reason in 37–41
and repression 42–3
and role of *psychē* 24–30, 34–44
Socrates on 23, 25–6, 27–30, 32–4, 35, 37–41, 43, 44–5, 46, 48
urban and environmental planning 50
Forms
and art 152–3
existence of 85–6
in flourishing 35–6, 38–9
freedom 39–41
Freud, Sigmund 41–2
friendship
and dialogue 121–2
and *philia* 122–9
Socrates on 122–3, 124

Genealogy of Morals, The (Nietzsche) 61
Glaucon 12, 25–6, 27, 29, 30, 40, 65, 73–4, 79, 88, 121
Goebbels, Joseph 45
Gorgias (dialogue)
on democracy 70–1, 96, 98–9
dialogue in 3, 11, 15
ethics of Socrates xxv
on geometry xix
kalon in 32
on mythology 158
on power 53–64
on rhetoric 51–3
on tyranny xix, 70–1
on women 81
writing of xx
Gorgias 51–3

Guardians
education of 78, 89–90
and flourishing 26–7
role of 80–4
Gyges Ring 73–4, 156

healthcare 49
Hector 104
Heraclitus xxii, xxv, 1, 86, 131
Hermocrates 163
Herodotus 163
heroism
and Achilles 102–5, 106, 107–13
definition of 116–17
and the gods 105–6
Homeric 102–5
memorials to 117–18
and *psychē* 118–20
Socrates as hero 114–16
Socrates on 101, 106–15
statues to 117–18
and warriors 112
Hesiod 106
hierarchy of flourishing 44
Himmler, Heinrich 168
Hippias Major 109–10
Hippias Minor 110–11
History of the Peloponnesian War (Thucydides) 2, 59–60, 82, 163
Homer 65, 102–7, 109, 110, 111, 115, 13
Homeric Hymns 144
Hylas and the Nymphs (Waterhouse) 154
ideal city
and degenerate cities 94–8
democracy in 92–4
education in 89–90
Guardians in 80–4, 89–90
in *Laws* 99–100
myths of 78–9
philia in 123–6
Philosopher-Rulers in 84–7, 89–90

INDEX

practicality of 90–2
slavery in 91–2
Socrates on 77, 78, 79–80, 81, 82–6, 89–98
Iliad (Homer) 65, 102, 103–5, 108, 109, 111, 112, 113, 153
Isocrates xxi

justice
Adeimantus on 74–5
in flourishing 25–30
Glaucon on 73–4
and rhetoric 51–3
Socrates on 64–8, 72–3, 74
Thrasymachus on 64–70
kalon 32–3, 54–5, 151–2

Kant, Immanuel 24

Laertius, Diogenes xix, xx
Lastheneia of Mantineia xx
Laws
on cataclysms 164
on dialogue 12–13, 121
on justice 70
on mythology 158, 160
Socrates in xxiv
Lee, Robert E. 117
love
Agathon on 135–6
Alcibiades on 144–7
Aristophanes on 131–5
Diotima on 137–40
and *erastēs/erōmenos* relationships 129–30, 140–1, 142–3, 149–50
and *erōs* 127–9, 130–4, 135–6, 137–9, 141, 142–3, 147–50
Eryximachus on 131
and *paiderastia* 129–30
Pausanias on 130–1
in *Phaedrus* 147–50
Phaedrus on 130
process of 140–3

Socrates on 128, 135, 136–7, 138–9, 143, 144–8
in *Symposium* 127–47
Lucretius 113–14
Lysis 122–3
Lysis 122–3

Macedonia 163–4
Marathon, Battle of xvi, 163
Marx, Karl xii
Megillus 121
Melian Dialogue 2
Melissus 85
memorials to heroism 117–18
Menexenus 82
Menexenus 122–3
mental health 36–7
Meno 81
Mill, John Stuart 24
More, Thomas xii, 91, 167
Mundus Novus (Vespucci) 167
Murdoch, Iris xii
Mycale, Battle of xvi, 163
mythology
and Atlantis 155–68
importance of 165–7
Socrates on 155–6, 157, 158, 159–60, 162–3, 165–6

Neoplatonism xii
New Atlantis (Bacon) 167
Nietzsche, Friedrich xii, 61

Odysseus 102, 103, 105–6, 107, 108, 109–12, 114
Odyssey (Homer) 65, 105, 109, 110, 153
oligarchies 95–6
On Duties (Cicero) 113
On Nature (Empedocles) 155
On Nature (Parmenides) 155
On the Nature of Things (Lucretius) 113–14

One Flew Over the Cuckoo's Nest   43
Oreithyia   166

paiderastia   129–30
Parmenides   xxv, 1, 85, 86, 155
Patroclus   104, 105, 107, 108, 113
Pausanias   130–1
Peloponnesian War   59, 82
Pericles   xvi, xvii, 82
Perictione   xvii
Persian Empire   xvi, 7, 8, 163
Phaedo   158
Phaedrus (dialogue)
    dialogue in   5, 20–1
    on love   147–50
    Freud's admiration for   41
    on mythology   166
    Socrates in   xxiii
Phaedrus   130, 166
Pharnabazus   8
Philebus   13
philia   122–9
Philolaus   31
Philosopher-Rulers
    education of   89–90
    role of   84–7
Philosophy for Children (P4C)
    movement   21
Philosophy in Prison initiative   21
Pindar   70
Plataea, Battle of   xvi, 163
Plato
    and the Academy   xx–xxii
    birth of   xvi
    death of   xxii
    and dialogue form   1–2, 3–17, 19–22
    early life of   xvii–xix
    and Forms   85–6
    and Homer   106–12
    importance of   169
    influence of Socrates on   xxii–xxvii
    and knowledge   86–7
    visits to Sicily   xix–xx
Polemarchus   65
Polus   15, 52–5
Popper, Karl   xii
Posidonius   161
Posterior Analytics (Aristotle)   105, 110
power
    dispute between Socrates and Callicles   55–64
    and rhetoric   51–3
Priam, King   104–5
Process and Reality (Whitehead)   xiv
Prodicus   130
Producers
    in flourishing   44
    role of   80
    women as   82
Protagoras   3, 9, 11
Protagoras   13, 102
psychē
    and abuse   43–4
    and heroism   118–20
    influence on Aristotle   42
    influence on Freud   41–2
    and psychic harmony   27–30, 34–7
    and reason   37–41
    and repression   42–3
    role in flourishing   24–30, 34–44
psychic harmony   27–32, 34–7
Purifications (Empedocles)   155
Pyrilampes   xviii

reason in flourishing   37–41
Report on Strategies to Reduce Inequalities in Access to Planned Care (NHS Strategy Unit)   49
repression   42–3
Republic, The
    dialogue in   4, 10, 12, 13, 16–17, 121
    on education   32–3, 48

INDEX

on ethics xxv
on flourishing 23, 26–30, 31, 32–4, 35, 37–41, 43–6, 48
Freud's admiration for 41
on heroism 101, 106–7, 108, 111–12, 115, 116, 118–19
on the ideal city 77–99
on justice 64–8, 72–5
on mythology 155–7, 158–9, 165–6
on *philia* 124, 125, 126–7, 143
on power 55, 59, 64
on sense-perceptions 87–9
on tyranny xix
women in xx, 13, 81–3
rhetoric
    and justice 51–3
    Socrates on 52, 53–5
Rosenberg, Alfred 168
Rulers 26
    role of 80–4
Rushdie, Salman 154

Salamis, Battle of xvi, 163
Satanic Verses, The (Rushdie) 154
Secret Doctrine, The (Blavatsky) 168
Sermon on the Mount xxvi
Sicily xix–xx, 163
Simile of the Sun 87
Socrates
    and Allegory of the Cave 88–9
    and art 152, 153–5
    and beauty 151
    and Callicles 55–64
    and censorship 153–5
    and democracy 92–3, 97–7
    and dialogue form 1, 2–3, 4–9, 10–14, 15–19, 20–1
    dreams about Plato xii
    and education 101
    ethics of xxv–xxvii
    and flourishing 23, 25–6, 27–30, 32–4, 35, 37–41, 43, 44–5, 46, 48

and friendship 122–3, 124
as hero 114–16
and heroism 101, 106–15
and the ideal city 77, 78, 79–80, 81, 82–6, 89–98
influence on Plato xxii–xxvii
and justice 64–8, 72–3, 74
and love 128, 135, 136–7, 138–9, 143, 144–8
and mythology 155–6, 157, 158, 159–60, 162–3, 165–6
and Polus 53–5
and rhetoric 52, 53–5
and women 81, 82–3
Solon 156–7, 159
Solzhenitsyn, Alexander 43
Sophist
    dialogue in 10
    Socrates in xxiv
Sparta xvi, xvii, 7, 8, 163
Statesman
    on cataclysms 164
    on democracy 99–100
    Socrates in xxiv
statues to heroism 117–18
Strabo 161
Symposium
    Alcibiades in 6–7, 8–9
    dialogue in 5, 6–7, 9, 121–2
    Freud's admiration for 41
    on love 127–47

Thales xxv
Theaetetus
    dialogue in 4, 14, 121
Theaetetus 11–12, 121
Theodorus 121
Thera 160–1
Thirty Tyrants xvii, xviii, 91
Thrasymachus 16–17, 20, 27, 59, 64–72
Thucydides 2, 7, 59–60, 82, 97, 162, 163

199

thumoeides 34–5, 40, 101–2, 112
Thus Spake Zarathustra (Nietzsche) 61
Timaeus 32, 156, 157, 159, 160, 162–3, 168
timarchies 94–5
Tissaphernes 7
Tusculan Disputations (Cicero) xxv
tyranny
  and democracy 96–8
  in *Gorgias* 70–1
  in Sicily xix

urban and environmental planning 50
Utopia (More) 91, 167

Vespucci, Amerigo 167
von List, Guido 168

Waterhouse, John William 154
Whitehead, A. N. xii
Will to Power (Nietzsche) 61
Wirth, Herman 168
women
  in *Republic* xx, 13, 81–3
  Socrates on 81, 82–3
Works and Days (Hesiod) 106

Young Plato (documentary) 21

Zeno 1
Zschaetzsch, Karl Georg 168